The ULTIMATE Book of
HOUSEHOLD
Hints & Tips

The ULTIMATE Book of
HOUSEHOLD
Hints & Tips

Cassandra Kent

DORLING KINDERSLEY

LONDON · NEW YORK · SYDNEY · MOSCOW

A DORLING KINDERSLEY BOOK

Project Editor Victoria Sorzano
Project Art Editor Jayne Carter
Designer Darren Hill
Senior Editor Stephanie Jackson
Managing Art Editor Nigel Duffield
Senior Managing Editor Krystyna Mayer
Senior Managing Art Editor Lynne Brown
Production Sarah Coltman
DTP Designer Raúl López Cabello

First published in Great Britain in 1996
by Dorling Kindersley Limited,
9 Henrietta Street,
London WC2E 8PS

Copyright © 1996
Dorling Kindersley Limited, London

A CIP catalogue record for this book is available
from the British Library

ISBN 0 7513 0265 1

Reproduced by Chroma Graphics, Singapore.
Printed and bound in Italy by Lego.

CONTENTS

INTRODUCTION 6

USING THIS BOOK   6
GETTING ORGANIZED   8

HOUSE CLEANING 10

GENERAL CLEANING   12
FLOORS   14
WALLS AND CEILINGS   18
FURNISHINGS   22
BATHROOMS   24
KITCHENS   26
CLEANING CHECKLIST   31

STAIN REMOVAL 32

TACKLING STAINS   34
FOOD STAINS   36
SPILLED BEVERAGES   39
BIOLOGICAL STAINS   42
PIGMENT AND SYNTHETIC STAINS   46
HOUSEHOLD PRODUCT STAINS   49
WEAR-AND-TEAR MARKS   52
OTHER STAINS   55

CLOTHES & LAUNDRY 56

WASHING CLOTHES   58
SPECIAL TREATMENTS   60
DRYING CLOTHES   62
IRONING CLOTHES   64
CARING FOR CLOTHES   66
SHOE CARE   69

CARE & REPAIR 70

WOOD	71
METAL	74
GLASS AND CHINA	78
ORNAMENTAL SURFACES	81
SOFT FURNISHINGS	82
AROUND THE HOME	84
ACCESSORIES	86

HOME IMPROVEMENTS 88

HOUSEHOLD TOOLS	90
HOUSE PAINTING	92
HOW TO PAINT	94
SPECIAL AREAS	96
FINISHING OFF	98
HANGING WALLPAPER	100
OTHER TECHNIQUES	104

HOME MAINTENANCE 106

PLUMBING	107
ELECTRICITY AND FUEL	111
HEATING AND COOLING	114
GENERAL REPAIRS	116
HOME SECURITY	118

FOOD & DRINK 120

FRUIT AND VEGETABLES	122
MEAT, DAIRY, AND EGGS	126
BREAD, PASTA, AND RICE	130
ALL THE EXTRAS	132
BAKING AND SWEETS	136
BEVERAGES	140

HOUSEKEEPING 142

HOUSE PLANTS AND FLOWERS	144
SEWING	148
CHILD AND PET CARE	150
HEALTH AND BEAUTY	154
CARS AND GARAGES	158
ENTERTAINING	160
MOVING HOUSE	162

HEALTH & SAFETY 164

ACTION IN EMERGENCIES	166
RESUSCITATION	168
TREATING INJURIES	170
COMMON INJURIES	173
COMMON AILMENTS	179

INDEX	182
ACKNOWLEDGMENTS	192

INTRODUCTION

THE KEY TO RUNNING A HOME well is organization. Keep clutter to a minimum, establish a cleaning routine that you can live with, and make time for regular repairs and maintenance. This book is filled with common-sense solutions, expert advice, and traditional tips that will help you do these things quickly and easily – so that you have more time to enjoy yourself at home.

USING THIS BOOK

KEEPING A CLEAN HOME
The first three chapters cover every aspect of keeping a home clean – from how to look after different types of floor surface, to how to remove red-wine stains. House Cleaning describes the correct procedures for looking after the different surfaces and rooms in your home. Clothes and Laundry demystifies washing instructions and procedures, and offers invaluable advice on caring for clothes, shoes, and accessories. Stain Removal is a complete, step-by-step colour guide that shows you exactly how to remove even the most stubborn mark from every type of surface.

How to remove stains
To find out what to do (and what not to do) to remove stains from clothes, furniture, and carpets, see pages 32-55.

REPAIRS AND RESCUES
Most well-run homes require a little more attention than simple cleaning. Care and Repair describes how to look after special objects and how to repair them if they get broken. Home Improvements features tips on performing decorating tasks quickly and efficiently, and Home Maintenance guides you through the home, pinpointing all the areas where things could go wrong and detailing the appropriate action in case they do. Accidents and emergencies occur even in the best-run homes, and it is vital to know how to deal with them. Health and Safety features Red Cross approved life-saving techniques and treatments for injuries and ailments.

Perfect painting
For tips on painting walls and ceilings, wallpapering rooms, and caring for tools, see pages 88-105.

HOMEMAKING MADE EASY

There is more to homemaking than cleaning and maintenance. For most people, cooking – whether a pleasure or a chore – is a major feature of home life. Food and Drink offers hundreds of tips on solving common kitchen problems, storing food, cooking meat and vegetables, and baking perfect cakes and pastry. Housekeeping provides short cuts and advice on specialized homemaking skills such as sewing, flower arranging, caring for plants and pets, and entertaining. Finally, the comprehensive index and chapter-by-chapter colour coding make it easy to find tips throughout the book.

Flower care
Knowing how to care for cut flowers can prolong their life. See page 147 for the relevant details.

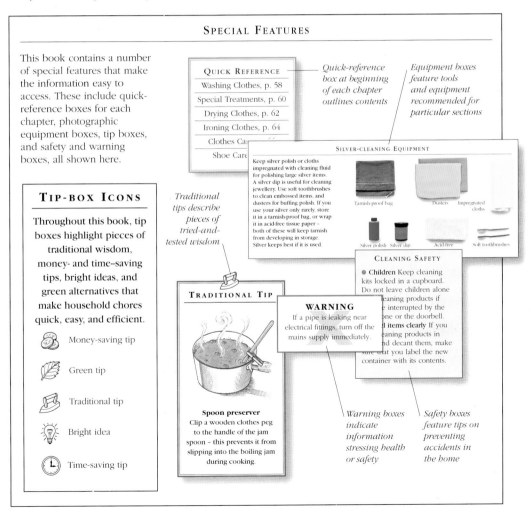

SPECIAL FEATURES

This book contains a number of special features that make the information easy to access. These include quick-reference boxes for each chapter, photographic equipment boxes, tip boxes, and safety and warning boxes, all shown here.

QUICK REFERENCE
Washing Clothes, p. 58
Special Treatments, p. 60
Drying Clothes, p. 62
Ironing Clothes, p. 64
Clothes Ca...
Shoe Care

Quick-reference box at beginning of each chapter outlines contents

Equipment boxes feature tools and equipment recommended for particular sections

SILVER-CLEANING EQUIPMENT

Keep silver polish or cloths impregnated with cleaning fluid for polishing large silver items. A silver dip is useful for cleaning jewellery. Use soft toothbrushes to clean embossed items, and dusters for buffing polish. If you use your silver only rarely, store it in a tarnish-proof bag, or wrap it in acid-free tissue paper – both of these will keep tarnish from developing in storage. Silver keeps best if it is used.

Tarnish-proof bag   Dusters   Impregnated cloths

Silver polish   Silver dip   Acid-free   Soft toothbrushes

TIP-BOX ICONS

Throughout this book, tip boxes highlight pieces of traditional wisdom, money- and time-saving tips, bright ideas, and green alternatives that make household chores quick, easy, and efficient.

Money-saving tip

Green tip

Traditional tip

Bright idea

Time-saving tip

Traditional tips describe pieces of tried-and-tested wisdom

TRADITIONAL TIP

Spoon preserver
Clip a wooden clothes peg to the handle of the jam spoon - this prevents it from slipping into the boiling jam during cooking.

WARNING
If a pipe is leaking near electrical fittings, turn off the mains supply immediately.

CLEANING SAFETY
● **Children** Keep cleaning kits locked in a cupboard. Do not leave children alone ...eaning products if ...e interrupted by the ...one or the doorbell. ...l items clearly If you ...eaning products in ...d decant them, make ...re that you label the new container with its contents.

Warning boxes indicate information stressing health or safety

Safety boxes feature tips on preventing accidents in the home

MAKING LISTS

Lists help you to get things done efficiently, without wasting time through forgetfulness. Make a master list of food and household items that you shop for regularly, and add or delete entries before each shopping trip (see right). Keep the master in your home log book (see opposite) and make copies to be stuck on the refrigerator door. Every year, write down the dates of birthdays on a large calender and add social events, holidays, and appointments. Have the whole household use the calendar to communicate their plans. Lists can also be used to plan your tasks for the week, prepare for holidays, and organize parties.

Shopping lists
Keep a copy of your general shopping list stuck to your refrigerator door, and cross off items as they run out.

Home office
Set up a filing system for your important paperwork, so that you can access documents easily when you need them.

PLANNING YOUR TIME

If you have a busy household, it is wise to approach managing it almost like running an office. Set aside a regular time each week to deal with correspondence and bills, and to plan your chores and appointments for the week ahead. When scheduling tasks, allow yourself extra time for travelling, queues at checkouts, and delay. Be sure to leave some free time for yourself each day, either to enjoy a little relaxation or to deal with any unexpected problems – you never know when a child may need to talk or a friend may require your help.

ATTACKING HOUSEHOLD CLUTTER

Nothing makes a home seem as disorganized as unnecessary clutter. Go through your home at regular intervals and dispose of things you do not need. These may include clothes you never wear, old magazines, and broken toys and gadgets. To dispose of undamaged items, hold a garage or car boot sale, or donate the items to a charity shop. Cut down on clutter by placing shelves near the front door, and allocating a shelf to each family member. They can leave frequently used items here when they come in, and they will always be able to find them easily when they are about to go out again.

Personalized shelves
Family members can leave much-used items such as toys, umbrellas, and boots on their shelf near the door.

MAKING A HOME LOG BOOK

A home log book is useful for keeping all the information about your home in one, easily accessible place. It is particularly handy for details that will slip the mind over a period of time – such as the telephone number of a certain repairman, or the solvents used to remove a particular stain. Use several notebooks, or a ring binder, to create a system to suit you. It helps if there is scope to add or remove pages, and also to include things like fabric or paint swatches. Dedicate a part of the log book to the items in your home: make a household inventory – this will prove invaluable if you have a fire or a theft. Keep a copy of all guarantees, instruction leaflets, and the dates of purchase of major items in this section.

A master diary of important dates and events is another vital part of your home log book.

Making a log book
Ring binders make ideal log books because they allow you to add and remove pages easily. Alternatively, use notebooks, one for each different area of your home life.

ADDITIONAL INFORMATION

Most homes require regular maintenance, so keep a note of what repairs were done when, as well as any details to do with decoration (see p. 99). You may wish to dedicate a section to health, with a list of emergency telephone numbers (see p. 165) and a record of every visit made to a doctor by a family member. A section devoted to local services and information is also useful – consult it as a guide to taxi services, area take-aways, or library opening times. Keep your log book in a sensible place where it is readily to hand, and make sure that all members of the household know where it is.

HOME LOG BOOK CONTENTS

The sections below are a rough guide to what a home log book could contain.

HOUSEHOLD DIARY
● Keep a list of dates such as birthdays, school terms, inoculations, and dates when things like insurance have to be paid. Update it each year, and transfer it to a calendar.

HOUSEHOLD INVENTORY
● List all valuable household items, and serial numbers where applicable. Take photographs of valuable items (see p. 119).
● Keep copies of guarantees, instruction booklets, and records of dates of purchase. If instruction booklets prove too bulky, keep them in a separate folder.

HOME MAINTENANCE AND DECORATING
● See page 99 for what to include in a decorating log.
● Note the names, addresses, and telephone numbers of anyone you employed for repairs or decorating.
● Write down where there are electrical cables, central-heating pipes, and any other items that might cause problems when decorating.

OTHER INTERESTS
● If you entertain frequently, make a record of the guests you invited to each gathering and the food that was served.
● Keen gardeners can set up gardening logs that contain essential planting details.
● Set up a car log with details such as insurance policy numbers, dates of repairs, and tyre pressures.
● Keep a cleaning file to record how you removed stains from items (see p. 11).

HOUSE CLEANING

QUICK REFERENCE

General Cleaning, p. 12

Floors, p. 14

Walls & Ceilings, p. 18

Furnishings, p. 22

Bathrooms, p. 24

Kitchens, p. 26

Cleaning Checklist, p. 31

*C*LEANING DOES NOT HAVE TO BE *hard work if you follow a few basic rules. Invest in the right equipment, and take care of it. Dusting is the key to a clean home, so keep that task on your regular agenda. Sensible use of the vacuum cleaner and all its attachments makes light work of many chores, not just cleaning carpets. Do not aim for hospital hygiene; a home need not be squeaky clean to look good.*

HOUSE-CLEANING EQUIPMENT

These are the essential items you will need for keeping your home clean. Buy a plastic storage box with a handle, which you can use for carrying equipment around. If your home has lots of stairs, consider investing in two sets of cleaning tools to save carrying them. Clean all equipment after use.

Household dusters

Chamois leather

Dustpan and brush

Sponge mop

Acrylic dusting brush

Cloths for wet work

Rubber gloves

Scrubbing brush

Floor-cleaning cloth

Bucket

Long-handled broom

HOUSE-CLEANING MATERIALS

Nowadays, there is a product to clean almost everything in your home. Although manufacturers would like you to believe that their products are essential, all you need are some key items. A cleaning kit that contains washing-up liquid, non-abrasive and abrasive household detergent, biological washing powder, furniture polish, and metal polish will look after all the surfaces in your home.

EXTRA ITEMS
● **For specific marks** Ammonia, household bleach, methylated spirit, rubbing alcohol, laundry borax, washing soda, and white spirit are useful for cleaning particular surfaces, and for removing difficult stains. Keep them away from children.
● **From the kitchen** Salt, lemon juice, glycerine, white vinegar, and bicarbonate of soda can be used as gentle, environmentally friendly household cleaners.
● **Specialist cleaners** Buy sugar soap for washing down very dirty walls. Keep a supply of hide food for feeding and protecting leather furniture.

MAKING RECORDS
● **A cleaning file** Make a record of how you cleaned special items, and what you used, to avoid trial and error the next time. Keep this file in your home log book (see p. 8–9).

 Household bleach
 Cream cleaner
 Spray cleaner
 Furniture polish
 Ammonia

 Methylated spirit
 Rubbing alcohol
 Liquid cleaner
 White spirit
 Washing-up liquid

 Laundry borax
 Floor and wall cleaner
 Biological washing powder
 Washing soda
Metal polish

 Bicarbonate of soda
 Salt
 Lemon juice
 Glycerine
 White vinegar

CLEANING AND SAFETY

● **Keep children safe** Keep your cleaning kit locked away in a cupboard. Do not leave children alone with cleaning products if you are interrupted by the telephone or the doorbell.
● **Label items clearly** If you buy products in bulk and decant them, make sure you label the new container clearly with its contents.

● **Protect your skin** Wear rubber gloves if you are using strong household cleaners. Avoid contact with skin, eyes, and clothes when using bleach or ammonia.
● **Beware of fumes** Open windows in the rooms you are cleaning (if possible) to provide ventilation. Avoid naked flames, as they may cause chemicals to ignite.

● **Do not mix cleaners** Some chemicals react adversely when mixed. If a cleaning product has not worked on a surface, rinse it off before using another cleaner.
● **Watch your step** If you are cleaning hard-to-reach places, always stand on a ladder or stepstool. Standing on a chair or table is dangerous, and could lead to an accident.

GENERAL CLEANING

LITTLE AND OFTEN is the best way to keep your home clean. If you leave things for weeks, you will find yourself with a major chore on your hands. Clean living rooms once a week; sinks and kitchen surfaces should be cleaned daily.

MAINTAINING EQUIPMENT

Keep your equipment in good condition, otherwise you will have to spend extra time getting it back into shape. Always clean equipment before you put it away, and store items properly. Wash cleaning cloths regularly, and discard any that are too dirty to reuse.

STORING EQUIPMENT

Tie plastic bag with string

Store used pads in soapy water

Use half a pad at a time

Broom care
Wash brooms in soapy water from time to time. Store upside down to prevent the bristles from bending – you can make a rack using two cotton reels.

Sponge mops
Rinse floor mops thoroughly after use (they should not need any extra washing). Store the heads in plastic bags so that they do not dry out and warp.

Steel-wool pads
Keep steel-wool pads in soapy water to stop them from rusting, or wrap them in aluminium foil. Save money by cutting them in half so that they go twice as far.

CLOTHS AND SPONGES
● **Cleaning and storage** Shake dusters well in the garden or out of a window after you have used them. Soak slimy sponges in vinegar and water. Store dusters and polishing cloths in plastic bags.

CHAMOIS LEATHERS
● **General care** Chamois leathers are expensive, but will last for years if well cared for. Wash in warm, soapy water, and rinse thoroughly. Allow to dry away from direct heat to preserve the skin's natural oils.

BRUSHES
● **Using toothbrushes** Old toothbrushes are perfect tools for cleaning intricate metal work, grouting, around taps, and awkward spaces. Save as many as you can, and keep them in your cleaning kit.

VACUUM CLEANERS

Use your vacuum cleaner for as many tasks as possible. The range of attachments can be used to clean curtains, furniture, and upholstery, as well as floors. Check the brushes and rollers before you start vacuuming – the machine will not work well if it is clogged up. A range of vacuum cleaners is available for carrying out different tasks. Hand-held vacuum cleaners are ideal for cars and for cleaning up spills.

● **Upright vacuum cleaners**
These are best for covering large areas of floor, but they cannot always get under furniture or into awkward corners.
● **Cylinder vacuum cleaners**
These are good for cleaning awkward areas, such as stairs and under low furniture, but can be cumbersome to use.
● **Wet-and-dry vacuum cleaners**
These suck up water as well as doing routine cleaning.

Dusting tool

Crevice tool

Upholstery tool

METHODS AND ROUTINES

Establish and maintain a cleaning routine so that all areas of your home receive regular attention and the work does not pile up. Use these tips to get around rooms efficiently and make your home appear tidy – even when you know it is not as clean as it could be.

CLEANING METHODS

Grasp a clean duster in each hand

Dust in direction of grain

Two-handed dusting
Using two dusters - one in each hand - will help you get around the surfaces in a room in half the time and with half the effort.

Two-bucket method
Wash floors and walls using two buckets: fill one with cleaning solution, and the other with water for rinsing the sponge or mop.

TIME-SAVING TIP

Cleaning in a hurry
If visitors are coming and you are unprepared, make do with cleaning the hallway, tidying obvious clutter, and throwing away dead flowers. Straighten cushions, chairs, and rugs to create an impression of order. Spray room freshener and dim the lighting or use candlelight.

TIME-SAVING DUSTER

Place duster in paraffin and vinegar

Wear gloves to protect your hands

1 To create a duster that literally lifts up dirt, soak a new duster in equal parts of paraffin and vinegar.

2 Remove the duster when it is fully saturated, and store it in a screwtop jar until you are ready to use it.

CLEANING ROUTINES
● **Daily cleaning** Kitchens and bathrooms should be cleaned daily (see p. 24–30).
● **Regular cleaning** Bedrooms and living rooms should be cleaned weekly. Begin by ventilating the room and tidying up. Starting at one side of a door, dust all items and surfaces, working around the whole room. Always dust higher surfaces first, since some dust may fall on to lower surfaces. Finally, vacuum or sweep the floor.
● **Occasional cleaning** Every few months, give all rooms a thorough going over. Take down curtains for cleaning, shampoo upholstery and carpets, and clean walls and windows. Tidy up cupboards, and dispose of any items that you no longer use.

ROOMS	CLEANING FREQUENCY
BATHROOMS AND KITCHENS	Clean these rooms daily to maintain good hygiene.
BEDROOMS	Air beds each morning, as we lose 250 ml (½ pint) of moisture every night. Clean rooms weekly.
LIVING ROOMS	Clean once a week. Vacuum floors twice a week if necessary.
OTHER AREAS	Vacuum halls twice a week. Clean little-used rooms monthly.

FLOORS

Dirt is transmitted to floors from outdoors, so lay a doormat inside all exterior doors to remove dirt from shoes. If you keep floors clean by sweeping or vacuuming regularly, you will cut down on heavy-duty cleaning.

CLEANING HARD FLOORS

Hard floors that are dusty look dirtier than unvacuumed carpets. Sweep, vacuum, or mop them regularly – particularly hallway, kitchen, and bathroom floors. Wood floors need polishing; marble, vinyl, and tiled floors require heavy-duty cleaning from time to time.

SWEEPING FLOORS

Removing dust
Sweep or vacuum hard floors every few days, paying special attention to corners, where dirt collects and builds up.

MOPPING FLOORS

Effective mopping
Damp mop all sealed floors weekly, using the two-bucket method. Do not use soap when mopping slate or stone floors.

SCRUBBING FLOORS

Heavy-duty washing
Scrub stone, concrete, and tiled floors with floor cleaner and a scrubbing brush occasionally to get rid of accumulated dirt.

POLISHING FLOORS

Give floors a good shine, and your home will look well cared for. Use the right type of polish for your floor, and remember that polish builds up and will need to be removed from time to time. Use floor cleaner, ammonia, or commercial wax remover to remove polish.

TYPES OF POLISH

SOLID-PASTE POLISHES
These solvent-based polishes are suitable for vinyl, wood, and cork. Application is difficult and must be done by hand, but the shine lasts a long time.

LIQUID-SOLVENT POLISHES
These are also suitable for vinyl, wood, and cork. They are easier to use than solid-paste polish, but they are not as long lasting.

WATER-BASED EMULSION POLISHES
These usually contain silicone. They can be used on all floors except vinyl, unsealed wood, and cork. They are easy to apply and long lasting.

Secure duster around broom head

Improvised polisher
Tie a duster around a soft broom, and use this instead of an electric polisher to apply and buff wax polish. Always clean floors thoroughly before you apply polish for the first time.

TYPES OF FLOORING

Hard floors can take a lot of heavy wear, but different types of surface need varying amounts of attention. Sweep hard floors daily if necessary, and clean them according to their type. Do not let dirt build up so that cleaning becomes a hands-and-knees job.

TYPE	TREATMENT
VINYL An easy-care floor covering that lasts well if cared for correctly.	● Sweep regularly. When dirty, wash vinyl with a solution of household detergent and warm water. Rinse with clear water. Apply a water-based emulsion polish, but do not allow it to build up. ● Never use a solvent-based polish on vinyl; it can destroy the surface. Remove stubborn marks with a little emulsion polish on a damp cloth.
LINOLEUM A tough flooring, but take care not to overwet, because this can cause damage.	● Wipe linoleum floors with a mop dampened in a weak solution of water and household detergent. Use an emulsion polish – which will not leave a watermark – on kitchen and bathroom floors, and a wax polish on floors elsewhere in the home. ● Remove scuff marks by rubbing with fine-grade steel wool dipped in turpentine or white spirit.
WOOD Treatment depends on whether or not the wood is sealed.	● Sweep or dry mop unsealed floors regularly to remove dust and dirt. Clean sealed wood floors with a mop dampened and wrung out. To give the floor a shine, polish with wax or emulsion polish. ● Use a damp cloth to remove sticky marks on unsealed floors. Remove wax polish from sealed wood floors with a cloth and white spirit.
CORK Needs regular sweeping, otherwise a build-up of dirt or polish will occur around the edges.	● Mop regularly with a solution of warm water and household detergent, and apply wax polish occasionally. Try to avoid a build up of polish around the edges of the room as this eventually results in a sticky deposit that attracts dirt. ● If laying cork tiles, ensure that the edges are sealed, otherwise water may seep in from the sides.
CERAMIC TILES This surface is as hard as nails, so anything dropped on it will break – take care.	● Clean with a solution of washing-up liquid applied with a sponge mop or a cloth, then wipe over with a chamois leather. Mop up spills immediately – wet floors are dangerously slippery. ● Do not polish ceramic tiles, since this will make them slippery. Clean grouting with a soft-bristled brush dipped in a strong solution of detergent.
QUARRY TILES Pretty, but porous unless sealed. Rub faded tiles with steel wool and white spirit, then apply coloured solid-paste polish.	● Glazed quarry tiles need mopping regularly with water and a little general-purpose cleaner. Scrub unglazed quarry tiles with this solution to remove dirt. Rinse thoroughly. Polish with liquid or solid-paste polish, preferably non-slip. ● Treat newly laid tiles with linseed oil. Do not wash them for at least two weeks afterwards.

SPECIAL FLOOR TREATMENTS

Avoid scuffing or scratching hard floors if possible, because these marks can be difficult to remove. Polish rocking-chair arcs to prevent them from scratching floors, and slip small mats underneath furniture when moving heavy pieces across a room.

REMOVING STAINS FROM WOOD FLOORS

● **Ink stains** Treat ink stains by dabbing them with neat household bleach, applied on a cotton-wool bud. Blot quickly with paper towels, and repeat if necessary.

● **Candle wax** Harden spilled candle wax with an ice cube, then ease off the wax with a blunt knife. Rub in a little liquid floor polish, then buff well, using a soft cloth.

REMOVING SCRATCHES FROM WOOD FLOORS

Rub scratch gently

1 Rub the scratch with fine steel wool. Be careful not to spread the rubbed area any further than necessary. Wear gloves when using steel wool.

2 Mix a little brown shoe polish with floor wax, and apply the mixture to the area. Rub in well, so that it blends with the rest of the floor.

REPAIRS TO FLOORS

● **Vinyl and cork** Remove burn marks by rubbing with fine sandpaper. If a burn is very noticeable, cut out the damaged part with a craft knife and insert a new piece.

● **Linoleum** These floors tend to crack with age. Cover any cracks with clear adhesive tape, then apply a coat of clear polyurethane varnish.

● **Broken tiles** Repair holes in tiles with wall or wood filler. Apply the filler slightly proud of the floor, and sand down when dry. Apply colour (shoe polish or artist's oils), then finish with clear floor seal.

● **Wood floors** Where a defective damp course is causing rising damp, a cheap and easy solution is to lift the flooring and paint the concrete sub-floor with a special waterproof coating.

QUARRY TILES

● **Restoring colour** If colour has faded, remove any old polish with steel wool and white spirit. Wash, rinse, and apply pigmented wax polish when dry. Buff well to make sure that the polish is not picked up on shoes.

Treating white patches
These are caused by lime in the sub-floor and will disappear eventually. Hasten the process by washing with a solution of 60 ml (4 tbsp) vinegar to 5 litres (9 pints) water. Do not rinse.

TRADITIONAL TIP

Keeping dust down
Sprinkle damp tea leaves on wood floors to help collect dust when sweeping. Damp tea leaves will also keep dust down when you are cleaning ashes out of fireplaces – this is particularly useful for people who have dust allergies.

VINYL AND LINOLEUM

● **Paint stains** Remove fresh emulsion by rubbing with a damp cloth. Rub fresh oil-based paint stains with steel wool dipped in solid-paste polish. Saturate dried paint stains with boiled linseed oil, let stand, then wipe off.

Wear gloves when using strong chemicals

Scuff marks on vinyl
Remove scuff and heel marks on vinyl floors with white spirit or turpentine, applied on a cloth. An eraser may also do the trick, or try rubbing the mark with a cloth dipped in emulsion polish.

FLOOR COVERINGS

Carpets and rugs are among the most expensive items of room decoration, so they should be well cared for to make them last. Always follow the carpet manufacturer's care instructions to ensure that your carpet stays in good condition as long as possible.

CLEANING CARPETS

● **Vacuuming** Vacuum regularly to remove dust and dirt, and keep the pile in good condition. Ideally, go over each area eight times – but fewer will do if you are in a hurry. Take advantage of all the attachments to clean around the edges of each room and under low furniture.

● **Shampooing** Apply carpet shampoo by hand to dirty patches. When the whole carpet is dirty, shampoo it using a machine, or call a professional cleaner. Shampoo fitted carpets in place – they may shrink if you take them up and wet them, and you will have to pay for relaying.

GREEN TIP

Dry shampoo
To freshen your carpet cheaply and ecologically, liberally sprinkle bicarbonate of soda all over it. Leave for 15 minutes, then vacuum thoroughly. Not only will your carpet be clean – you will have discouraged pests and neutralized odours.

FURNITURE MARKS ON CARPETS

Damp carpets
If you need to replace furniture before a recently shampooed carpet is fully dry, place squares of foil beneath the furniture legs to prevent the furniture from marking the carpet.

Raising crushed pile
To raise indentations in carpets caused by the weight of heavy furniture, place an ice cube in the dent, and leave the ice cube to melt. Let the area dry naturally, then vacuum.

RUGS AND MATS

● **Cleaning** Beat rugs outside with a carpet beater or an old tennis racquet. Vacuum natural floor coverings (rush, sisal, coconut matting); when dirty, scrub with salty water, rinse, then leave them to dry away from direct heat.

HOUSEHOLD PESTS AND SMELLS

Carpets and rugs are susceptible to pests such as carpet beetles, and they also pick up and hold smells from cigarette smoke, frying food, and pets.

● **Carpet beetles** A tell-tale sign of carpet beetles is their sloughed-off skins, usually around carpet edges. These pests are difficult to eradicate because they get into well-hidden places. Kill as many as you can by sprinkling laundry borax around the carpet edges, and also over the padding before a new carpet is laid.

● **Cigarette smoke** The smell of smoke lingers in carpets and soft furnishings. Put a bowl of water in a discreet place if you are expecting smoking visitors. Lighting candles also helps. Line the bottoms of ashtrays with baking soda to prevent butts from smouldering.
● **Vinegar air freshener** A small container of vinegar left in any room of the house keeps the room smelling fresh, even if the house is closed up for a while. Add vinegar to the water in humidifiers occasionally – it will keep the air fresher.

Creeping rugs
Prevent rugs from sliding around on hard floor surfaces by sticking pieces of heavy-duty, double-sided tape around the edges. Use pieces of Velcro to prevent rugs from creeping on carpet.

WALLS AND CEILINGS

Unless you live in a heavily polluted area or have a houseful of smokers, you do not need to clean your walls and ceilings more than once a year. Do not tackle more than a room at a time – this task is physically demanding.

WALL COVERINGS

Dust non-washable wallpaper regularly to prevent dirt from building up. Never use water because it will loosen the paper from the wall. Sponge washable wall coverings with a washing-up liquid solution, working from bottom to top. Rinse clean with warm water.

CLEANING NON-WASHABLE WALLPAPER

Removing marks
Rub marks with a scrunched up piece of crustless, white bread, or an eraser. Rub gently to avoid damaging the wall covering – it may take several attempts before the marks begin to disappear.

Removing grease marks
Apply a warm (not hot) iron over brown paper to absorb grease marks. Repeat using clean parts of the brown paper until all the grease is absorbed, then apply an aerosol grease solvent.

CLEANING VINYL

General care
Wash vinyl wall coverings occasionally, using a detergent solution applied on a sponge. Start from the bottom and work your way up, and rub gently so as not to damage the surface.

PATCHING WALLPAPER

1 Badly marked wallpaper may need to be patched rather than cleaned. Tear a matching piece, pulling away from you as you tear to create an uneven edge (which will show up less obviously than a cut edge).

2 Stick the new patch into position with wallpaper paste, making sure that the pattern matches. If you are patching old wallpaper, leave the new piece in the sun to fade for a few days before patching.

SPECIALTY WALL COVERINGS

● **Grasscloth** Clean carefully, since the grasses can come loose very easily. Simply dusting is sufficient – use a soft-brush vacuum-cleaner attachment on low suction. Be careful not to place furniture against grasscloth; it may rub the grasses loose and leave unsightly marks.
● **Hessian** Dust regularly, using a vacuum-cleaner attachment. The dyes in hessian tend to run, so do not wet. Remove marks by rubbing with a piece of crustless white bread.

PAINTED SURFACES

Painted walls and ceilings can be kept in good condition for a long time with regular cleaning. But marks such as heavy tobacco stains can be difficult to eradicate. If this is a problem, redecorating may be a better solution than trying to scrub off the stains.

CEILINGS
● **Cleaning** Do not wash ceilings – a fresh coat of paint is more effective. Dust with the improvised duster shown below, a long-handled brush, or the upholstery attachment on your vacuum cleaner.

Making a ceiling duster
Tie a clean duster loosely around a broom head, and use this to dust ceilings thoroughly from time to time. Remember to give the broom a shake at intervals.

WALLS, DOORS, AND TRIMMINGS
● **Cleaning walls** Use a warm solution of washing-up liquid to clean walls. Do not stop in the middle of cleaning – you will create a tidemark that is difficult to remove. Wash one wall at a time completely.

Wall-washing method
Always start at the bottom of a wall and work upwards. This may sound like extra work, but it is easier to wipe dirty trickles off a clean surface than off a dirty one.

● **Very dirty walls** Clean with a solution of sugar soap (follow the manufacturer's instructions for dilution) before using other cleaners.
● **Doors and skirting boards** Wash with a solution of washing-up liquid (not detergent, which can affect paint colour). Rinse with clear water, and pat dry.

MARKS ON WALLS
● **Tackling stains** Most marks come off painted walls, but treat them gently to avoid damaging the paintwork. Rub fingerprints and pencil marks gently with an eraser. Wash food stains off with neat, non-abrasive household cleaner. Where furniture has knocked into a wall and left a mark, first use an eraser then household cleaner.

OTHER WALL TYPES

Ceramic tiles often show dirt in the grouting between the tiles. Wood-panelled walls need frequent dusting (you can use your vacuum cleaner for this) and polishing once a year. Marks on bare brickwork are difficult to remove, so dust these walls frequently.

CERAMIC-TILE WALLS

Cleaning grouting
Use an old, clean toothbrush dipped in a bleach solution to clean grouting between tiles. If the grout is filthy, it may be easier to apply new grouting.

WOOD PANELLING

Removing polish
When the polish on wood walls builds up, remove it using fine steel wool and white spirit. Rub gently but firmly, following the direction of the grain.

BRICKWORK

Sealing brick walls
Apply a sealer to bare brickwork so that the brickwork will just require dusting and damp wiping. Use a soft paint brush, and make sure the wall is clean.

WINDOWS

Dirty windows spoil the look of a home. Clean the outsides as often as necessary, depending on the area in which you live, and wash the insides two or three times a year. Do not forget to dust windows when you clean each room. Use a soft, acrylic brush.

WASHING WINDOWS

Homemade cleaner
Make your own solution for washing windows by adding vinegar to water in a plant-spray bottle. Vinegar cuts grease, and brings up a good shine,

WIPING WINDOWS

Using newspaper
Wipe newly washed windows clean with crumpled newspaper. This is a cheap alternative to a chamois leather, and the ink will give the glass an extra shine.

TIME-SAVING TIP

Protecting curtains
To avoid removing curtains when cleaning windows, loop them over a hanger.

SMEAR-FREE WINDOW CLEANING

● **Window-washing weather** Wash windows on dull days, when they are damp and every fingerprint and mark shows up. Sunny days are less ideal for window washing, since the windows dry too quickly, leaving smeary marks.

● **Smear finder** When cleaning the outside and inside of a window, use horizontal strokes on one side and vertical strokes on the other. This way you can easily tell which side of the window still has the odd smear left.

MIRRORS

When cleaning mirrors, avoid using water, which can trickle down behind the glass and damage the silvering. Instead, use a commercial glass cleaner, then buff the mirror well.

ELECTRIC FIXTURES

Clean plastic wall sockets and light switches by wiping them with methylated spirit on a clean cloth. Metal fixtures need the appropriate metal polish. Light bulbs should be dusted and cleaned regularly – dirty bulbs can reduce lighting efficiency by up to 50 per cent.

CLEANING FIXTURES

● **Using templates** To avoid getting cleaner or polish on walls when cleaning fixtures, make a template that fits around the fixture, and hold it in place during cleaning.

WARNING
Turn off electricity before cleaning electrical fixtures. Do not clean light bulbs while they are in their sockets.

CLEANING LIGHTS

● **Light bulbs** Before removing a light bulb for cleaning, switch off the electricity. If the light has been on, wait for the bulb to cool down. Dry it thoroughly before replacing. Never use water on a bulb that is still in its socket.
● **Scented bulbs** Wipe a little vanilla extract on the tops of light bulbs with a soft cloth. When you turn on the lights, the scent will be released.

Swivel the bulb in the cloth

Cleaning light bulbs
Hold light bulbs by the base and carefully wipe over with a well-wrung-out, damp cloth.

RADIATORS AND HEATERS

Clean radiators once a week in winter and less often when not in use. Wipe with a washing-up liquid solution, and clean behind them with a vacuum-cleaner attachment or a radiator brush. Wipe heaters with a washing-up liquid solution.

CARE AND UPKEEP

● **Heating and air vents** These attract dust, so keep a sharp eye on them before they become clogged up. A bottle brush is the best way to remove grime as it builds up.
● **Protecting flooring** Place sheeting underneath radiators during cleaning so dust and liquid do not fall on the floor.
● **Marks above radiators** Rising hot air creates dust marks on walls above radiators. Fitting shelves above radiators will help prevent this, and will also direct heat into the room.

CLEANING BEHIND RADIATORS

Vacuum cleaning
Use the crevice tool of your vacuum cleaner to either suck or blow accumulated dust from behind radiators.

Improvised brush
Cover a broom handle with a sponge, then an old sock. Use to clean behind radiators; change the sock when it gets dirty.

FIREPLACES

An open fire is very cheering, but fireplaces will grow dirty with a build up of soot unless you act before the soot becomes ingrained. See page 54 for treatment of soot marks. Clean the fire surround thoroughly each year as soon as the fire-lighting season is over.

CLEARING GRATES

● **Removing ashes** Remove coal ashes weekly, but leave wood ashes in the grate – they will act as a good base for your fire all winter.

METAL PARTS

● **Polishing** To clean the metal on fireplaces, use blacking or a commercial cleaner.

Applying blacking
Wearing gloves, apply blacking on a piece of steel wool. Polish the blacking with a soft cloth.

DAMPENING ASHES

● **Keeping dust down** Put damp tea leaves on to the ashes when you are cleaning out a grate. This will help to stop the dust from rising.

CLEANING SURROUNDS

● **Brick** Scrub well with a hard scrubbing brush and clean water. Sponge burn marks with vinegar, and rinse.
● **Ceramic tile** Wash with a solution of washing-up liquid or household detergent, and rinse. Use a non-abrasive household cleaner on soot marks (see also p. 54).
● **Marble** Sponge with a soapflake solution, then rinse and dry with an old towel. If polished, use a product specially designed for marble. Products are also available for repairing damaged marble; see page 81 for treating stains.

DISPOSING OF ASHES

● **Hot embers** Always use a metal container when carrying ashes to the rubbish bin, as any undetected hot embers will burn through plastic.

TRADITIONAL TIP

Making a scented fire
Throw pieces of dried citrus peel on to a fire to scent a room pleasantly. Pine cones have the same effect.

FURNISHINGS

THE UBIQUITOUS VACUUM CLEANER and its attachments are useful for keeping most furniture and soft furnishings dust free. More specialist cleaning can usually be carried out infrequently, but remove stains when they occur (see p. 32–55).

WOODEN FURNITURE

Well cared for wooden furniture lasts for years, even centuries. Dust wood often, always working along the direction of the grain. Be careful not to wet unsealed wood – it will swell. See pages 71–73 for special treatments for wood and wooden furniture.

DUSTING WOOD

Carved wood
Dust with a synthetic fluffy duster. Rub the duster first to increase static collection. A soft paint brush also works well.

EVERYDAY PIECES
● **Basic care** Clean wooden furniture with a detergent solution applied on a damp cloth. Rinse and buff to a shine. Occasionally, use an aerosol or trigger polish.
● **Teak furniture** Modern teak furniture only needs dusting. Polish these items with teak oil or cream, used sparingly, once or twice a year.
● **Painted wood** Wipe with a solution of washing-up liquid (unless antique or fragile), then rinse with clear water, and dry. Use neat washing-up liquid to remove marks.

VALUABLE PIECES
● **Antique furniture** Keep away from direct heat and sunlight, which cause damage. Dust regularly. Remove sticky marks with a little vinegar and water. Use a beeswax polish on antique furniture once or twice a year (see p. 71).
● **French-polished wood** Buff in the direction of the grain, using a soft duster. Occasionally, use a wax polish, and rub in well. Remove sticky marks and fingerprints with a little white spirit. If the French polish is damaged, call a professional.

OTHER HARD FURNITURE

Wicker and cane furniture require regular dusting with a brush or vacuum-cleaner attachment. Marble and metal furniture require a bit more care. Plastic furniture is easy to keep clean – just wipe with detergent solution occasionally, then rinse with clear water.

MARBLE FURNITURE
● **General care** Marble just needs dusting with a cloth or soft brush. Occasionally, wipe with soapy water, and rinse before buffing the surface. Do not use polish on white marble. See page 81 for removing stains on marble.

WICKER FURNITURE
● **Cleaning** Use a vacuum cleaner in reverse to blow out dust. Scrub wicker furniture occasionally with a nail-brush dipped in washing-up liquid solution. Rinse, and dry.

CANE FURNITURE

Apply salty water with a sponge

Thorough cleaning
Scrub cane furniture from time to time with a soapflake solution. Rinse with salty water to keep the cane stiff.

METAL FURNITURE

Removing rust
Use a stiff wire brush to remove rust on metal furniture. Coat metal furniture that is kept outdoors with rust-proof paint.

SOFT FURNISHINGS

Dust upholstered furniture with the dusting tool attachment of the vacuum cleaner. Feel down the backs and sides of chairs and sofas for items before using the crevice tool to remove dust. See page 82 for advice on caring for leather and making repairs to upholstery.

REGULAR CARE

● **Slip covers** Remove covers when dirty, and wash them according to fabric. While the covers are still damp, put them back on the furniture, and press with a cool iron. Glazed chintz covers can be washed, but the glaze may be removed.
● **Upholstery** Clean this yourself using upholstery shampoo (always follow the manufacturer's instructions), or call in a professional firm. When removing marks, be careful not to overwet.

REMOVING LINT

Using adhesive tape
To remove lint and pet hair from upholstery, wind adhesive tape around your fingers (sticky side out) and brush it over the fabric.

LEATHER AND VINYL

● **Leather care** Dust leather frequently. Apply hide food occasionally. Rub it in well so it does not stain clothes.
● **Dirty leather** Wipe with a damp cloth wrung out in a soapflake solution (take care not to overwet). Do not rinse. Allow to dry naturally, then polish as usual.
● **Vinyl upholstery** Dust and wipe with a damp cloth regularly. Use a soapflake solution to clean dirty vinyl.

CURTAINS AND BLINDS

Expensive curtains and blinds should be dry cleaned by a professional: an expert will measure them before taking them down and ensure that they are returned fitting as well as they did originally. See page 83 for additional tips on caring for curtains.

CURTAINS

● **Washing** Always have lined curtains professionally dry-cleaned, even if they are washable – the different fabrics may shrink at varying rates if you wash them yourself. Wash large curtains in your bath, since they are too heavy for a machine and could cause damage.

General care
Dust curtains frequently, using the upholstery attachment of your vacuum cleaner. Stand on a stepstool to reach the top.

BLINDS

● **Roller blinds** Vacuum with the upholstery attachment or dusting tool. If the blinds are spongeable, wipe them with a solution of washing-up liquid, then rinse with a damp cloth. An application of aerosol blind stiffener will help keep them clean. (It is best to apply this outdoors.)

Venetian blinds
Dust by running hands encased in cotton gloves along the slats. Wash blinds in the bath (keep the roller mechanism dry).

● **Festoon blinds** Vacuum folds regularly. Unfold blinds occasionally, and wash or dry clean according to the fabric.

BRIGHT IDEA

Marking the spot
When removing curtain hooks, mark their spaces with nail varnish. This way you will not have to spend time guessing the correct spacing when replacing the hooks.

BATHROOMS

THESE ROOMS NEED cleaning daily. Encourage members of your household to clean sinks and baths after they have used them. Dirty bathrooms are unattractive and unsanitary. They are also difficult to clean if left dirty.

BATHROOM-CLEANING KIT

Store your bathroom-cleaning kit in the bathroom ready for everyone to use after they have finished. Rinse sponges, cloths, and toilet brushes after each use. If bathroom sponges become slimy from a build up of soap, soak them in white vinegar and water. Flush toilet cleaner away before you use the toilet, otherwise a chemical reaction may cause splashes that will damage the skin.

Sponge

Cloths

Toilet brush

Toilet cleaner

BATHS, SHOWERS, AND SINKS

Washing-up liquid is just as good as a specialist cleaner for cleaning baths, showers, and sinks. Wipe around immediately after use to keep these areas clean. Prevent condensation in bathrooms by running cold water into baths before running the hot water.

ACRYLIC BATHS

Removing scratches
Rub with metal polish. For deep scratches, rub with ultra-fine wet-and-dry sandpaper, then finish off with metal polish.

BATHROOM SINKS
● **Drainholes** Pay special attention to plugholes and overflows. Clean with a bottle brush, and pour a little bleach down them once a week.

OTHER BATH TYPES
● **Enamel and porcelain** Clean with a non-abrasive cleaner – harsh abrasives will dull the bath's surface. Rub stubborn marks with turpentine or white spirit. Rinse with a hot solution of washing-up liquid.
● **Glass-fibre** Treat carefully, as the colour is in the surface coating only. Use washing-up liquid – avoid abrasives, metal polish, and harsh cleaners.

SHOWERS
● **Shower doors** Remove hard-water deposits by wiping with white vinegar. Leave for 30 minutes, then rinse.
● **Shower curtains** These tend to develop mildew, which can be removed by soaking in a bleach solution, rinsing, and hand or machine washing. Remove soap build up by soaking in warm water with a little fabric softener.

STAINS ON BATHS AND SINKS

● **Blue-green marks** These are caused by the minerals in water from dripping taps. Use a vitreous enamel cleaner to clean enamelled surfaces.
● **Rust marks** Remove using a commercial bath-stain remover that contains scale remover.

● **Hard-water marks** Use a vitreous enamel cleaner on enamelled surfaces, and cream cleaner on acrylic surfaces.
● **Tidemarks** Rub heavy marks on enamel and acrylic with white spirit, then rinse with a washing-up liquid solution.

FIXTURES

Clean taps regularly so that dirt does not build up. For chrome taps, remove greasy marks with washing-up liquid, and serious marks with metal polish; restore dulled old chrome with special chrome cleaner for cars. Clean rubber plugs with turpentine.

CLEANING BATHROOM TAPS

● **Removing scale** Where scale builds up on chrome taps, rub well with half a lemon until the scale disappears. Rinse thoroughly, then buff dry.

● **Gold-plated taps** Wipe with a barely damp cloth after each use. Do not rub. Never use metal polish, because it will damage the finish.

SHOWER HEADS

● **Cleaning** Unscrew shower heads from time to time and rinse out hard-water scale. Rub deposits with white vinegar.

Submerge shower head completely

Descaling tap nozzles
Tie a plastic bag or a yoghurt pot containing vinegar or descaler over the tap nozzle. Leave until the scale is dissolved, then rinse.

Cleaning tap bases
Use an old, clean toothbrush dipped in cream cleaner to get rid of the deposit and grime that builds up behind taps.

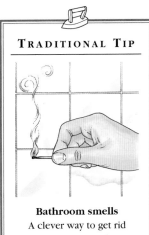

Clogged shower head
Soak in a bowl of warm, neat vinegar or commercial descaler. Use a toothbrush or darning needle to clear blocked holes.

TOILETS

Brush toilets thoroughly each day. Wipe the seat, cistern, and the outside of the bowl weekly, and clean the bowl with a commercial toilet cleaner. Do not regularly use bleach to clean a toilet; if left for any length of time it may cause crazing or cracking in the glaze.

HEAVY-DUTY CLEANING

● **Dirty toilets** Use a toilet brush with a cloth tied firmly over the head to push the water out of the bowl. Bale out the last bit, then clean the bowl thoroughly with bleach. Flush immediately.

● **Damaged surfaces** Treat hard-water deposits with a paste of laundry borax and white vinegar. Leave for a few hours, then rinse. Cracked and crazed bowls harbour germs and should be replaced.

TRADITIONAL TIP

Bathroom smells
A clever way to get rid of a smell in the bathroom is by striking a match. The flame literally burns away noxious gases.

OTHER BATHROOM TIPS

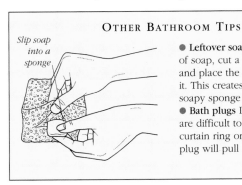
Slip soap into a sponge

● **Leftover soap** To use up ends of soap, cut a slit in a sponge, and place the soap pieces into it. This creates a delightful soapy sponge for the bath.
● **Bath plugs** If rubber plugs are difficult to remove, slip a curtain ring on to the top – the plug will pull out easily.

KITCHENS

Like bathrooms, kitchens need daily cleaning, since dirty food-preparation surfaces or equipment can cause food poisoning. Keep pets away from surfaces where food is prepared – or work strictly on chopping boards.

KITCHEN-CLEANING EQUIPMENT

Keep these items by your kitchen sink. Do not use dirty kitchen-cleaning equipment. Wash steel-wool and scouring pads after each use, and get rid of cleaning cloths when they become worn or dirty. A washing-up brush is more effective than a sponge, and it can be useful for getting into corners of pans and dishes.

Steel-wool pads

Scouring pads

Washing-up brush

Cleaning cloth

Washing-up liquid

SINKS AND SURFACES

Keep sinks and surfaces in the kitchen squeaky clean for sanitary reasons. Clean laminated counter tops with a damp cloth dipped in bicarbonate of soda or cream cleaner. Avoid harsh abrasives and cleaners containing bleaches, which can be poisonous.

PORCELAIN SINKS
● **Easy clean** Fill your sink with hot water and a few drops of household bleach. Wearing a protective glove, pull the plug out, and replace it upside down. The water will drain slowly, giving everything a good cleaning. Rinse well.

STAINLESS-STEEL SINKS
● **Restoring shine** Clean sinks daily with washing-up liquid. Use surgical spirit or white vinegar to remove water spots. Give the sink a good shine by rubbing with soda water or using stainless-steel polish. Rinse thoroughly.

Sparkling white sinks
Place a layer of paper towels across the bottom of the sink, and saturate with diluted household bleach. Leave for five minutes, then remove towels (wearing gloves). Rinse well before use.

Removing limescale
Limescale tends to build up around drainholes in hard-water areas. Rub the deposit vigorously with the cut side of half a lemon. Alternatively, use a commercial scale remover.

KITCHEN SURFACES

● **Kitchen cupboards** Clear out cupboards several times a year, discarding anything that is no longer fresh. Wash the interiors with a mild detergent solution, then rinse. Wipe the base of each item before replacing.
● **Wooden kitchen tables** Scrub unsealed wood tables that are used for meals or food preparation regularly to keep grease and germs at bay. Sealed wood tables just need frequent wiping.

COOKERS

Wipe cooker exteriors over from time to time with a damp cloth. Clean off spills with washing-up liquid or household cleaner.

If you are cooking food that may bubble over in the oven, place the dish on a baking tray; the tray is easier to clean than the oven floor.

CLEANING OVENS

● **Basic care** Keep ovens clean by wiping them out – while still warm – with a damp cloth dipped in bicarbonate of soda. Use abrasive household detergent to remove stains on ovenproof glass, but wait until the glass is completely cold.

● **Dirty ovens** Clean with a commercial oven cleaner (this does not apply to self-cleaning ovens). Clean up any spills on oven floors to prevent them from becoming encrusted.

MICROWAVES

● **Basic cleaning** Wipe out after each use. If the cavity smells, microwave a bowl of water with a little added lemon juice on high for one minute, then wipe out.

COOKER HOBS

● **Cleaning** Wipe hobs after you finish cooking. Where food has burned around burners, cover with a cloth wrung out in washing-up solution. Leave for a couple of hours before cleaning.

Preventing burns
Pouring salt on to food spills that occur during cooking will prevent the spills from burning; this works inside ovens as well.

REMOVABLE PARTS

● **Shelves and grills** Oven shelves can be cleaned in the dishwasher. Or, place dirty shelves and grills in the bath, and soak in a solution of biological detergent and hot water. Use old towels to protect the bath surface.

● **Grill pans** Wash after each use, otherwise the build-up of fat may become a fire hazard.

Lining grill pans
Place foil inside grill pans so that you can simply discard the foil when it becomes dirty, rather than having to wash the pan.

REFRIGERATORS AND FREEZERS

Use bicarbonate of soda and warm water to wipe out the insides of refrigerators and freezers – soap or washing-up liquid will leave

a smell and can taint food. If you need to defrost your freezer, store food in cool boxes, or borrow space in a neighbour's freezer.

CLEANING AND DEFROSTING

An old towel on refrigerator floor will soak up liquid from cleaning or defrosting

If defrosting freezer, place baking tin on floor to catch drips

Use a hairdryer to speed up defrosting – keep it away from plastic

Cleaning refrigerators
Once every few months, remove all the food, switch off the refrigerator, and wipe down all the surfaces. Defrost the freezer at the same time if necessary.

REFRIGERATOR SMELLS

● **Deodorizing refrigerators** Leave a bowl filled with cat litter or charcoal to absorb smells in refrigerators that are going to be left switched off for any length of time.

● **Persistent smells** Wipe all non-metal parts with a capful of baby-bottle sterilizer in 1 litre (35 fl oz) of water to remove persistent smells.

WASHING DISHES

Do it straight away is the golden rule if you wash your dishes by hand (people with dishwashers have a little more leeway). When you cannot wash dishes at once, remember to soak everything you can. Change washing-up water as soon as it starts to look dirty or greasy.

GENERAL TIPS

- **Smells on hands** Immersing hands that smell from food preparation into hot water will set the smell. Prevent this by rubbing vinegar over hands before doing the dishes.
- **Stained china** Remove tea and coffee stains on cups, and cigarette burns on china by rubbing with a damp cloth and bicarbonate of soda.

WASHING-UP SEQUENCE

- **Glassware** Wash first. Rinse glasses used for milk or alcohol in cold water before washing. Place a rubber splash guard on your tap to reduce the risk of glasses being chipped.
- **Cutlery** Wash after glassware. Do not leave items with wood, bone, china, or plastic handles in water for any length of time.
- **Crockery** Wash after cutlery. Scrape or rinse off all food debris. Do not use hot water on egg-, milk-, or starch-based foods, otherwise they will set.
- **Pots and pans** Wash last. Leave to soak while washing other items. Use the methods described opposite to clean burned pots and pans.

WASHING GLASSWARE BY HAND

Preventing cracks
To ensure that glasses do not crack when you place them in hot water, slip them in sideways instead of bottom first. Always be sure to check the water temperature *before* you put on rubber gloves.

Crystal and fine china
Place a towel on the bottom of the sink to act as a cushion when washing crystal and fine china. Alternatively, use a plastic washing-up bowl to prevent items from knocking against the hard surface of the sink.

GREEN TIP

Cut through grease
Add a little vinegar to the rinse water. It cuts through grease and leaves dishes sparkling clean.

DISHWASHERS

These are the ultimate kitchen tools. Always use the recommended type and amount of detergent – too much detergent makes too many suds and prevents the machine from cleaning properly. Check the dishwasher's inlet and outlet hoses periodically for blockages.

BASIC CARE

- **Cleaning** Wipe dishwasher exteriors regularly, and clean the inside with household detergent. Run the dishwasher empty occasionally, using a special interior cleaner.
- **Choosing cycles** Try out all the cycles on a dishwasher; a shorter cycle may clean just as well as a longer one.

WASHING ITEMS

- **Not dishwasher safe** Wash valuable glassware, china and glassware with a metal strip, fine or delicate china, and antique china by hand – never wash them in a dishwasher.
- **Cutlery** Never put stainless steel with silver or silver-plated cutlery – the silver may become pitted or stained.

WASHING PROBLEMS

- **Dishes not clean** If food specks remain on dishes after washing, you may have overloaded the dishwasher, not used enough detergent, or used the wrong cycle.
- **Cloudy glasses** This is the result of hard-water deposits. Use more detergent and – if suitable – rinse aid and salt.

POTS AND PANS

Soaking pots and pans after use makes them easier to clean. Some non-stick surfaces just need to be wiped over with paper towels. To remove persistent smells from a pan, fill the pan with water and 30 ml (2 tbsp) of white vinegar, and bring this mixture to a boil.

ALUMINIUM

Use apple skins only

Removing discolouration
Boil natural acid – try an onion, lemon juice, rhubarb, or apple peel – in discoloured aluminium pans. Do not soak aluminium (or stainless steel) pans for long or leave food in them because they will discolour and pit.

COPPER

Dip lemon in salt to make it mildly abrasive

Removing tarnish
Rub the exteriors of copper pots with the cut side of half a lemon dipped in salt to remove tarnish. Alternatively, fill a spray bottle with vinegar and 45 g (3 tbsp) salt, and spray on to the copper. Let sit, then rub clean.

CAST IRON
● **Cleaning** Dry cast iron thoroughly after washing to prevent rusting. Rub a little oil around the inside to keep it seasoned. Clean the outside with commercial oven cleaner.

BURNED POTS AND PANS
● **Soaking burns** Fill a badly burned pan with a solution of biological detergent. Leave for a couple of hours, then bring to the boil, and remove as much deposit as possible. This treatment may need to be repeated several times before the burn disappears.
● **Thick burns** Allow the burn to dry, pick off as much of the deposit as possible, then use the treatment above.

EQUIPMENT AND APPLIANCES

Take care of your kitchen equipment, and it will last for years. Do not put equipment away with any specks of food still adhering to it. If an item needs serious cleaning to keep it functioning, make time to do it. Wash and dry wooden items immediately after use.

HARD-TO-CLEAN ITEMS

Scrub with washing-up liquid

Cleaning graters
Get debris out of graters and sieves with an old toothbrush. Boil a few old toothbrushes to sterilize them, and keep them in your kitchen-cleaning kit.

SMALL APPLIANCES
● **Blenders** Rinse the jar as soon as you have used it. Pour in a little washing-up liquid and warm water, and blend thoroughly to clean. Repeat with water to rinse.
● **Food processors** These usually have several parts, some of which can be washed in a dishwasher. Check the manufacturer's instructions; some plastic parts should be washed only on the top rack.
● **Coffee makers** Keep the internal parts clean by running neat vinegar through them, as if making coffee. Run clean water through the cycle twice afterwards to rinse away the vinegar and remove the smell.

WOODEN ITEMS

Rub with cut lemon

● **Chopping boards** After chopping foods such as fish or garlic, remove smells by rubbing chopping boards with half a lemon.
● **Rolling pins** Sprinkle with salt, and rub with your hand to loosen particles of pastry. Then wash, rinse, and dry.
● **Wooden bread bins** To stop mildew from developing, wipe bread bins with white vinegar on a cloth. Dry open.

KITCHEN WASTE

Keeping your kitchen free from waste is important for health as well as aesthetics. If waste is left around, particularly in hot weather, smells build up and create further problems. To discard fat, freeze it in an old can, then throw the can in the rubbish bin.

DISPOSAL UNITS

Cleaning and care
Stop electric waste-disposal units from becoming smelly by grinding citrus peel in them. Clear any food debris by pouring a bucket of hot water with a handful of washing soda down them from time to time.

RECYCLING WASTE
● **Plastic containers** Keep plastic margarine and cottage cheese containers – they can be used for freezing food, and come in handy around the house when mixing glue or cleaning paint brushes.
● **Plastic bags** Save and use as bin liners. Always use lunch bags more than once.

Clean foil with a damp cloth

Reusing kitchen foil
Recycle kitchen foil, which is rarely worn out after just one use. Wipe with a damp cloth, or – if it is very dirty – soak it in a hot solution of washing-up liquid. When clean, rinse and smooth out with a cloth.

SINK OUTLETS
● **Weekly clean** Put a capful of washing soda down the plughole once a week, and follow it with a kettleful of boiling water. This keeps the sink clean and removes blockages that have built up.
● **Grease and fat** If you pour fat down the sink by accident, follow it immediately with a kettleful of boiling water. Repeat the treatment until it clears. You can pour used fat down an outdoor drain, but follow it with some washing soda and boiling water.
● **Sink plugs** If your rubber plug tends to come out during washing up, roughen the plug edges with steel wool.

SCENTED KITCHEN

Cinnamon sticks

● **Baking scent** Cook brown sugar and cinnamon on a very low heat on a pan on the stove – this will make your kitchen smell as if you have been baking all day.
● **Simmering cloves** To create a delicious smell around the house and increase humidity, simmer some cloves in water.

DEALING WITH PESTS AND SMELLS

ANT DETERRENTS

● **Ant-free cupboards** Hang sprigs of dried penny royal, rue, or tansy in kitchen cupboards to keep ants away from your foods and dishes.
● **Keeping ants out** If you know where ants are coming in, sprinkle dried mint, chilli powder, or laundry borax across their trail. Plant mint near windows and doors.

● **Ants' nests** Mix together one part laundry borax with one part icing sugar. Scatter the mixture over a piece of wood near the site of the nest. The ants will be attracted by the sweet sugar and will then be poisoned by the laundry borax.

OTHER PESTS
● **Cockroaches** Leave a mixture of equal parts of flour, cocoa powder, and laundry borax; or a mixture of equal parts of bicarbonate of soda and icing sugar in shallow dishes. Keep away from children and pets.

FOOD SMELLS
● **Burned food** Boil a few slices of lemon in a saucepan to clear the air of burned food smells.
● **Fried food** Place a small bowl of white vinegar next to the stove when you are frying foods, since this helps clear the air of unpleasant fat smells.

CLEANING CHECKLIST

THIS CHART CONTAINS brief guidelines for cleaning the different surfaces found in the home. For more detailed instructions on caring for various household items and surfaces, and undertaking minor repairs, see pages 70–87.

SURFACE	BASIC CLEANING METHOD	SPECIAL NOTES
TILES	Wipe with household detergent, and rinse to remove residual traces. Clean dirty grouting with a household bleach solution.	Remove soap splashes with a solution of one part white vinegar to four parts water. Rinse.
BRICK	Scrub with a solution of washing-up liquid, taking care not to overwet since bricks are porous. Rinse, and dry.	Sponge burn marks with vinegar, and rinse. See p. 54 for removing soot marks from brick.
CONCRETE	Dissolve a cup of washing soda in a bucket of warm water, and wash. Sweep concrete floors regularly.	See p. 158 for removing oil stains from concrete garage floors.
LEATHER	Wipe with a damp cloth rubbed on a bar of glycerine soap. Apply a thin coat of hide food occasionally.	See p. 23 and 82 for cleaning and caring for leather furniture.
GLASS	Use a window-cleaning product on glass surfaces. Do not get it on carpets; it will stain.	Try to avoid touching glass, as it shows fingerprints. Use vinegar to remove greasy marks on glass.
MARBLE	Sponge with a soapflake solution, and rinse. Use specialist products for any further treatments needed.	See p. 22 for caring for marble furniture, and p. 81 for removing unsightly stains on marble.
SLATE	Clean with a washing-up liquid solution. Rinse with a damp cloth, then buff to a shine.	Use marble polish on smooth slate. Scrub textured slate with a brush and washing-up liquid solution.
PLASTIC	Wipe over with washing-up liquid. Use an aerosol cleaner to protect plastic from dust.	Soak smelly plastic containers overnight in a bicarbonate of soda and warm water solution.
STAINLESS STEEL	Wash and dry immediately after use. Polish occasionally. See p. 26 and 76 for additional care advice.	Tends to discolour and pit, so immerse it in water for as short a time as possible.
SILVER	Polish regularly. If stored, keep items in tarnish-proof paper or bags. See also p. 74–75.	Never mix silver and stainless steel in a dishwasher's cutlery basket. Egg will stain silver cutlery.
WOOD	Dust, sweep, and mop regularly, and polish only occasionally. Do not wet unsealed wood.	See p. 14–16 for wood floors, p. 22 for wooden furniture, and p. 71–73 for caring for wood.

STAIN REMOVAL

QUICK REFERENCE

Tackling Stains, p. 34

Food Stains, p. 36

Spilled Beverages, p. 39

Biological Stains, p. 42

Pigment Stains, p. 46

Product Stains, p. 49

Wear and Tear, p. 52

Other Stains, p. 55

THE SECRET OF REMOVING STAINS is to treat them at once – or as soon as possible after they occur. Stains that are left to soak in and dry are more difficult to remove and may, in some cases, be impossible to get out. Keep a kit with stain-removal equipment, cleaners, and solvents handy, so you can act quickly when accidents happen. Here you will find essential information on stain-removal equipment and methods, as well as specific treatments for the most common stains.

STAIN-REMOVAL EQUIPMENT

These are the items that you will need for your stain-removal kit. Together with the cleaners and solvents on the opposite page, they will enable you to tackle stains effectively. Keep your kit in a separate box, and replace items as necessary.

● **To absorb grease** Use brown or blotting paper, together with an iron, to remove grease.
● **To blot stains** Use anything that is disposable, such as paper towels. Never use anything with its own dye.
● **To apply solvents** Use cotton wool or a white cloth. Never use coloured cloth, which may transfer dye to stained items.
● **To dilute stains** Use a sponge to apply clean water to stains, or use a soda syphon, which will flush stains out of carpets.
● **To scrape up deposits** Use an old spoon or a metal ruler to lift off stain deposits.
● **For protective covering** Rubber gloves protect your hands when you use harsh cleaners or toxic solvents. Always wear gloves when using ammonia and bleach.

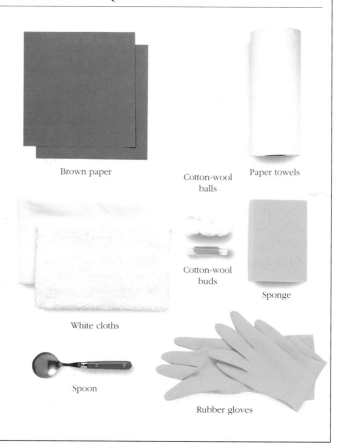

Brown paper

Cotton-wool balls

Paper towels

Cotton-wool buds

Sponge

White cloths

Spoon

Rubber gloves

CLEANERS AND SOLVENTS

The cleaners and solvents shown here will remove most household stains. Keep the items that you use most in your stain-removal kit. Ammonia, methylated spirit, rubbing alcohol, laundry borax, hydrogen peroxide, white spirit, and acetone are toxic. Lemon, eucalyptus oil, glycerine, and vinegar are all natural stain remedies. Carpet shampoo, biological detergent, and talcum powder are helpful for treating stains on carpets, clothes, and furniture respectively.

DILUTION FORMULAS
● **Ammonia** Add 5 ml (1 tsp) to 500 ml (1 pint) of cold water.
● **Laundry borax** Add 15 g (1 tbsp) to 500 ml (1 pint) of warm water.
● **Hydrogen peroxide** Dilute one part to six parts cold water.
● **Glycerine** Dilute with equal parts warm water.

Methylated spirit

Rubbing alcohol

Carpet shampoo

Ammonia

Laundry borax

Biological washing powder

Talcum powder

Lemon

Eucalyptus oil

Hydrogen peroxide

Glycerine

White spirit

Washing-up liquid

Acetone

White vinegar

COMMERCIAL CLEANERS

Specialist laundry products (for example pre-wash sticks and sprays), proprietary stain removers, and stain solvents are ideal for removing marks on fabric and carpets. You can also buy grease solvents for grease and oil marks, and commercial upholstery- and carpet-spotting kits, which contain small bottles of different chemicals that you mix together to treat stains.

Pre-wash stick

Foam stain remover

Aerosol stain remover

Pre-wash spray

Stain solvents

TACKLING STAINS

TREAT STAINS AT ONCE, but test the method on a hidden part of the item first. To avoid spreading a stain, dab at it instead of rubbing it, and always work from the outside to the centre. Never use hot water, which will set stains.

TYPES OF STAIN

Stains can be divided into two main types: built-up stains and absorbed stains. Some substances, such as blood and egg, produce a stain that is a combination of the two. Always treat these "combination stains" as built-up stains first, then treat them for absorption.

BUILT-UP STAINS

Removing deposits
Built-up stains are made by thick substances that need to be scraped off before treatment. Scoop them up quickly so that they do not penetrate far.

ABSORBED STAINS

Blotting up liquid
Thin liquids will sink quickly into a surface. Blot the area with paper towels or a white cloth immediately. Launder or sponge to remove the rest of the stain.

OTHER STAINS

● **Mystery stains** If you do not know the cause of a stain, proceed with caution. Soak washable items, then launder them according to fabric. Sponge non-washables with clear, warm water. If staining persists, apply a hydrogen peroxide solution (see p. 33).
● **Dried stains** To loosen dried stains, use a glycerine solution (see p. 33). Sponge off this initial treatment before using another chemical that may react with the glycerine.

DIFFERENT SURFACES

Stains should be treated not only according to type, but also according to the surface on which they fall. The three methods below outline the basic treatments that can be used for stains on carpets, stains on non-washable fabrics or upholstery, and stains on clothes.

CARPETS

Apply shampoo on a sponge

Shampooing carpets
After removing any deposit, treat the remaining mark with a solution of carpet shampoo. If this leaves a startlingly clean spot, you will need to shampoo the entire carpet using either a manual or an electric machine.

UPHOLSTERY

Absorbing stains
Scrape up any deposit, and blot the stain well. Apply talcum powder, and leave until it appears discoloured, having absorbed the stain. Wipe away with a cloth. Apply more talcum powder if the mark persists.

CLOTHES

Dab mark, rather than rubbing it

Dabbing away stains
Treat stains on washable clothes as soon as they occur, and always before you launder the item. Use lukewarm or cold water and a cloth to dab the mark. Alternatively, soak the garment if recommended.

STAINS ON WASHABLE FABRICS

Laundering a stained garment can set the stain, making it very difficult to remove. Always treat stains before laundering, using one of the three methods below. Observe the guidelines for different fabrics, and invest in any laundry aids you think might be useful.

GENERAL TREATMENT

Rinsing off stains
Rinse stains in cold or lukewarm water as soon as possible after they occur. Alternatively, sponge with clear water until the stain fades. Never use hot water on stains; it will cause them to set.

PROTEIN STAINS

Soaking items
Stains made from substances such as milk and blood respond best to soaking in biological detergent. Do not soak items for longer than recommended; always immerse the whole item.

PERSISTENT STAINS

Applying a solvent
If stains persist after rinsing or soaking, use a stain or grease solvent before laundering. Place a white cloth under the stain to avoid transferring the stain to another layer, then dab.

LAUNDRY AIDS

● **Detergents** These come in varying strengths, and many contain additives to remove stains. Some stains require extra treatment with one of the substances below.
● **Biological detergent** This works well on stains that contain proteins, such as egg yolk, blood, and sweat. It is often a constituent of ordinary detergents, but is best used separately for stain removal.
● **Bleach** This has a whitening effect, so it should be used with care on coloureds. Avoid contact with your skin and clothes. (See also p. 58.)
● **Laundry borax** This rather old-fashioned laundry aid is an excellent stain remover. Dilute for sponging or soaking (see p. 33), or sprinkle directly on to stains (see p. 41).
● **Other aids** Stain solvents and pre-wash sticks and sprays help remove marks on clothes (see p. 33). Soapflakes are the best treatment for ink stains.

FABRICS	TREATMENT NOTES
COLOUREDS	Treat stains with care to avoid producing bleached patches. Soak the whole item when using a bleaching treatment such as laundry borax.
WHITES	Natural fabrics can usually be bleached. Synthetics and mixtures can yellow with this treatment and may respond better to the correct detergent.
NATURAL FABRICS	Because these can be washed at high temperatures, rinsing or pre-soaking items before laundering is usually enough to remove most stains.
SYNTHETIC FABRICS	These are easily damaged by some chemicals, so test any treatment on a hidden part before tackling the stain.
DELICATES	These fabrics should always be treated cautiously. Avoid using strong chemical treatments on delicate fabrics.

FOOD STAINS

Most food stains can be removed using the basic methods shown on pages 34–35, provided you act quickly. The worst culprits are those featured here – stains from greasy foods, egg, and foods containing strong colourings.

OIL, FAT, AND GREASE STAINS

Grease stains are straightforward to remove from fabric, but they may cause more of a problem on carpets and furniture. Ties and scarves are susceptible to grease spots; spray non-washable items when new or newly dry cleaned with a fabric-protection spray.

ON CARPETS

1 Place a piece of brown paper over the grease mark. Apply the tip of a warm iron until the grease is absorbed into the brown paper.

2 Apply a solution of carpet shampoo to the remaining mark, using a sponge. Rub into the carpet gently but firmly for a few minutes.

3 Wipe off the foam with a clean sponge or cloth. Inspect the mark; if it remains or reappears later, repeat the treatment from the beginning.

ON FURNITURE

Cover stain with talcum powder

Brush off talcum powder with dry, fluffy cloth

1 Sprinkle talcum powder thickly over the grease mark, and leave until the grease begins to be absorbed.

2 After 10 minutes, brush off the talcum powder. If the mark still appears to be greasy, repeat the treatment.

ON CLOTHES

● **General treatment** Blot excess grease, using paper towels. Dab gently, taking care not to spread the stain. For non-delicate fabrics, which can be washed at reasonably high temperatures, laundering will remove residual marks.

● **Delicate fabrics** Dab delicate fabrics with a little eucalyptus oil, then either hand wash them, or machine wash at a low temperature. If the item is dry clean only, sponge with clear, warm water – this will help to get rid of any smell.

GREASE ON SHOES

Repair adhesive

● **Leather shoes** Apply a little bicycle puncture repair adhesive to grease spots. Leave overnight, then peel off. Use shoe polish or hide food to finish off. Well-cleaned leather shoes will resist grease – just wipe over with a paper towel

● **Suede shoes** Blot well, then rub with a block suede cleaner. Treat bad stains with a pad of white cotton wool dampened with lighter fuel. Check first on a test area to make sure that the colour is not adversely affected.

OTHER GREASY STAINS

Foods such as avocado, peanut butter, and those listed below contain oil or fat, and may leave behind a grease patch. Tackle the grease stain before dealing with any remaining colour. Substances such as car oil, ointments, and lotions should also be treated as grease.

MAYONNAISE
● **On washable fabrics** Sponge with warm water, then soak in a solution of biological detergent before laundering.
● **On non-washable fabrics** Wipe with a damp cloth, then use an aerosol grease solvent.

ICE CREAM
● **On washable fabrics** Wipe with a damp cloth, then soak in a detergent solution.
● **On non-washable fabrics** Blot, then wipe with a damp cloth wrung out of warm water. Use a grease solvent.

GRAVY
● **On washable fabrics** Soak overnight in tepid water, then launder according to the fabric. Soak dried marks in biological detergent if the fabric permits.
● **On non-washable fabrics** Use an aerosol stain remover.

Mayonnaise on carpets
Scrape up as much as possible, then blot. Use a general stain remover for light marks, and the carpet treatment, opposite, to remove heavier stains.

Ice cream on carpets
Scrape up the deposit, and wipe the area with a damp cloth. Clean with a solution of carpet shampoo. Use a stain remover or grease solvent if marks remain.

Gravy on carpets
Scoop up what you can with a spoon, or blot the area dry with paper towels. Treat with a liquid stain remover followed by an application of carpet shampoo.

EGG STAINS

Egg is a tricky stain. The merest drop of hot water causes it to set and form a crusty deposit that is much harder to remove than a fresh stain. If you cannot treat an egg stain immediately, cover it with a damp cloth to keep it moist and prevent it from setting.

ON FURNITURE

Wipe spills as soon as they occur

Remove the deposit
Use a damp white cloth to remove the spilled egg. If only egg white has been spilled, or you manage to clear the yolk, sponge with cold, salty water. For yolk alone, dab with lather from a washing-up solution.

ON CARPETS
● **Basic treatment** Scrape up the deposit, then use a liquid stain remover to tackle what remains. If a mark is still visible when dry, apply a carpet-shampoo solution.

ON CLOTHES
● **Washable fabric** Sponge with cold, salty water. Rinse off when it looks as if the stain has disappeared. Soak in a biological detergent solution if necessary (and appropriate).
● **Non-washable fabric** Sponge with salt water, then sponge off with clear water, and blot dry. Use an aerosol stain remover on remaining marks.

TRADITIONAL TIP

Stains on cutlery
Egg, especially boiled egg, stains cutlery black. Wipe fresh egg off cutlery after use. Rub black stains with salt, applied on a damp cloth.

COLOURED FOOD STAINS

Colour is the last thing you treat when dealing with a food stain. Get rid of the deposit first, then treat any grease element. Finally tackle the colour, which may require several attempts. Specific treatments for well-known "difficult" food stains appear below.

FOOD TYPE	ON WASHABLE FABRICS	ON OTHER SURFACES
TOMATO SAUCE Treat tomato sauce and other thick, bottled sauces in the same way.	Hold fresh stains under cold, running water, and rub between your fingers. Apply a pre-wash treatment, then launder according to fabric.	On carpets, remove deposit, and sponge with warm water. Blot dry, apply carpet shampoo, and wipe off. When dry, use a spray stain remover. Follow these steps for non-washable fabrics, omitting the shampoo.
MUSTARD Mustard powder can be brushed off. Ready-mixed mustard produces a stain that is difficult to remove.	Rub fresh stains between your fingers in a mild detergent solution, then sponge with an ammonia solution (see p. 33). Soften dried stains with a glycerine solution (see p. 33), and leave for at least an hour.	Sponge carpets and furniture with a mild detergent solution, then an ammonia solution (see p. 33). Avoid overwetting, and finish by sponging with clean water. Stubborn stains require professional cleaning.
JAM AND PRESERVES These leave sticky residues that should be scooped up and wiped with a damp cloth.	Laundering should remove stains. Soak dried marks for half an hour in a laundry borax solution (see p. 33).	Sponge furniture with a warm washing-up liquid solution. Sprinkle laundry borax on the mark, and sponge off after 15 minutes. On carpets, use carpet shampoo, then methylated spirit on remaining marks.
CURRY AND TURMERIC These are two of the worst stains. Do not get them on wall coverings, where the only solution is a patch.	Rinse stains in tepid water. Rub in a glycerine solution (see p. 33), leave for half an hour, and rinse. Launder in biological detergent, if suitable. Use a hydrogen peroxide solution (see p. 33) on persistent stains.	Sponge carpets and furniture with a laundry borax solution (see p. 33). If this does not work on furniture, have the covers dry cleaned (if possible). A laundry pre-wash stick may also be effective on carpets.
BEETROOT This stain is difficult to remove because the colour is deep and persistent.	Rinse under cold, running water until as much colour as possible has come out. Soak coloured fabrics in a laundry borax solution (see p. 33). For whites, use the treatment for dried tea stains shown on p. 41.	Do not attempt to remove stains on non-washable fabrics or furniture yourself. Have both slip covers and upholstery professionally cleaned.
CHOCOLATE Dropped pieces of chocolate are a problem once they get warm or if someone sits on them.	Allow to set, then scrape the dry deposit with a blunt knife. Soak, then launder in biological detergent if suitable; otherwise launder as usual. For persistent stains, use the treatment for dried tea stains shown on p. 41.	Allow to set, then scrape up with a blunt knife. Apply a lather of carpet shampoo (for both furniture and carpets), rubbing in gently. Wipe off with a damp cloth, and use a liquid stain remover when dry.

SPILLED BEVERAGES

BLOTTING IS THE GOLDEN RULE for removing stains caused by spilled drinks. Always use a white cloth, tissues, or paper towels. Never use coloured paper towels, which may bleed dye into the stain and make matters worse.

RED-WINE STAINS

Red wine is one of the most common carpet stains. Salt is effective for preventing stains on table linen from spreading, but on carpets it creates a permanent damp patch that attracts dirt to the area. Use the three-step treatment below or, as an alternative, use white wine.

ON CARPETS

1 Blot the spill immediately, then sponge repeatedly with warm water. If you have a soda syphon, use this to flush the stain – the soda water plus the spraying action will shift the stain effectively.

2 Blot dry, then apply the foam from some made-up carpet shampoo on a sponge, working it in well. Sponge again with clear water, and repeat the treatment as often as necessary until clear.

3 Cover any remaining stain with a glycerine solution (see p. 33), and leave for up to an hour. Sponge off with clear water, and blot well. Apply a little methylated spirit on a sponge to reduce old stains. Use the method as right for a quick rescue when you cannot treat stains properly.

DRIED STAINS ON FURNITURE

1 Apply a glycerine solution (see p. 33) to loosen the stain. Leave the solution on for at least 30 minutes.

2 Sponge off with a weak, warm solution of washing-up liquid. Wipe with a cloth wrung out in clear water.

FRESH STAINS ON FURNITURE

1 Blot, sponge with warm water, and blot again. Repeat if necessary. Cover persistent marks with talcum powder while still damp.

2 Brush the talcum powder off after a few minutes, using a soft brush or cloth. Continue the treatment until the mark disappears.

QUICK ACTION

Pour white wine on to red-wine spill immediately

Pour some white wine over a red-wine spill as soon as it occurs. Blot both liquids well, sponge with clear, warm water, then pat the area dry.

ON CLOTHES

● **General treatment** Rinse fresh wine stains in warm water. If the stain persists, soak the garment in a laundry borax solution (see p. 33) or a heavy-duty detergent, then launder according to fabric type.

● **Delicate fabrics** Bleach stains on white wool or silk with a hydrogen peroxide solution (see p. 33). Rinse, then hand wash.

ON TABLE LINEN

● **Fresh stains** Bleach white cotton and linen items. Soak coloured items in a heavy-duty detergent solution, then launder as usual. Alternatively, use the treatment for dried tea stains shown on page 41.

BEER AND SPIRITS STAINS

Beer and spirits stains are fairly easy to remove from most surfaces (unless they are highly coloured or sticky liqueur stains). Old beer and spirits stains are another matter, however, and require more drastic treatment if they are to come out satisfactorily.

ON CLOTHES
● **Beer and spirits** Rinse or soak in tepid water, then launder according to fabric type. On whites, use a hydrogen peroxide solution (see p. 33) to bleach any remaining marks. On coloureds, sponge with a white vinegar solution – 30 ml (2 tbsp) vinegar to 500 ml (1 pint) water.

ON FURNITURE
● **Beer** Blot thoroughly, then sponge with a cloth wrung out in clean, warm water. Treat remaining marks with an aerosol stain remover.
● **Spirits** Sponge with clean, warm water until all traces of stickiness are removed, then use an upholstery-spotting kit. Have delicate fabrics that might watermark professionally dry cleaned.

ON CARPETS
● **Beer** Sponge with clean, warm water, or flush with a soda syphon, then blot. If marks remain, use a solution of carpet shampoo.
● **Spirits** Use the treatment above, acting quickly to prevent colour from soaking in. If coloured marks remain, sponge with methylated spirit applied on a damp cloth.

Old beer stains
Gently wipe old beer stains on carpets with methylated spirit until the mark begins to fade.

LIQUEUR STAINS

These tend to be stickier than other spilled alcohol drinks. If any stains from highly coloured liqueurs remain after treatment, use a stain remover or methylated spirit on the mark, testing first on an inconspicuous area.

● **Carpets** Flush stain with a soda syphon to dissipate stickiness, and blot the residue with paper towels. Apply carpet shampoo.
● **Upholstery** Sponge with warm water until all traces of stickiness are gone. Take care not to overwet. Apply carpet shampoo; use an upholstery-spotting kit on any remaining marks. Professionally dry clean any loose covers that might watermark.
● **Clothes** Rinse the mark in warm water, then wash or dry clean the item as usual.

FRUIT-JUICE STAINS

Fruit juices cause problem stains because of the colour residue they leave – especially dark-coloured fruits such as red berries and blackcurrants. If they are allowed to dry they can be difficult to remove and – unless treated carefully – will leave a permanent mark.

FRESH STAINS
● **Clothes** Rinse under cold, running water until as much of the mark as possible is removed. Treat any remaining colour with methylated spirit or a stain remover.
● **Carpets** Blot with paper towels. Rub the area with a laundry pre-wash stick, and leave for a few minutes. Rinse off, blot dry, and shampoo. Treat any remaining colour with methylated spirit.
● **Furniture** Sponge with cold water, and blot dry. Use a liquid stain remover.

DRIED STAINS
Loosen stain with glycerine solution

Treating old stains
Hold a clean cloth under the stain and apply a glycerine solution (see p. 33) with a second cloth. Leave for one hour, rinse, then treat as for fresh stains (see left).

GREEN TIP

Nature's stain remover
Rub the cut side of half a lemon on fresh fruit-juice stains - lemon juice is a natural bleaching agent.

TEA, COFFEE, AND COCOA STAINS

These stains tend to be a combination of the colouring of the drink and grease from any added milk. Blot the whole stain initially, then attack the grease, and finally use a method that will get rid of the colour. Dried tea stains on fabric require special treatment.

ON FABRIC

● **Fresh tea stains** Rinse stains on clothes in lukewarm water, then soak in a laundry borax solution (see p. 33). Rinse stains on blankets at once in warm water, then launder. Rinse table linen immediately under a cold tap, then soak and launder, preferably in a biological detergent.
● **Coffee and cocoa** Rinse in warm water. Soak in a warm biological detergent solution (if suitable), or in a laundry borax solution (see p. 33).

ISOLATING A STAIN

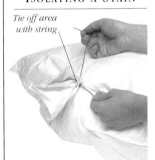

Tie off area with string

On a duvet or pillow, push the filling down and tie off the stained area, then wash it. This way you do not have to wash the entire item.

DRIED TEA STAINS

If treating linen or cotton, water should be boiling

1 Drape the stained item over a bowl or basin. Sprinkle with laundry borax until the whole stain is thickly covered.

2 Pour a kettleful of hot water around the stain, working towards the centre. Repeat treatment if necessary.

ON CARPETS

● **White coffee and cocoa** Sponge with tepid water, or flush with a soda syphon. Apply a little carpet shampoo, and – when dry – use a liquid stain remover (but not on foam-backed carpets).
● **Black coffee** Sponge the stain repeatedly with tepid water, or flush it several times with a soda syphon, then blot.
● **Tea** Blot with paper towels, then sponge with tepid water, or apply a squirt from a soda syphon. Use a little carpet shampoo, and use an aerosol stain remover when dry.

ON FURNITURE

● **White coffee and cocoa** Blot the stain with paper towels, then sprinkle with biological detergent. Wipe off with a damp sponge.
● **Black coffee** Blot, sponge and, if necessary, shampoo. Lubricate dried stains with a glycerine solution (see p. 33). Rinse, and blot well. Use an aerosol stain remover on any remaining marks.
● **Tea** Sponge with a laundry borax solution (see p. 33), then wipe with a damp cloth. When dry, use an aerosol stain remover.

MILK STAINS

If milk is not treated immediately after it is spilled on carpet, it will dry and leave a smell that is virtually impossible to remove. Move fast with the treatment, or you could find yourself having to replace an expensive item because of the permanent smell.

ON CLOTHES

● **Fresh stains** Rinse in tepid water, then launder as usual. Use a liquid stain remover if a grease mark persists.
● **Dried stains** Soak the item in biological detergent if the fabric is suitable.

ON FURNITURE

● **General treatment** Sponge with tepid water (but do not overwet padded upholstery). Blot dry with paper towels or a white cloth. Treat any remaining marks with an aerosol stain remover.

ON CARPETS

● **Fresh stains** Sponge with clear, warm water, then apply an aerosol cleaner.
● **Dried stains** If a stain is allowed to dry, the smell may return after cleaning. Use a professional carpet cleaner.

BIOLOGICAL STAINS

REAT BIOLOGICAL STAINS IMMEDIATELY, since they can be difficult to remove if they are allowed to set. Also, they invariably carry unpleasant smells, which tend to linger if the stain is not cleaned up as quickly as possible.

BLOOD STAINS

Blood is a combination stain that soaks into surfaces and leaves a deposit on the top. The deposit is not as thick as some biological stains and therefore cannot be scraped off, but it should be wiped or brushed off immediately. After that, treat the coloured stain.

ON CLOTHES

Fill bucket with cold water

Add a generous handful of salt

1 Add a handful of salt to a bucket of cold water. Soak the stained item of clothing for 15 minutes, making sure it is completely immersed.

2 Soak the item in biological detergent next (if suitable), then launder as usual.

ON MATTRESSES

1 Follow the three steps in the box below. Next, apply a thick paste made up of bicarbonate of soda and water to any stains that remain.

2 Leave the paste to dry, then brush it off with a dry cloth. Repeat if necessary.

ON CARPETS

● **General Treatment** Sponge the area with cold water, and blot dry. Repeat until the stain disappears. If this does not work, use a carpet-spotting kit, followed by an application of carpet shampoo.

DRIED BLOOD STAINS

● **On clothes** Soak in a hydrogen peroxide solution (see p. 33) with 2.5 ml (½ tsp) added ammonia. (Do not use on nylon.)
● **On carpets** Use a glycerine solution (see p. 33), then treat as for fresh stains.
● **On untreated wood** Bleach stains with diluted household bleach, then recolour the wood to its original shade.

REMOVING STAINS FROM MATTRESSES

1 Turn the mattress on its side (this may take two people). Prop it up to prevent the stain and treatment from soaking in.

2 Position a towel directly beneath the stain. Always wear rubber gloves when treating biological stains.

3 Sponge the mark, repeating until it disappears. Hold the towel in place beneath the stain so that nothing trickles down.

URINE STAINS

Urine is an unpleasant stain that can leave a permanent mark and smell if it is not treated properly immediately. However, correct treatment is usually successful, so if your household is prone to this type of accident, keep the remedy to hand.

ON LEATHER SHOES
● **Fresh stains** Wipe polished shoes with a cloth wrung out of warm water. When dry, buff shoes well, then polish.

● **Dried stains** Wipe with a damp cloth to bring salts to the surface. Apply a product designed to remove salt stains.

ON SUEDE SHOES

Removing marks
Wipe gently with a damp cloth. Brush the damp area with a suede brush. On dry marks, use a salt stain remover. Brush with a suede brush between applications.

Wipe with a cloth wrung out in warm water

GREEN TIP

Neutralize urine smells
Using a plant-spray bottle, squirt a solution of one part vinegar to five parts water on to pet stains on carpets to help remove the smell.

ON CARPETS
● **Fresh stains** Use a carpet cleaner containing deodorant. Alternatively, sponge with cold water, pat dry, then rinse with a little antiseptic added to a bowl of cold water.
● **Dried stains** Treat as for fresh stains to remove the smell and the mark. Raise any faded colour by sponging with a mild ammonia solution.

ON CLOTHES
● **Coloured fabrics** Rinse in cold water, then launder according to fabric type.
● **Pale fabrics** Bleach dried urine stains with a hydrogen peroxide solution (see p. 33), to which a few drops of ammonia have been added. Alternatively, soak the item in biological detergent, or use a proprietary stain remover.

DRYING MATTRESSES

Clean urine off mattresses using the method opposite. Stand the mattress on its side, then prop it leaning slightly forwards so no liquid soaks in further. Speed up drying with a hairdryer on a cool setting.

VOMIT STAINS

With vomit, it is vital to get rid of all the deposit before tackling the underlying stain. Use the bowl of a spoon to lift off as much as possible, and use a metal ruler to scrape up the final traces. Take care not to spread the stain. Wear rubber gloves.

ON CARPETS
● **Removing stains** Sponge with laundry borax solution (see p. 33), then with clear, warm water that includes a few drops of antiseptic. If any discolouration remains, work in the lather from some carpet shampoo with a sponge, or use an aerosol foam cleanser.
● **Removing smells** If the smell persists, continue rinsing with clear water and antiseptic until it disappears.

ON FURNITURE
● **Upholstery** Sponge the area with warm water containing a little ammonia, then pat dry. Or, use an upholstery cleaner that contains a deodorizer. Clean expensive or delicate items professionally.
● **Mattresses** Remove stains by following the method shown opposite. Sponge with a warm solution of washing-up liquid. Sponge off with warm water that contains a little antiseptic.

ON CLOTHES
● **Removing stains** Rinse the area under cold, running water until the mark begins to fade, rubbing the fabric gently between your hands to help the process. Soak, then launder in biological detergent if the fabric is suitable. Alternatively, launder the garment as usual according to fabric type.
● **Removing smells** If the smell persists after laundering, launder the item again.

MUD STAINS

The key to removing any mud stain is to let it dry completely before tackling it. Do not be tempted to apply any treatment whatsoever until the deposit has become hard and you can brush it off easily. After that, you can tackle the stain that has been left behind.

ON CARPETS
● **Persistent marks** Use either a carpet-spotting kit or a little methylated spirit to remove traces of colour that remain after removing the deposit.

ON FURNITURE
● **Basic treatment** Remove the deposit, then sponge the area with a weak, warm solution of washing-up liquid or mild detergent. Wipe, then pat dry.

ON CLOTHES
● **Coats and jackets** Remove dry mud with a soft brush. Apply a proprietary dry-cleaning product to any stains that do not brush off.

REMOVING DRIED MUD DEPOSITS

Brush mud off with a dry cloth

Vacuuming carpets
Leave the mud to dry (this usually takes one or two hours), then vacuum up the deposit. If necessary, use a stiff brush to loosen the dried mud first.

Brushing furniture
Use a soft brush to clear mud deposits on furniture without damaging the upholstery. Remove any remaining traces with a vacuum cleaner.

Wiping clothes
Brush dried mud off clothes with a dry cloth or a soft clothes brush. Launder to remove the remaining marks. Use methylated spirit on persistent mud stains.

GRASS STAINS

Grass stains are inevitable if your household includes any games enthusiasts or small children. They are quite tricky to remove and may take some time and trouble. As a rule, soak white cottons in bleach; a proprietary stain remover will deal with other fabrics.

ON WASHABLE FABRICS
● **Light stains** Provided the fabric is suitable, these stains should respond to a soak followed by laundering in biological detergent. If marks remain, follow the treatment for non-washable fabrics.
● **Heavy stains** Rub the stain with a heavy-duty hand cleaner – the kind used after serious do-it-yourself jobs. Apply a little methylated spirit or a commercial stain remover to the area (testing first), then rinse in cool, clean water before washing the garment according to fabric type.

ON NON-WASHABLES
● **White flannel** This fabric usually requires professional dry cleaning. Between visits to the cleaner, rub a mixture of equal parts of cream of tartar and table salt into the stains. Leave for half an hour, then brush the mixture off.
● **Canvas shoes** Scrub grass stains with a nail-brush dipped in a solution of washing-up liquid and warm water. Wash the shoes in the washing machine, or on the top rack of the dishwasher (making sure all grit is removed first). Allow the shoes to dry naturally.

TRADITIONAL TIP

Treating old stains
Use egg white and glycerine in equal parts to loosen old grass stains on whites, then treat as for fresh stains.

OTHER BIOLOGICAL STAINS

Combat these stains on clothes by soaking in biological detergent (if the fabric is suitable). Buy some disposable plastic gloves, or use a plastic bag over your hand when dealing with unpleasant deposits. Discard the bag or gloves after you have used them.

STAIN	SURFACE	TREATMENT
POLLEN STAINS	● These stains occur mainly on clothes and wall coverings, and can be very difficult to remove. Wear an apron when picking or arranging flowers, and keep floral arrangements well away from wallpapered walls.	● Normal laundering will remove light stains on clothes. Failing this, dab lightly with methylated spirit, then sponge off with warm water. ● Rub stains on wallpaper with a ball of white, crustless bread or a rubber. If this treatment fails, the wallpaper may need patching (see p. 18).
FLY SPECKS	● These tend to occur on lampshades, furnishings, and windows. Treat fabric lampshades with care.	● Wipe plastic lampshades with a washing-up liquid solution. Use an aerosol stain remover on fabric lampshades, or apply a warm detergent solution with a soft toothbrush, rubbing gently. ● Use methylated spirit on windows, and a proprietary stain remover on upholstery.
PERSPIRATION STAINS	● This appears as a yellowish or discoloured patch in the armpit area of clothes.	● Sponge washable fabrics with an ammonia solution (see p. 33), then rinse. Where dye has run, sponge with 15 ml (1 tbsp) white vinegar diluted in 250 ml (½ pint) water.
PET STAINS	● These are urine, vomit, and faecal stains that occur mainly on carpets and furniture.	● See p. 43 for treating urine and vomit stains and for getting rid of unpleasant smells. See below for treating faeces.
FAECAL STAINS	● Always scrape up the deposit from carpets, furniture, and clothes with the bowl of a spoon immediately, taking care not to spread the stain.	● Sponge stains on carpets and furniture with a solution of warm water and a few drops of ammonia. Soak clothes in biological detergent if suitable.
BIRD DROPPINGS	● Clothes drying on a washing line may frequently become soiled by bird droppings.	● Remove the deposit, and relaunder washable fabrics. A bleach or hydrogen peroxide solution (see p. 33) may work on white and pale garments.
TOBACCO STAINS	● Nicotine can stain smokers' hands and fingernails with a yellowish tinge.	● Rub a pad soaked in babies' nappy sterilizing fluid over the stained areas. Use smoker's toothpaste on fingernails.

PIGMENT AND SYNTHETIC STAINS

THE VARIOUS PAINTS, PENS, and crayons used around most homes produce marks that can be difficult to eradicate, especially since it is not always clear which dyes they contain, and therefore what will remove them.

PAINT STAINS

Every household will suffer at one time or another from spilt paint stains, especially when homes are undergoing redecoration. Unfortunately, paint stains are often left until the end of the day. Dried paint stains can be removed satisfactorily, but you must take care.

ARTIST'S PAINTS
● **Fresh stains on clothes** Blot water-based paint stains with paper towels, then wash under a tap with soap and water. Launder as usual. Dab at oil-based paints with white spirit, holding a white pad beneath the stain. Sponge off, then launder as usual.

EMULSION PAINTS
● **Fresh stains on fabric** Blot immediately, sponge with cold water, then launder.
● **Dried stains on fabric** Recently dried stains should respond to a proprietary stain remover. Apply methylated spirit to older stains (testing first), then launder as usual.

OIL-BASED PAINTS
● **On clothes** Dab with white spirit, then sponge with cold water. You may need to repeat this several times. Do not launder until all the paint has gone – if you do, you will set the stain. Bad stains and acetate and viscose fabrics need professional treatment.

Use a pad of absorbent white cloth

Dried stains on clothes
Hold a pad under the stain. Dab at the mark with a stain remover or methylated spirit. For oil-based paints, use a paint solvent (available from art shops).

Sponge carpet with clear water

Spills on carpet
Using a sponge and cold water, dab at the stain, taking care not to spread it further. Work from the outside inwards. When clear, apply carpet shampoo.

Oil-based paint on carpet
Blot fresh spills with paper towels, then treat the area with carpet shampoo. For old stains, try using a proprietary solvent, or snip off the top of the pile.

DYE STAINS

Dried dye never comes out, so mop up spills immediately. Use a dry cloth to wipe spills on hard surfaces – water will dilute and spread the mark. Wear protective clothing, and cover surrounding areas when using dye. Lemon juice will remove dye from skin.

ON CARPETS
● **Basic treatment** Add a few drops of household ammonia to some methylated spirit in a small container. Apply on a white pad, repeating several times if necessary, then apply carpet shampoo.

ON CLOTHES
● **Colourfast fabrics** Soak in a biological detergent solution, then launder the item as usual.
● **Non-colourfast fabrics** Sponge with, or soak in, a hydrogen peroxide solution (see p. 33) for 15 minutes.

OTHER DYE STAINS
● **Laundry colour run** If you accidentally include an item that runs in a load of wash, relaunder the whole load (but not the offending item!) using a commercial colour-run remover instead of detergent.

BALLPOINT-PEN MARKS

These are particularly difficult stains to remove. For bad stains, it may be worth contacting the pen's manufacturer for a remedy for the type of ink used, since they may sell their own solvent. Dried ballpoint-pen ink is especially difficult to get out, so act quickly.

ON FABRIC

Dab lightly at mark

Blot the stain
Press paper towels against the stain to absorb as much of it as possible. Then apply methylated spirit using a cotton-wool bud.

ON WALL COVERINGS

Treat immediately
Scrub vinyl wall coverings immediately with soap and water. Ordinary wall coverings may need patching (see p. 18).

ON OTHER SURFACES

● **Suede** Rub the stain with a fine emery cloth, emery board, or a proprietary suede-cleaning block. Take professional advice before cleaning valuable items.
● **Vinyl surfaces** Treat marks on vinyl immediately by gently rubbing the area with a nail-brush and soapy water. If the ink is allowed to remain on the vinyl surface, it will merge into the plasticizer and leave a permanent mark.

FOUNTAIN-PEN INK MARKS

Most fountain-pen ink is washable, and it is worth making sure that the brand you use definitely is. Always screw on the cap of your pen firmly, especially when carrying it around with you. If you use ink from a bottle, rather than a cartridge, keep the top screwed on well.

ON CARPETS

1 First dilute the stain by sponging repeatedly with clean water, or squirting with a soda syphon. Blot the area well with paper towels.

2 Make a hot, thick solution of soapflakes, and apply liberally on a white fabric pad. Leave for 15 minutes.

3 Wipe off the solution. If the mark persists, repeat Step 2 until it disappears.

ON SKIN

● **Removing marks** Scrub with a nail-brush dipped in vinegar and salt. Or rub marks with the inside of a banana skin.

TRADITIONAL TIP

Natural ink removers
Traditional wisdom recommends treating ink stains with milk or tomato. Cover the stains with a little milk, or rub with the cut side of half a tomato. Rinse both treatments out well.

DRIED STAINS ON CLOTHES

1 If a fountain-pen ink stain remains after you have washed a garment, rub the mark with half a lemon, or squeeze lemon juice on to it.

2 Press the stained area between two pieces of white cotton cloth. Repeat as necessary, then rinse. Launder according to the fabric.

FELT-TIP PEN STAINS

Homes with small children are particularly susceptible to felt-tip pen marks on walls and furniture. Felt-tip pens also often leak into pockets of suit jackets – never attempt to tackle this yourself, but take the jacket to a dry cleaner and explain what the problem is.

ON FABRIC
● **Small marks** Press a paper towel on marks on clothes or furniture to remove as much ink as possible. Dab with methylated spirit on a cotton-wool bud, then launder using soapflakes, not detergent. (Soap is more effective than detergent on all types of ink.)
● **Large marks** Use an aerosol stain remover, repeating applications as necessary. Alternatively, buy a specific commercial stain remover.

ON WALL COVERINGS
● **Vinyl** Apply a non-abrasive household cleaner to marks, or use methylated spirit.
● **Wallpaper** The best solution is to cover marks with a new patch of wallpaper (see p. 18).

ON OTHER SURFACES
● **Carpets and furniture** Blot stains with cotton-wool buds and paper towels, then dab with methylated spirit.

Stains on vinyl
Wipe marks on vinyl surfaces such as toys with a white cloth wrapped around one finger and moistened with neat washing-up liquid. Rinse with clear water.

OTHER PIGMENTS

● **Correction fluid** Leave to dry, brush off, then launder.
● **Crayon** Use a non-abrasive household cleaner for marks on vinyl. Painted walls may need to be repainted, and ordinary wall coverings may require patching (see p. 18).
● **Pencil** Use an eraser on walls and furniture. Sponge marks off clothes, then launder according to fabric.

STICKY SUBSTANCES

Chewing gum and coloured plastic putty can be difficult to remove, especially from fluffy fabrics and carpets where rough removal can leave a bare patch. Freezing is the trick to removing chewing-gum stains; use a liquid stain remover on any marks that are left behind.

PLASTIC PUTTY

● **On clothes** Plastic putty does not freeze, so pick off as much as you can with your fingernails. Next, hold a folded white pad underneath the mark, and – using another white cloth – apply liquid stain remover until the deposit is dissolved. Rinse, then launder as usual.
● **On carpets** Pick off the deposit with your fingernails. Remove any residue with liquid lighter fuel (test on a hidden area, since lighter fuel may damage synthetic fibres). Do not overwet or allow the lighter fuel to reach the carpet backing.

CHEWING GUM ON CARPET

Use your fingers to lift gum

1 Hold a plastic bag filled with ice cubes over the chewing gum to harden it.

2 Pick off the hardened deposit, taking care not to remove the carpet pile.

CHEWING GUM ON CLOTHES

1 Place the stained garment in a plastic bag in the freezer for an hour, so that the chewing gum hardens.

2 Remove the item from the freezer. Bend the fabric across the stain to crack the gum. Pick off the pieces.

HOUSEHOLD PRODUCT STAINS

CLEANERS, MEDICINES, AND ADHESIVES are household substances that can cause difficult stains, particularly on carpets. Stains from cosmetics and candle wax are common in some homes. Tar and creosote stains require careful treatment.

POLISH STAINS

Try to avoid spilling liquid household cleaners or getting polishes on to surfaces which are not intended for their use. Put caps on firmly when cleaners are not being used. Always store household cleaners in an upright position, away from direct sunlight.

SHOE POLISH
● **On carpets** Scrape off the deposit with a metal ruler. Apply white spirit or a liquid stain remover to dissolve any traces. Rinse with clear water, then use methylated spirit to remove any remaining colour. Apply carpet shampoo.
● **On fabrics** Washable fabrics will respond to either a stain remover or a little ammonia added to the rinsing water when washing. Treat non-washable fabrics as for carpet.

METAL POLISH
● **On clothes** Clean off any deposits with paper towels. Use a liquid stain remover, then launder as usual.

On carpets
Spoon and blot up as much polish as you can. Dampen the area with white spirit, and allow to dry. Brush off the dried deposit with a brush or cloth, then apply carpet shampoo.

● **On furniture** Sponge with warm water, leave to dry, and brush well. Apply an aerosol stain remover.

Use a stiff-bristled brush

MEDICINE STAINS

These cause sticky, coloured stains that should be treated quickly so that they do not set into a solid deposit. Ask your pharmacist what is in a particular medicine if you cannot get the stain out. Iodine is one of the worst offenders when it comes to medicine stains.

OINTMENTS

Spills on clothes
Ointments leave behind an oily residue. Scrape off the deposit, then treat the area with a grease solvent. If any colour remains, apply methylated spirit on a cotton pad (test first). Hold a pad beneath the stain to prevent any colour transferring through.

LIQUID MEDICINE
● **On clothes** Laundering should remove most medicine stains from clothes. If any colour remains, apply a little methylated spirit. Hold a pad beneath the stain as you apply the methylated spirit, testing this treatment on a hidden part of the item first.
● **On carpets and upholstery** Scrape up the deposit, then wipe the area with a damp cloth. Apply carpet shampoo.
● **Preventing stains** Keep a roll of paper towels nearby when giving liquid medicine. Use a bib made from a kitchen cloth when giving medicine to small children.

IODINE STAINS
● **On carpets** To remove stains, use a solution of photographic hyposulphite (this is a chemical used in photography development, which you can purchase at photographic shops). Dilute 2.5 ml (½ tsp) in 250 ml (½ pint) warm water. When clear, apply carpet shampoo.
● **On washable fabrics** Wash clothes by hand in soapflakes and water, with a few drops of ammonia added. Wear rubber gloves.
● **On non-washable fabrics** Have items professionally cleaned, or use a commercial tea-and-coffee stain remover.

COSMETICS STAINS

Cosmetics get spilled on and around the dressing table, they come off on clothes and bedding, and they frequently leak inside handbags. Unfortunately, no all-purpose stain-removal technique exists for cosmetics stains. You must treat each item individually.

NAIL VARNISH

Apply nail-varnish remover on cotton wool

On fabric
Hold a white, absorbent pad beneath the stain, and dab with non-oily nail-varnish remover.

MASCARA
● **On clothes** Use an aerosol or liquid stain remover to remove mascara stains. If any marks remain after treatment, sponge, allow to dry, then apply a solution of one part ammonia to three parts cold water. Rinse, and launder.

● **On carpets** Blot up as much as possible with paper tissues. Apply non-oily nail-varnish remover on a ball of cotton wool, testing at the edge of the carpet first, since the backing can be damaged if the solvent soaks through. Treat any remaining traces of colour with methylated spirit applied on a white pad. Finally, apply carpet shampoo.
● **On furniture** Blot well, then apply non-oily nail-varnish remover, testing carefully first.

LIPSTICK
● **On clothes** Sponge with methylated spirit, then neat washing-up liquid. Launder.
● **On walls** Rub marks gently with a damp cloth wrung out of a warm detergent solution. Use household cleaner on stubborn lipstick marks.

BRIGHT IDEA

Preventing spills
Make sure cosmetic bottles do not spill in luggage when travelling by taping the lids shut, or applying nail varnish to the edges of the caps.

FOUNDATION CREAM
● **On clothes** Wipe off the excess cream, then soak in an ammonia solution (see p. 33). Launder according to fabric.

SCENT, SPRAY, AND LOTION STAINS

Sprays and scents tend to be cocktails of chemicals, usually containing some alcohol. They need to be treated with care in case they react with the chemicals used for removal. Creamy lotions usually contain oil or grease and should be treated accordingly.

PERFUME
● **On washable fabrics** Rinse out immediately, then launder the item. Apply a glycerine solution (see p. 33) to dried stains. Leave for an hour, then launder. Alternatively, rub with a laundry pre-wash stick.
● **On non-washable fabrics** Apply a glycerine solution (see p. 33) as soon as possible. Leave for one hour before wiping with a damp cloth. Take care not to wet any padding on furniture. Expensive items should be cleaned professionally.

DEODORANT
● **All surfaces** Blot, then sponge the area with warm water. Repeat if necessary. Use a commercial stain remover on remaining marks.

LOTION
● **Cleansing lotions** Blot with tissues, then treat the area with a grease solvent. Launder clothes; use carpet shampoo on carpets and upholstery.
● **Toning lotions** Squirt the area with soda water, or sponge with warm water. Allow to dry naturally.

HAIRSPRAY

On mirrors
Hairspray leaves a sticky deposit on mirrors, producing a blurred effect. Wipe off with a little methylated spirit on a cloth.

CANDLE-WAX STAINS

These are almost unavoidable if you enjoy candlelight. The wax is easy to remove, but coloured candles may leave dye stains, and these need to be treated after the wax has been cleared. Wax does not set hard, so these stains do not require immediate treatment.

ON CARPETS

Scoop up wax while it is soft

Place iron on a warm setting

1 Scrape up as much of the wax deposit as you can with a spoon. If the wax is hard, use your fingernails.

2 Place brown paper over the remaining wax. Iron with a warm iron until the wax melts into the paper.

ON OTHER SURFACES

● **Clothes** Use the treatment for carpets, left. Treat any residual colour marks with methylated spirit (testing first). Hold an absorbent, white pad under the stain as you apply the methylated spirit.
● **Furniture and wallpaper** Use the treatment for carpets, left, without lifting any wax first. Use methylated spirit to remove colour on furniture, and an aerosol stain remover for marks on wallpaper.
● **Wood** See page 16.

ADHESIVE MARKS

Adhesives stick to you as well as to whatever is being glued. Scrape up fresh spills immediately, then use the appropriate solvent. Dried stains are extremely difficult to remove. If you are doing a lot of gluing, buy the appropriate solvent when buying the adhesive.

FRESH ADHESIVE

● **Appropriate solvents** Use non-oily nail-varnish remover on clear adhesive. Remove contact adhesive with a manufacturer's solvent. Use a stain remover on model-making cement, liquid grease solvent on latex adhesive, and lighter fuel on epoxy resin.
● **On hard surfaces** Use white or methylated spirit. Allow latex adhesives to set, then roll off with your finger.
● **On skin** Use lemon juice.

DRIED ADHESIVE

Hold scissors as horizontal as possible

On carpets
The best way to remove dried adhesive is to trim the top of the pile with a pair of scissors.

Apply solvent on cotton wool

On hard surfaces
To remove label residue marks, rub with methylated or white spirit, or cellulose thinners.

CREOSOTE AND TAR STAINS

These substances are best left outside, but they often creep in on shoes, swimwear, and beach towels – not to mention clothes. Because stains from creosote and tar are difficult to remove, take great care not to let them transfer on to any further surfaces.

● **On carpets** Blot gently, then apply a glycerine solution (see p. 33), and leave for one hour. Rinse with clear water, then use a carpet-spotting kit.

● **On clothes** Place an absorbent, white pad on top of the stain. Apply eucalyptus oil from below the stain with a piece of cotton wool.

● **On shoes** Use lighter fuel, but check for affected colour.
● **On furniture** Expensive furnishings should be dry cleaned professionally.

WEAR-AND-TEAR MARKS

Wear and tear is inevitable around the home. However, some problems, such as mildew, need to be kept in check; otherwise they may require professional treatment and can cause permanent damage to household items.

MILDEW PATCHES

Mildew tends to occur in damp parts of the home and should, if possible, be caught in the early stages. It appears as an unsightly growth of spores, which makes surfaces look as if they are covered in small, dirty patches. Left unchecked, mildew develops a deposit.

ON CLOTHES
● **Whites** Bleach mildew with a hydrogen peroxide solution (see p. 33); do not use this treatment on nylon. Soak natural fabrics in a household bleach solution (see p. 58).
● **Coloureds** Dampen, then rub with a bar of hard soap. Leave to dry in the sun before laundering. Repeated washing will get rid of any remaining marks, and a specialist stain remover can be used on white and colourfast fabrics.

ON LACE

Cover mildew with soap

Using household soap
Rub the lace with soap so that a film develops. Leave in the sun for several hours, then rinse.

ON SHOWER CURTAINS

Removing marks
Sponge curtains with either a detergent solution, or a weak bleach solution (wear gloves).

ON WALLS
● **General treatment** Wash the whole wall (even areas where mildew does not show) with a mild detergent solution. Wipe the wall with a solution of proprietary bactericide (a paint pad is good for this).

ON FURNITURE
● **Removing marks** Remove mildew spores as described below. If marks remain, have loose covers dry cleaned. Apply a hydrogen peroxide solution (see p. 33) to fixed covers, then rinse thoroughly.

ON LEATHER
● **General treatment** Leather shoes, furniture, bags, and luggage all attract mildew in storage. Remove using the treatment below, then apply a coat of hide food or shoe polish. Rub in and buff well.

Tackling corners
Sponge carefully into corners of rooms. Take extra care near windows in bathrooms and kitchens, where condensation could form pools that encourage mildew growth to develop.

Killing mildew spores
Brush off as many of the spores as possible, then spray the item with a proprietary solution designed to kill the spores. Do this outdoors so that the spores do not transfer to other items.

Treating leather bags
Sponge mildew with 5 ml (1 tsp) disinfectant diluted in 500 ml (1 pint) of warm water. Alternatively, apply an antiseptic mouth wash, neat, on a cotton pad. Wipe dry, and buff well.

WATER MARKS

Water marking is caused by minerals in water, and often occurs after an area of a garment has been sponged. To prevent water marks from forming after removing a stain, sprinkle the damp area with talcum powder, cover with a dry cloth, then iron dry.

ON HIDES AND WOOD

● **On leather** Wipe off rain spots on shoes and handbags before they dry with a clean cloth. Allow to dry naturally. If salt marks appear or water marks persist, redampen the area with a sponge or cloth, then dry by rubbing with a soft, absorbent cloth.
● **On suede** Allow rain spots to dry, then brush with a soft-bristled brush, or use a suede-cleaning pad or stick.
● **On wood** See page 72.

ON FABRIC

Rub towards centre of mark

1 Hold the marked area over the steam from a boiling kettle. Take care not to burn your hands or the fabric.

2 Remove from the steam. Rub the area with a cloth over your finger. Start at the edge and work inwards.

SCORCH MARKS

Scorch marks are usually the result of an accident with an iron left on clothing for too long, or cigarette and other tobacco burns. For severe burns on carpet, you may need to trim the top of the carpet pile, or to replace the burned area with an offcut (see below).

ON FABRIC

● **Washable fabrics** Rub the mark under cold, running water, using another piece of the fabric rather than your fingers. Soak in a laundry borax solution (see p. 33), rubbing gently until clear.
● **Non-washable fabrics** Apply a glycerine solution (see p. 33). Leave for two hours, then sponge with warm water.

ON CARPETS

Cigarette burns
Rub burns with fine sandpaper, using gentle, circular motions until the mark disappears.

TRADITIONAL TIP

Natural alternatives
To treat light scorch marks on carpets, boil together 250 ml (½ pint) white vinegar, 50 g (2 oz) unscented talcum powder, and two coarsely chopped onions. Leave the mixture to cool, then spread over the stain. Leave to dry and then brush off. To remove small burns on polished wood, rub the area gently with very fine steel wool, then rub in a little linseed oil. Leave for 24 hours, then polish well.

TREATING SEVERE SCORCH MARKS

1 Place a new piece of carpet over the burned area, and cut both layers together.

2 Insert the new patch into the space. Stick it down with double-sided tape.

RUST MARKS

Rust and iron mould appear to be difficult marks to remove, but in fact they do not require any drastic treatment. Lemon juice is useful as a gentle treatment for rust stains. If you do not have any fresh lemon to hand, lemon juice from a bottle works just as well.

ON CLOTHES

Cover mark thickly with free-flow salt

1 Hold a white, absorbent pad under the rust stain, and apply lemon juice from the cut half of a lemon.

2 Cover the lemon juice with salt, and leave to dry for an hour (if possible, in the sun). Rinse off, then launder.

OTHER SURFACES

● **On carpets** Remove rust marks with a proprietary rust remover, following the instructions carefully.
● **On non-washable fabrics** Use a proprietary rust remover, then wipe with a damp cloth. A little lemon juice may help (be careful not to overwet the area).
● **On baths** Use a commercial cleaner that contains a rust remover. See page 24 for treating other bath stains.

SOOT MARKS

These are a common problem in homes that have open fires. Treat brick and stone fire surrounds as below; see page 21 for cleaning other fire-surround surfaces. Soot marks should wash out of clothes easily – but use an aerosol stain remover on any persistent stains.

LIGHT MARKS

Dusting off soot
Keep soot marks at bay by cleaning your fireplace surround regularly, either with a vacuum-cleaner attachment or a brush.

ON CARPETS
● **Basic treatment** Vacuum well, or shake the carpet or rug. Do not brush the area because this will spread the mark. If this is not effective, apply unscented talcum powder, then vacuum. Have any large stains on carpets professionally dry cleaned.

SOOT STAINS

Scrubbing marks
If soot marks cannot be brushed or vacuumed away, scrub them vigorously with clean water, using a stiff scrubbing brush.

ON STONEWORK
● **Stubborn marks** Use a weak solution of washing-up liquid on stubborn soot marks on stonework, then scrub the whole area with clear water. Treat heavy soot marking with a concentrated solution of household bleach, then rinse the area thoroughly.

PERSISTENT STAINS

Using acidic cleaners
Apply neat white vinegar on a sponge or brush to tough stains. Rinse well. If marks persist, treat with spirit of salts (see below).

WARNING
Spirit of salts is a solution of hydrochloric acid in water, and is poisonous and highly corrosive. Wear rubber gloves and protective goggles when handling this substance.

OTHER STAINS

M OST STAINS CAN BE REMOVED using the methods described previously. If you are faced with an obscure stain, follow the treatment for the most similar substance, testing carefully first. Refer to page 34 for removing mystery stains.

STAIN	TREATMENT	STAIN	TREATMENT
BABY FORMULA	Treat as for milk, p. 41. Do not allow the stain to set.	HAIR OIL	On wooden headboards, rub with white spirit.
CARBON PAPER	Dab with methylated spirit or aerosol stain remover.	HEAT MARKS	See scorch marks, p. 53, and marks on wood, p. 72.
CHUTNEY	Treat as for jams and preserves, p. 38.	NEWSPRINT	Apply methylated spirit on a cloth, then rinse well.
COAL	Brush off marks. Launder clothes in warm water.	SHELLAC	Act quickly. Dab with methylated spirit.
COLA DRINKS	Blot spill, then treat as for fruit juice, p. 40.	SORBET	Remove deposit, then treat as for fruit juice, p. 40.
COPIER TONER POWDER	Brush off deposit, then wash item in warm water.	SOUP	Rinse or blot spill, then treat as for grease, p. 36.
CREAM	Treat as for oil, fat, and grease, p. 36.	SOY SAUCE	Treat as for tomato sauce, p. 38. Do not allow to set.
DUPLICATING INK	Dab marks with neat washing-up liquid.	TOMATO	Blot, rinse, then treat as for tomato sauce, p. 38.
EMBROIDERY TRANSFER	Dab with methylated spirit, then launder as usual.	TREACLE	Treat as for jams and preserves, p. 38.
FRUIT	Rinse stain, then treat as for fruit juice, p. 40.	YOGHURT	Scoop up deposit, then treat as for milk, p. 41.

STAINS ON DIFFICULT SURFACES

ON WOOD
● **Unvarnished wood** Stains on unvarnished wood are almost impossible to remove. Bleach what you can, then wash the area with detergent solution. Seal the surface with varnish to prevent future marks.
● **Varnished wood** See page 72 for treating marks on furniture; see pages 15–16 for special treatments for wood floors.

ON SKIN AND HAIR
● **Paint stains** Use white spirit to remove paint from skin and hair; or try vegetable oil on skin as a gentler alternative. Protect your hair with a cap when painting.
● **Ink stains** Scrub ink marks on the skin with a nail-brush dipped in vinegar and salt.
● **Other stains** Use pure lemon juice to remove dye stains and adhesive marks on skin.

ON OTHER SURFACES
● **Paper** Remove grease spots by laying a piece of blotting paper over the mark and ironing with a warm iron.
● **Glass** Use white vinegar to remove grease marks on glass.
● **Leather and suede** See page 47 for removing ink stains; see page 53 for treating water marks; and see page 83 for care and minor repairs to leather and suede.

CLOTHES & LAUNDRY

QUICK REFERENCE

Washing Clothes, p. 58

Special Treatments, p. 60

Drying Clothes, p. 62

Ironing Clothes, p. 64

Caring for Clothes, p. 66

Shoe Care, p. 69

PROLONG THE LIFE of your clothes and your household linen by ensuring that they do not become heavily soiled before washing. Take advantage of the variable programming of modern washing machines to clean at the right temperature and spin speed. Do not neglect the launderette – it is the best bet for washing heavy items such as pillows, which could damage your domestic machine.

DETERGENTS AND LAUNDRY AIDS

In addition to liquid or powder detergents for machine washing, use the the following aids to keep clothes looking their best.

● **Fabric softener** Use either a commercial fabric softener, or add 30 ml (2 tbsp) white vinegar to the final rinse.
● **Starch** This keeps cotton shirts and table linen crisp and clean (see p. 63).
● **Bleach** For use on whites. Always dilute household bleach. Lemon juice is a natural alternative to bleach.
● **Biological detergent** Use for treating built-up protein stains.
● **Soapflakes or hand-washing detergent** Use these for hand washing delicate items.
● **Laundry borax** This removes stains. Commercial pre-wash sprays or sticks are also useful.

Fabric softener

Liquid detergent

Spray starch

Bleach

Powder detergent

Biological detergent

Soapflakes

Laundry borax

INTERNATIONAL FABRIC CARE SYMBOLS

The symbols on care labels fall into five categories. An "X" through a symbol means that a specific treatment should be avoided. Most detergent packets feature a complete list of the symbols and their meanings.

Washing symbol

Bleaching symbol

Ironing symbol

Dry-cleaning symbol

Drying symbol

FABRIC CARE

Certain fabrics need more careful treatment than simply machine washing. Check the care label – if it says hand wash or dry clean, follow these instructions. Use a dry cleaner for tailored clothing, items with special finishes, and anything made of more than one fabric.

FABRIC	WASHING	DRYING AND IRONING
ACETATES Temperamental fabrics. Never use biological detergent.	Machine or hand wash at a low temperature. Do not wring or fast spin in a washing machine.	Do not tumble dry. Allow acetate items to dry naturally, and iron while still damp.
ACRYLIC Needs frequent washing since it can smell of perspiration.	Usually machine washable, but check the care label. Wash items at a low temperature.	Pull into shape after washing, and remove excess water (see p. 60). Dry flat or line dry.
BROCADE Take care not to flatten the raised pile when washing.	Hand wash at cool temperature or dry clean, according to the care label. Do not wring.	Iron on the wrong side with the pile over a towel (see ironing embroidery, p. 65).
CASHMERE Expensive, so it merits the specialist care that it needs.	Hand wash in cool water in well-dissolved soapflakes. Rinse well. Do not wring.	Dry naturally, either flat or on a jumper rack. Iron inside out while damp with a cool iron.
CORDUROY Tough in wear but needs care in washing to avoid crushing pile.	Always wash inside out. Hand or machine wash, according to the care label instructions.	Iron inside out while evenly damp, then smooth the pile with a soft cloth.
COTTON When mixed with other fibres, wash as for the most delicate.	Machine wash cotton at a high temperature, always keeping whites separate from coloureds.	Tumble or line dry. Do not allow items to dry completely, as they will be difficult to iron.
DENIM A strong fabric, but prone to shrinking, fading, and streaking.	Wash separately until you are sure there is no colour run (see p. 59). Wash items inside out.	Tumble dry or line dry. Iron denim items while still very damp, using a hot iron.
LACE An extremely delicate fabric. Wash and dry carefully.	Treat stains before hand washing in a mild detergent. Never use bleach – it causes yellowing.	Dry flat on a white towel away from direct sunlight. Iron, if you must, over a white towel.
LEATHER AND SUEDE Surprisingly washable, but check the care label.	Protect items with a specialist spray after hand washing so that marks do not build up.	Rub suede with another piece of suede or a suede brush to keep the nap looking good.
LINEN A tough fabric that withstands the highest temperatures.	Machine wash according to the label. Test coloured linen items for colourfastness (see p. 60).	Iron while still very damp. Starch will prevent some creasing (but not on bed linen).
SILK A delicate fabric that requires special care to prevent damage.	Hand wash in warm water. Some silk items can be machine washed on the delicate cycle.	Line dry naturally, and iron while damp. Use a pressing cloth to protect the fabric.
WOOL Wash and dry carefully, since items easily lose their shape.	Some woollens can be machine washed, others must be done by hand. Check the care label.	Wool can be dried flat, line dried, or dried on a jumper rack. Do not tumble dry.

WASHING CLOTHES

ALWAYS READ THE CARE LABEL before washing clothes to establish which method of cleaning is most suitable for the item. Soak heavily soiled clothes before washing. Treat stains as soon as they occur, then launder.

SOAKING CLOTHES

A good soak before washing loosens the dirt from clothes. Biological detergent is best for protein-based stains. Soak clothes in the bath or in a bucket, keeping them completely immersed. Ensure that biological detergent is fully dissolved before you soak clothes.

DARK COLOURS

● **Black garments** When these develop a "bloom" and do not look black any longer, it is because of a build up of soap. Either soak the item in warm water with a little white vinegar, or add water softener (instead of detergent) to the machine's regular wash.
● **Colour runs** Always wash dark colours separately until you are sure that the dye does not run (see washing coloureds, opposite). If dye from dark clothes runs on to pale fabrics in the wash, you can use a commercial dye-run remover to eradicate colour from the lighter items.

DENIM ITEMS

Preserving colour
To prevent a new pair of jeans from fading when washed, soak them in 60 ml (4 tbsp) of vinegar mixed with 5 litres (8 pints) of water for about 30 minutes.

BRIGHT COLOURS

Push items under water with a wooden spoon

Preventing fading
To keep coloured clothes bright, soak them in cold, salty water before washing them for the first time. Use a solution of a handful of salt to a bucketful of water.

WHITENING DISCOLOURED CLOTHES

Submerge socks with a wooden spoon

White cotton socks
Return white socks to pristine condition by boiling them in a saucepan with a few added slices of lemon. The lemon is a natural bleach. Dishwasher detergent also whitens socks – just add it to the regular washload.

● **Cotton or linen** Soak items for 15 minutes in a solution of 15 ml (1 tbsp) household bleach to 10 litres (16 pints) cold water. Rinse thoroughly before washing as usual.
● **Wool** Soak discoloured wool overnight in one part hydrogen peroxide to eight parts cold water. Rinse, and wash according to care label.
● **Nylon** Soak nylon items in the following mixture: 90 ml (6 tbsp) dishwasher detergent and 45 ml (3 tbsp) household bleach to 5 litres (8 pints) very hot water. Allow the mixture to cool to room temperature, then soak the nylon items in it for at least 30 minutes.

USING BLEACH

Always dilute bleach before you use it – neat bleach will "burn" holes in fabric. Follow the manufacturer's instructions for dilution. If in doubt, add an egg cup of bleach to a bucketful of cold water to make a standard bleach solution.

MACHINE WASHING

Sort clothes into matching loads, based on care label instructions. If you need to wash mixed fabrics together to make up a full load, set to the lowest recommended temperature. Do not be tempted to use more detergent than instructed – it will not get clothes any cleaner.

WASHING SYMBOLS

The washtub symbol contains details of the temperature and type of cycle to be used.

The figure indicates the maximum recommended water temperature.

Broken bars beneath the tub recommend using a gentle cycle.

The hand in the tub means that the item should always be hand washed.

WASHING COLOUREDS

Checking for colour run
Place an old, white handkerchief with coloured garments to pick up any colour run. When it stays white, all the loose dye has run out, and the coloured items can be washed with white ones.

MACHINE BASICS

● **Cleaning machines** From time to time, clean your washing machine by running it empty on a hot cycle with a little white vinegar in the detergent compartment. This will clear any detergent deposits that may have built up over a period of time.
● **Detergent quantities** Using too little detergent results in clothes remaining dirty; if you use too much, it will not rinse out of clothes properly.
● **Washing times** Whites may yellow if washed for too long at too high a temperature, and natural fibres may shrink.

SORTING CLOTHES

Close zips and do up buttons on garments before you machine wash them. Leaving these open results in their getting battered, and they may not close properly when the wash cycle is finished. To avoid ending up with grey whites, do not mix whites and strong colours.

PREPARING CLOTHES FOR THE WASH

● **Checking pockets** Be sure to go through pockets before you put items in the wash – tissues disintegrate, pens leak, and money can be damaged.

Place tights and scarves in pillowcase, then fasten at top

Pin socks at tops

Keeping socks in pairs
Use safety pins to keep pairs of socks together in the wash, so that individual socks do not get lost. Leave the pins in while the socks dry (either in the tumble dryer or on a clothes line).

Protecting delicates
Place small or delicate items such as tights and scarves in a pillowcase for machine washing. This will prevent them from snagging and from becoming tangled up with larger garments.

MONEY-SAVING TIP

A stitch in time . . .
Mend holes and tears in clothes before you machine wash them. The machine's agitating action makes the damage worse, and you may have to replace items or have them professionally repaired. Fixing loose buttons before you launder an item ensures that the buttons do not get lost in the wash.

SPECIAL TREATMENTS

Set aside time each week to deal with delicate and unusual items that cannot be washed in the machine. Treat household linen with care to prolong the life of individual items. Air bedding regularly to keep it in good condition.

HAND WASHING

Hand wash wool, delicate fabrics, and any items that continue to run. Use warm water for hand washing; if you use soapflakes, make sure that they are thoroughly dissolved. Do not skimp on rinsing: washing machines rinse clothes several times, and so must you.

COLOURFAST TEST

Using a steam iron
If you suspect that an item is not colourfast, steam iron an area between two layers of white fabric. If dye transfers on to the white, the item is not colourfast.

DELICATE FABRICS
● **Lace** Make a paper template of delicate lace items before you hand wash them. If they lose their shape, you can use the template to reshape the items correctly as they dry.
● **Silk** Add two lumps of sugar to the rinse water to give silk body; add a little lanolin to protect and restore silk.

RINSING TRICKS
● **Removing soap** Add 15 ml (1 tbsp) of white vinegar to the final rinse to remove soap.
● **Preventing freezing** Add a handful of salt to the final rinse to prevent clothes from freezing on the line in winter.

TIME-SAVING TIP

Getting rid of suds
If you have too many suds when hand washing, sprinkle them with talcum powder to make them disperse. This saves having to let water out and add more clear water.

DRY CLEANING

This is essential for fabrics that cannot take water. Use a specialist dry cleaner for expensive items; cheaper garments can be cleaned in a coin-operated machine. The following tips will help to minimize dry cleaning.

● **Outdoor clothes** Clean dirt from outdoor clothes as soon as you get home. Use an aerosol dry cleaner on coat and jacket collars and cuffs, which tend to get dirty faster than the main fabric.
● **Airing clothes** Hang non-washable items to air before you put them away. Never wear them two days running.

WOOLLEN CLOTHES

Drying woollens
Woollens can be distorted by machine spinning. After hand washing, roll them gently in a clean towel to remove excess water, then dry them flat on a rack or a dry towel (see p. 63).

Heat from hairdryer shrinks fibres on cuff

Reshaping stretched cuffs
Dip sweater cuffs in hot water, then dry them with a hair dryer on a hot setting. For a more permanent solution, stitch two or three rows of knitting elastic loosely around the cuffs.

BEDDING AND LINEN

Towels and bed linen get dirty quickly and require frequent laundering. Wash duvets and pillows only if absolutely necessary. When making beds, reverse the pillows each time to reduce wear on one side, and turn sheets from top to bottom – they will last twice as long.

PILLOWS

● **Hand washing** Wash pillows in the bath, using a soapflake solution. Knead vigorously, and rinse several times.

Drying pillows
Wet pillows are very heavy and may damage domestic machines. Remove all excess water before tumble drying, and add a clean tennis shoe to balance the load.

DUVETS

● **Dry cleaning** Duvets are too heavy to wash in domestic machines, and are too large to be washed by hand easily. Take them to a launderette or to a professional cleaner.

BATHROOM AND KITCHEN TOWELS

● **General care** Wash towels frequently, using a hot wash programme, to get rid of the debris that collects in the pile.

Vinegar removes soap residue

Soapy face cloths
Soak well-used face cloths in 15 ml (1 tbsp) vinegar or lemon juice and 500 ml (1 pint) water before machine washing. This will remove all traces of soap.

STORING AND CARING FOR SHEETS

● **Laundering** Wash sheets according to the care labels. Mixed-fibre sheets do not need ironing – simply fold them when dry. Natural-fibre sheets look better if ironed.

● **Removing the "bloom"** Use a water-softening powder to remove any soap build up and to restore fading colours.

Sterilizing kitchen cloths *No*
Get rid of lingering bacteria in kitchen cloths by placing them, newly washed, in a microwave. Turn on at a high setting for five minutes, then remove the cloths.

● **Storing** After laundering, place white linen or cotton sheets at the bottom of the pile in the linen cupboard. Regular rotation and use will prevent sheets from yellowing.

REMOVING DIRTY MARKS

Remove marks from clothes before washing, since laundering may cause stains to set. Use pre-wash sprays or sticks, soak items in biological detergent if the fabric is suitable, or use the relevant stain-removal technique recommended on pages 32–55.

● **Collars and cuffs** Follow the method shown right to remove dirt from around collars and cuffs; alternatively, apply hair shampoo to these areas before washing. Using starch or an ironing spray will keep collars and cuffs clean between washes.

Rub mark with soap

1 Rub a piece of damp soap or a pre-wash stick along the mark or stain. Make sure that the mark is well covered.

Scrub the soap well

2 Use a wet toothbrush to work the soap into a lather. Rinse the area in warm water, then launder the item.

DRYING CLOTHES

IF YOU DRY CLOTHES PROPERLY, you can cut down considerably on ironing. After line or tumble drying, fold clothes or put them on hangers. When hanging items on the line, try to keep seams and creases in the right places.

LINE DRYING

Hang clothes to dry outdoors whenever the weather permits – this will save electricity, and is gentler on clothes than tumble drying. Sunlight makes white clothes whiter. If you are short of outdoor space, hang two lines parallel to each other, and drape items across them.

DRYING SYMBOLS

The four variants to the square symbol indicate which drying method should be used.

 Tumble dry (any dots in the circle indicate settings).

 Drip dry items on a line.

 Hang dry items after removing excess water.

 Dry items flat after removing excess water.

PREVENTING PROBLEMS

● **Fading** Turn coloured T-shirts inside out, and hang them in the shade so that they do not fade in the sunlight.

Cleaning washing lines
Dirt collects on washing lines and may transfer to fabric. To clean lines, run a damp sponge or a split cork along the length of the line from time to time.

DRYING TRICKS

● **Belts** To dry belts without creating a peg mark, loop them around the washing line and fasten the belt buckle.
● **Pleated skirts** After washing, hang on the line from the waistband. Clip clothes pegs at the bottom of each pleat so that the pleats dry in place.

DRYING JUMPERS

Tights hold jumper in place

Preventing stretching
Jumpers will not stretch on a clothes line if you string an old pair of tights through the arms, and peg the tights – rather than the jumper itself – to the line.

TIGHTS AND SOCKS

● **Reducing snags** Clip clothes pegs to the feet of stockings or tights. This prevents them from blowing around and tangling or snagging.

Drying socks
To save space on lines, peg pairs of socks on a hanger. This will also enable you to remove the socks quickly if it starts to rain.

Quick-drying sheets
Peg the sheet at both ends first, then peg each side one-third of the way along. This "bag" shape allows air to circulate easily.

MONEY-SAVING TIP

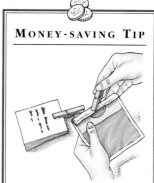

Handy helpers
Use ordinary clothes pegs around the house to clip things together. They reseal food packets and hold notes and telephone messages together as effectively as gadgets sold for the purpose.

TUMBLE DRYING

Tumble dryers work best when the drum is only half full – clothes will dry most quickly if they can move around freely. Do not let tumble-dried items become bone dry – if you do, you will find they are difficult to iron. Clean the tumble-dryer filter after each use.

USING TUMBLE DRYERS

● **Avoiding creases** Certain items require little ironing if tumble dried – in particular clothes made from polyester and cotton mixtures. Remove items as soon as the dryer stops, and fold or hang them.

● **Fabric-softener cloths** Use these in the tumble dryer to keep items from creasing – particularly items that you do not wish to iron, such as towels. Use half a sheet – it is as effective as a whole one.

● **Spin drying** You can use your tumble dryer to spin dry items you have hand washed. Put woollens in pillowcases to prevent them from stretching.

FABRIC SOFTENER

A cheap softener

For a money-saving alternative to commercial fabric-softener cloths, soak a face cloth in a solution of fabric-softener liquid and water for a few minutes. Squeeze out excess liquid, then add the face cloth to the clothes being dried in the tumble dryer.

FLAT DRYING

Lay jumper on dry towel

Clothes made from delicate fabrics should always be dried flat. Roll them in a towel to remove excess moisture, then stretch them into shape, and leave to dry on a towel (as shown above). Do not expose coloured items to direct sunlight while drying them, since this may cause fading.

AIRING AND STARCHING

Large items are best aired along parallel washing lines, which will not only take the weight but allow air to reach the entire area of fabric. Air items such as pillows and blankets on the washing line. To improvise an airing rack indoors, use the method shown below.

Tie two parallel lines of cord to each pair of chairs

Drape item over parallel lines

Place books on chairs to stabilize them

Make sure item does not trail on floor

Homemade airing rack

To air or dry large items if you do not have a clothes line, stretch strong cord between two chairs. Using parallel lines allows air to reach both sides of an item, and will not leave creases or peg marks. Use this system for blankets, duvets, towels, and curtains.

Use plastic chairs, if possible, since wooden chairs can stain damp items

USING STARCH

Apply starch to right side of fabric

Starching clothes and bed linen makes them crisp and helps reduce soiling. Rinsing kitchen cloths used for drying dishes in a weak starch solution will prevent fluff from coming off on glasses. Always apply starch to the right side of fabric, once the item is dry and just before it is ironed. Spray starch is easier to use then starch dip, but it does not last as long.

IRONING CLOTHES

ALWAYS IRON FABRICS that need the coolest setting first, and work up to the hottest setting. Iron as many items as possible at once, since irons use up a lot of electricity heating up. Ironing is easiest if clothes are slightly damp.

IRONING BASICS

Use long, smooth strokes when ironing, and iron clothes until they are dry. Freshly ironed clothes crease easily, so hang them carefully afterwards – do not simply drape them over chairs (especially not over wooden ones, which can transfer colour on to clothes).

IRONING SYMBOLS

There are four ironing symbols: hot, warm, cool, and do not iron.

Hot iron: 210°C (410°F).

Warm iron: 160°C (320°F).

Cool iron: 120°C (248°F).

Do not iron.

EQUIPMENT
● **Iron safety** Check the flex frequently to make sure you have not accidentally burned it with the iron and destroyed the protective coating.
● **Steam irons** Empty steam irons after each use to prevent them from becoming clogged. Descale using a commercial descaler or white vinegar.
● **Ironing boards** Choose an ironing board that can be adjusted to your height, as ironing at the wrong height can cause backache. Starch your ironing-board cover so that it stays clean and crisp.

GREEN TIP

Energy-efficient ironing
Place aluminium foil under ironing-board covers to reflect heat on to garments.

SIMPLE IRONING TECHNIQUES
● **Fastenings** Iron around – not over – zips and buttons. Metal zips could otherwise damage the iron, and nylon zips and buttons could melt.

● **Seams and hems** To avoid creating a line over seams and hems, iron the garment inside out, and stop just short of the seam or hem line.

CLEANING IRONS

Unplug your iron before you clean it. Unless your iron is non-stick, clean the base (the sole plate) with toothpaste, applied on a soft cloth. Rub persistent marks gently with fine-grade steel wool. Clean non-stick sole plates with a sponge dipped in a detergent and warm water solution, or use methylated spirit.

Protecting delicates
Iron delicate fabrics over a clean cloth or tissue paper to avoid damaging the fabric. Make sure the garment is evenly damp.

Ironing collars
Always iron collars on both sides, wrong side first. Iron inwards from the point to avoid pushing any creases to the tip.

SPECIAL ITEMS

Some fabrics need special attention when ironing. Acetates, triacetates, and some polyesters should be ironed on the wrong side when evenly damp. Iron acrylics from the back when dry. Always iron corduroy and crêpe on the wrong side, covered with a damp cloth.

HOUSEHOLD LINEN

- **Time-saving technique** Fold large items such as sheets and tablecloths double, and iron one side. Fold in half again and iron the other two sides. This also works for smaller items such as kitchen cloths, napkins, and handkerchiefs.
- **Large items** Stop sheets and other large items from trailing on the floor by putting the ironed half over a chair back. Cover wooden chairs with a towel to prevent stain from transferring from the wood.

PLEATED SKIRTS

Slip kirby grips over hem

Hold pleats in place
Use kirby grips to keep pleats firmly in place. Press all but the hem, then remove the kirby grips and finish ironing.

HEAVY FABRICS

Use a pillowcase if you do not have a pressing cloth

Preventing shininess
Iron heavy fabrics such as wool and viscose rayon over a damp pressing cloth to prevent the fabric from becoming shiny.

IRONING SMALL AND UNUSUAL ITEMS

- **Trimmings** If items have trimmings that need a cooler setting than the main fabric, iron these first, before ironing the rest of the garment.

- **Hair ribbons** To "iron" in a hurry, grasp both ends and pull the ribbon back and forth against a metal kettle that has just been used to boil water.

Cut template to match shape of tie

Creaseless ties
Slip a cardboard template into ties before ironing, so that the impression of the seam does not show through to the front.

Invert embroidery over towel

Ironing embroidery
Lay the piece of embroidery face down on a towel, and iron the reverse side. This way you will not flatten the embroidery.

DAMPENING ITEMS

Items that are too dry are difficult to iron. Use a plant-spray bottle to dampen dry clothes. Alternatively, put all the clothes into the tumble dryer together with a wet towel, and run the dryer on a no-heat setting. If you cannot finish a load of ironing, keep it damp by putting it in the freezer in a plastic bag.

ALTERNATIVES TO IRONING

- **Tumble-dry clothes** Take synthetic fabrics (cotton and polyester mixtures) out of the dryer as soon as the drying cycle is finished. Hang the items on coat hangers while they are still hot; creases will drop out as the items cool.

- **Drip-dry clothes** Straighten collars, seams, and pleats while still damp to ensure that they dry straight.
- **Velvet and silk** Hang silk and velvet items in a steamy bathroom to dry – the steam will make creases drop out.

- **Caught without an iron?** If you must press something but have no iron, put the item under your mattress overnight. Your body heat and weight will give it a thorough pressing. Dampen any creases on trousers with a wet towel first.

CARING FOR CLOTHES

CLOTHES NEED ATTENTION if they are to remain in good condition. Hang them properly after you take them off. Brush, remove stains, and make any repairs before wearing again. Never wear clothes or shoes two days running.

SOLVING PROBLEMS

Loose buttons, stuck zips, and runs in tights are common clothes problems. If a zip is stuck, remember that it is best to pull the zip down, ease out the material, and start again. For back zips that are difficult to do up, thread string through the tab, and pull.

BUTTONS

Long-lasting buttons
Buttons will not come off easily if you dab the threads of the buttons on new garments with clear nail varnish. Sew children's buttons on with dental floss.

ZIPS

Fixing sticking zips
Rub an ordinary pencil over a sticking zip – the graphite will help the zip to slide smoothly. See page 149 for repairing zips damaged close to the base.

CARING FOR TIGHTS

To prolong the life of tights, wet them when new, and place them in a plastic bag in the freezer for a few hours. To stop runs from spreading, apply clear nail varnish or rub with damp household soap.

MINOR REPAIRS

Prevention is always better than cure, so do not rush into wearing new garments when a simple treatment might keep them looking better longer. Mend holes and remove stains as they occur – and always before washing a garment. See pages 148–149 for sewing tips.

RING MARKS

Hold water mark over steam

Steaming off marks
Sponging a small area of a garment often leaves behind a ring mark. Hold the stained area in the steam of a boiling kettle until the mark disappears.

SHINY PATCHES

Sponging with ammonia
Areas that get a lot of wear, such as knees and elbows, often become shiny. Sponge with 15 ml (1 tbsp) ammonia diluted in 250 ml (½ pint) of water.

RECYCLING ITEMS

Turn old tablecloths into a set of napkins. Pillowcases can be made from worn sheets; flannelette sheets are ideal for making children's nightwear. Use old plastic raincoats to cover school books.

LOOKING AFTER CLOTHES

Storing and hanging clothes properly is essential to keep them looking good. After wearing clothes, hang them to air before putting them in a cupboard. Remove lint from clothes with a piece of adhesive tape wrapped around one finger, or with a damp sponge.

CREASELESS CLOTHES
● **Drawer storage** Fold clothes across their width when storing in drawers. Creases will drop out more quickly than if folded lengthways.

SPACE SAVERS FOR CUPBOARDS
● **Hanging items** Slip shower curtain hooks on the rod in your cupboard and hang belts and bags from them. Hang a string bag to hold socks.

● **Odds and ends** Plastic shoe containers with pockets can be hung in the cupboard and then used for storing socks and other small items.

SCARVES

Roll scarf on flat surface

Tube should be at least as wide as scarf

Storing in drawers
Roll silk scarves around the paper tubes from kitchen foil or clingfilm. This will prevent the scarves from creasing when they are stored in drawers.

LONG DRESSES

Proper hanging
Prevent a long evening dress from trailing by sewing loops at waist level inside the dress. Turn the bodice inside out, and hang the loops from a hanger.

BRIGHT IDEA

Storing skirts
If you do not have any room in your cupboard to hang skirts, roll them around plastic bags or tissue paper to prevent creasing, then store them in a drawer.

ADAPTING HANGERS

Wind rubber bands around hanger

Non-slip hangers
Prevent clothes from slipping off wire hangers by winding two or three rubber bands around the ends of the hangers.

Cut away from yourself when using craft knife

Making a skirt hanger
Cut V-shaped notches near the ends of a wooden hanger to hold skirt loops securely. Use a craft knife to cut the notches.

ACCESSORIES

Never throw away good-quality accessories – they take little space to store and may come back in fashion.

● **Hats** Store in large plastic bags. Blow the bags up and seal them with sticky tape.
● **Gloves** Marks on pale gloves can often be removed by rubbing with a pencil eraser. Wash gloves in special glove shampoo and put them on your hands while they dry – this restores the shape.
● **Buttons** When throwing out garments, snip off the buttons and save them. Keep sets of buttons in small plastic bags so that you know how many you have.

CARING FOR FURS AND SKINS
● **Suede** Pick up threads and fluff on suede bags and shoes by rubbing the suede with a piece of velvet fabric. This also works for dark clothes.

● **Fur care** When wearing furs, always wear a scarf to prevent make-up from rubbing off on to the collar. Do not spray perfume on when wearing fur.

STORAGE

Do not allow clothes in your cupboards to become crowded – if they do, they will not air properly and will become creased. Make space in cupboards by storing out-of-season clothes elsewhere. Alternatively, use a free-standing dress rail kept in a spare room.

DAMP CUPBOARDS

● **Cure for damp** Fill a coffee can with charcoal briquets. Punch holes in the cover, and place the can in the cupboard.

Using chalk
Tie 12 pieces of ordinary chalk together, and hang them inside a damp cupboard. The chalk will absorb moisture from the air.

STORING BED LINEN

● **Avoiding yellowing** Establish a separate cupboard for linen items – linen may yellow if stored in airing cupboards.

Scented linen closets
Store unwrapped soap in linen cupboards – the soap scents the linen and, at the same time, hardens to become long lasting.

HOLIDAY PACKING

When packing for holidays, put make-up and toiletry bottles, no matter how tightly closed, into plastic bags with twisted ties. Mix family members' clothes in different bags – if a bag is lost, no one has to do without clothes.

● **Saving space** Use small items such as underwear and socks to fill shoes which should, in their turn, be packed in plastic bags.
● **Planning ahead** Pack two large plastic bags for the trip home – one for dirty laundry, the other for damp items.
● **Suitcase storage** When you return home, put a couple of sugar lumps in your empty suitcase to absorb smells.

MOTH PROOFING

Moths breed in dust and dirt, so clean and air items before you store them. Clean cupboards and drawers out annually. Do not line drawers with ready-pasted wallpaper, which attracts moths. See page 52 for tackling mildew, which also affects items in storage.

NATURAL MOTH DETERRENTS

Citrus peel and cloves
Scatter dried citrus peel among clothes and shoes in cupboards and drawers. Put whole cloves in the pockets of coats before storing them, and into plastic bags for woollen jumpers.

Tie top of muslin bag with ribbon

Lavender sachets
Make your own lavender bags by tying a handful of lavender into a square of muslin. Place the bags in drawers and chests. They help keep moths away and also scent clothes and linen.

BED LINEN

● **Heat cure** If you suspect moth eggs are in your bed linen, hang the items in bright sunlight for a few hours or put them in your tumble dryer on the appropriate cycle.
● **Moth-proofing mixture** For washing a blanket for storage, mix together 45 ml (3 tbsp) eucalyptus oil, 225 ml (8 fl oz) methylated spirit, and 225 g (8 oz) soapflakes in a jar, and shake well. Add 15 ml (1 tbsp) of this mixture to 4.5 litres (1 gallon) of warm water, and soak the blanket, agitating until it is clean. Do not rinse. Spin dry, then hang in fresh air. Save mixture for later use.

SHOE CARE

S HOES ARE A VITAL AND EXPENSIVE PART of any wardrobe. Keep them well cleaned, inspect them regularly, and repair them at the first sign of damage. Air shoes after wearing and use shoe trees to help shoes maintain their shape.

CLEANING SHOES

W ell-cleaned leather shoes resist marking. Apply polish, leave overnight, then buff in the morning. White canvas shoes benefit from being starched. Nail a metal bottle top to the back of your shoe brush, and use this for removing dirt and mud from heels and soles.

PATENT LEATHER

Buff with a soft cloth

Raising a shine
Rub patent leather shoes with petroleum jelly – this shines the shoes and prevents them from sticking together. Buff well.

SUEDE

Ensure that shoe is dry

Use a clean eraser

Erasing marks
Use an eraser to remove mud and surface soil, and to raise crushed pile on suede shoes. Use a stain remover on grease.

CANVAS

Rub in shampoo until it creates a foam

Using carpet shampoo
Clean dirty canvas shoes with a toothbrush dipped in carpet shampoo. Treat new canvas shoes with fabric protector.

LOOKING AFTER SHOES

C oat new leather soles with castor oil or linseed oil to preserve them. Store your shoes and boots away from direct sunlight (particularly rubber boots, which may perish). Touch up scuff marks on shoes with a felt-tip pen or a wax crayon of the same colour.

USING NEWSPAPER

Stuff wet shoes and boots with newspaper to speed the drying process. Stretch tight shoes by stuffing them with wet newspaper and leaving them overnight. Improvise boot trees by stuffing rolls of newspaper into boots to help them keep their shape.

COMMON PROBLEMS

● **Muddy shoes** Let the shoes dry thoroughly, then scrape off the mud with a blunt knife or a piece of wood. Sponge any marks with a damp cloth, and stuff with newspaper or shoe trees to keep the shoes in shape. Polish when dry.

● **Polish substitute** If you run out of shoe polish, try using a similarly coloured furniture polish instead. Buff well.

● **Heel preserver** Paint the heels of new and newly repaired shoes with clear nail varnish – this prevents scuffing the finish and will stop cork heels from being damaged.

GREEN TIP

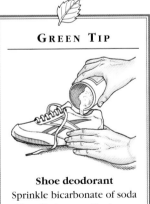

Shoe deodorant
Sprinkle bicarbonate of soda liberally into smelly shoes. Leave overnight, then shake out the bicarbonate of soda before wearing.

CARE & REPAIR

QUICK REFERENCE

Wood, p. 71

Metal, p. 74

Glass and China, p. 78

Ornamental Surfaces, p. 81

Soft Furnishings, p. 82

Around the Home, p. 84

Accessories, p. 86

*S*OME OF THE OBJECTS *and surfaces in your home require more attention than a regular cleaning routine provides. Make it a rule always to repair damage and mend items as soon as you can – leaving problems makes them worse, and you may lose pieces that have broken off. During regular cleaning, look out for problems that may need remedial action. Keep a kit of the repair equipment and specialist cleaners you are likely to use.*

CARE AND REPAIR EQUIPMENT

In addition to your cleaning kit (see p. 10–11), it is a good idea to assemble a kit of items that you might need for specialist cleaning and repairs. A selection of adhesives, sandpaper, and brushes is useful, as are different types of solvent and polish.

- **Brushes and wire wool** Use clean, soft paint brushes, old toothbrushes that have been sterilized, and wire wool to apply and remove substances.
- **Sandpaper** Keep a supply of different grades that can be used for a variety of tasks.
- **Adhesives** Use the correct adhesive for the material that you are mending. Adhesives are difficult to remove, so keep the appropriate solvent to hand during use. See page 51 for removing adhesive marks.
- **Solvents** Keep ammonia and methylated spirit or rubbing alcohol for cleaning. Store these substances out of the reach of children. Always wear gloves when handling ammonia.
- **Oil and polish** Linseed oil is a useful all-purpose treatment for wood, and also feeds leather. Metal polish will clean various metals, and remove scratches from glass and acrylic surfaces.

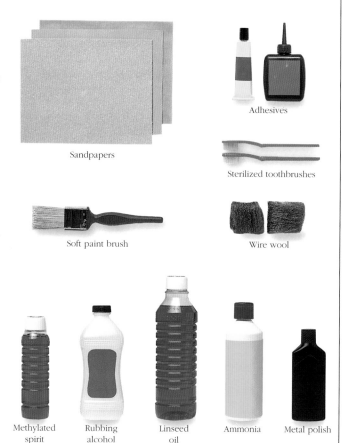

Sandpapers

Adhesives

Sterilized toothbrushes

Soft paint brush

Wire wool

Methylated spirit

Rubbing alcohol

Linseed oil

Ammonia

Metal polish

WOOD

Most homes contain wood surfaces, furniture, and objects, finished in a variety of ways. Although tough, wood is easily damaged. Polish protects wood, but will build up after time. Antique wood needs special care.

CARING FOR WOOD

Different types of wood vary in terms of hardness and colour, but all can be damaged by a dry atmosphere and exposure to sunlight. Position wooden furniture out of direct sunlight. Humidify rooms with house plants and hidden bowls of water.

TEAK

Wear gloves when handling wire wool

Applying teak oil
Once or twice a year, rub teak furniture with a small amount of teak oil or cream, applied with fine wire wool. Buff well with a soft cloth. Dust regularly.

OAK

Apply polish with a soft brush

Homemade polish
Polish oak with a mixture of 600 ml (1 pint) beer, a small lump of melted beeswax, and 10 g (2 tsp) of sugar. Buff well with a chamois leather when dry.

CONDITIONING WOOD
● **Mahogany** To remove the bloom from mahogany, mix 15 ml (1 tbsp) each of linseed oil and turpentine in 1.14 litres (2 pints) of water, and wipe. Rub well, and polish.
● **Ebony** To revive dull ebony, apply petroleum jelly, leave for half an hour, and rub off.
● **Other woods** Pine, beech, elm, and walnut need dusting regularly. Polish occasionally with wax polish that matches the colour of the wood. To keep oak in good condition, wipe occasionally with warm vinegar. Dry before polishing.

MAKING BEESWAX POLISH

Polish antique furniture with natural beeswax polish; silicone polish gives antiques an unnatural sheen and is difficult to remove. Use the recipe below to make your own beeswax polish. Store it in a wide-necked jar so that you can dip a cloth into it. If the polish becomes hard, stand the jar in warm water.

Use coarse part of grater

1 Coarsely grate 50 g (2 oz) of natural beeswax. If the beeswax is too hard to grate, warm it in a microwave on low for several seconds.

Pour turpentine on to beeswax

2 Place the grated beeswax in a screwtop jar. Add 150 ml (5 fl oz) of turpentine (do not use turpentine substitute), then place the lid loosely on the jar.

Water should be hot, not boiling
Cover jar loosely

3 Stand the jar in a bowl, and pour hot water in the bowl to melt the beeswax. Shake the jar gently so that the mixture forms a paste. Leave to cool.

REMOVING MARKS FROM WOOD

Wood is easily damaged by heat and scratching. Avoid placing hot objects directly on to wood – always use a mat. Wipe up spills quickly. Check that ornaments do not have bases that could scratch a surface. If necessary, fix adhesive felt pads to their bases.

MARK	NOTES	TREATMENT
ALCOHOL STAINS	Alcohol damages polished wood surfaces and leaves white marks. Spills should be blotted or wiped immediately; apply treatment as soon as you can.	Rub the area vigorously with your usual polish. If this does not work, rub along the grain of the wood with cream metal polish on a soft cloth.
SLIGHT BURNS	Slight burns on solid wood can usually be repaired. On veneered surfaces, you may need to cut out the damage and insert a new piece of veneer.	Rub with metal polish. If the wood is rough, scrape and sand the surface. Place wet blotting paper over the mark, and cover with clingfilm. Leave overnight.
SERIOUS BURNS	These need more drastic treatment than light burns. Do not attempt to repair expensive pieces yourself; they require professional attention.	Scrape out the burned wood with a sharp knife. Fill with matching wood filler. When dry, sand, then paint the area to match the colour of the grain with artist's paints.
HEAT MARKS	If hot dishes are placed on wood surfaces they can cause white marks to appear. Use table mats to protect wood from hot dishes and saucepans.	Rub cream metal cleaner along the grain. Alternatively, apply a paste of vegetable oil and salt. Leave for a couple of hours, then apply polish.
DENTS	Treat as soon as possible. Dented veneer may split, in which case you will have to cut out the damaged piece and replace it with a new one.	Fill the hollow with warm water, and leave it to swell the wood. Alternatively, cover with damp blotting paper, and apply a warm iron to the dent.
SCRATCHES	These must be filled. You can buy scratch-disguising sticks in a variety of shades to match different woods. Alternatively, use the treatment at right.	Rub with beeswax polish and a little linseed oil. Rub over the scratch, and buff well. Alternatively, use a coloured wax crayon or suitable colour of shoe polish.
WATER MARKS	Water marks wood and causes unvarnished wood to swell. Mop up as soon as possible, and allow the surface to dry before applying any treatment.	Rub with cream metal polish along the grain of the wood, or mix a little cigarette ash with petroleum jelly, and rub it over the marked area.
GREASE MARKS	Spilled grease will leave a permanent dark patch on wood unless treated quickly. Remove excess grease at once, using paper towels or a kitchen cloth.	Use neat vinegar to dissolve the grease, then wipe over the surface with a cloth wrung out with a solution of equal parts vinegar and warm water.

WOODEN FURNITURE

Modern furniture is not always solid wood, but may consist of blockboard or plywood covered with veneer. Minor repairs, such as fixing sticking drawers and wobbly legs, are relatively easy and do not take much time. Major repairs require expert attention.

SPECIAL TREATMENTS

● **Reviving dull polish** Use a mixture of 30 ml (2 tbsp) each of turpentine, white vinegar, and methylated spirit, and 15 ml (1 tbsp) of linseed oil. Shake, and apply on a cloth.

● **Surplus polish** Use vinegar and water to remove a polish build up. Rub off at once. This also removes finger marks.

● **Stuck paper** Moisten paper that is stuck to wood with baby oil. Leave for a few minutes, then roll paper off.

● **Cane chairs** If the seat of a cane chair is sagging, saturate it with very hot water, then leave it to dry in the sun.

WOBBLY TABLES

Cut cork to match shape of leg

Lengthening a short leg
If a table is wobbly because one leg is shorter than the others, cut a piece of cork to the right depth and width. Attach the piece to the bottom of the leg with woodwork adhesive.

STICKING DRAWERS

Greasing the runners
If a drawer does not slide in and out smoothly, rub the runners with soap or candlewax. If the drawer still sticks badly, rub the runners with fine sandpaper, and reapply the soap or candlewax.

WOODEN OBJECTS

Most homes contain a variety of wooden objects, such as ornaments, kitchen utensils, and musical instruments. These items need regular attention to prevent the wood from drying out and cracking. Keep them out of direct sunlight, which may cause fading.

CARING FOR KITCHEN UTENSILS

● **New utensils** Soak new wooden utensils in cider vinegar overnight to prevent them from picking up food smells. Dry on paper towels.

● **Old tableware** Restore stained tableware by rubbing along the grain with fine steel wool (wear gloves to protect your hands). Apply a little vegetable oil, and rub in well.

OTHER OBJECTS

● **Boxes** Give ornamental wooden boxes a sheen and scent by rubbing them with lemon-balm leaves. Sanding wooden boxes lightly will bring back their natural scent.

Salad bowls
Rub new wooden salad bowls with a little olive oil on a soft cloth. Do not clean with soap. Instead, rinse in warm water, and reapply olive oil when dry.

Cover whole board

Chopping boards
Seal splits in a chopping board (caused by the wood drying out) by covering it with a damp cloth for several hours. This will make the wood fibres swell.

Pour in a handful of dry rice

Musical instruments
Remove dust inside stringed instruments, such as guitars and violins, by pouring rice through the centre. Shake gently, then tip the rice out on to newspaper.

METAL

METAL ITEMS MUST BE CLEANED regularly, or they will tarnish and, on some metals, verdigris may appear. This is much harder to remove than a layer of dirt. If you do not have time to clean thoroughly, there are ways to restore shine.

CLEANING SILVER

Silver tarnishes easily so must be cleaned frequently. There are a number of different methods to choose from, some more suitable for particular types of silver than others. You may need more than one product, depending on the sizes of your silver objects.

SILVER-CLEANING EQUIPMENT

Keep silver polish or cloths impregnated with cleaning fluid for polishing large silver items. A silver dip is useful for cleaning jewellery. Use soft toothbrushes to clean embossed items, and dusters for buffing polish. If you use your silver only rarely, store it in a tarnish-proof bag, or wrap items in acid-free tissue paper – both of these will keep tarnish from developing in storage. Silver keeps best if it is used.

Tarnish-proof bag   Dusters   Impregnated cloths

Silver polish   Silver dip   Acid-free tissue paper   Soft toothbrushes

BASIC CLEANING TECHNIQUES
- **General care** Wash your silver regularly in hot water and washing-up liquid, and you will not have to polish it very often. Dust and wash ornaments once a week.

Scrub blackened areas gently but firmly for several minutes

Cleaning embossed silver
Use a soft toothbrush to apply silver polish to embossed silver. Alternatively, apply polish on a cotton-wool bud, or on a cuticle stick wrapped with cotton wool.

- **Dos and don'ts** Clean silver near an open window to stop fumes from collecting. Do not rub hallmarks too hard – you will wear them away and reduce the value of the piece.

Gloves prevent fingerprints

Handling clean silver
After you have cleaned silver, wrap it in acid-free tissue paper or place in a tarnish-proof bag if you plan to store it. Wear gloves to avoid leaving finger marks.

KEEPING SILVER CLEAN
- **Preventing tarnish** Do not store silver items in plastic bags or clingfilm. These trap condensation, which will encourage tarnishing.
- **Alternative cleaners** To remove bad tarnish from silver objects, first dissolve a handful of washing soda in hot water in an aluminium pan. Place the objects in the solution, and remove them as soon as the tarnish disappears. Rinse, and polish. Alternatively, use a paste made from salt and lemon juice. Brighten up silver quickly with a drop of white spirit on a soft cloth.
- **Homemade cleaning cloths** Make your own impregnated cloths by saturating cotton squares in a solution of two parts ammonia, one part silver polish, and ten parts cold water. Leave to drip dry.

PROTECTING SILVER OBJECTS

Polish silver at the first hint of tarnish. Buy a tarnish-proof bag with compartments for each piece of sliver – or make your own from baize. Avoid overcleaning antique silver – its charm lies in its slightly aged look; there is no need to make it look brand new.

SILVER TABLEWARE

● **Salt shakers** Do not put salt directly into a silver shaker – fit a glass interior. Remove the salt after each use.
● **Coffee pots** Remove stains from silver coffee-pot interiors by rubbing them with a piece of fine steel wool dipped in neat white vinegar and salt.
● **Teapots** To clean tea-stained interiors, fill teapots with boiling water, and add a handful of washing soda. Soak overnight, then rinse.
● **Candlesticks** Remove wax by pouring hot water over the candlestick. Melt wax on the base with a hair dryer.

STORAGE

Sugar lumps absorb damp

Preventing mustiness
Place a couple of white sugar lumps inside a silver coffee pot between uses to prevent a stale smell. Store with the lid off.

TRADITIONAL TIP

Silver tarnishers
Salt, egg yolk, broccoli, and fish are all notorious enemies of silver – they cause it to tarnish. Wash silverware immediately after it has been in contact with any of these foods. Then rinse and dry the silver thoroughly.

CLEANING SMALL ITEMS

Nail varnish will prevent allergic reaction

Silver earrings
Paint clear nail varnish on the posts of earrings to stop tarnish from causing ear infections.

Use toothpaste as a mild abrasive

Napkin rings
To clean intricate engravings on silver napkin rings, rub in a little toothpaste with a soft cloth.

SILVERPLATED ITEMS

● **Cleaning** Treat silverplated items as if they were solid silver – but with more care, since the coating can come off. Do not polish silver gilt; you may rub off the gold. Just dust occasionally.
● **Restoring silverplate** Dip worn silverplate in a special solution that applies a silver coating to it. This will wear off with polishing and must be reapplied. Do not use the solution on valuable pieces.

CARING FOR SILVER CUTLERY

Cover all the silver with water

Always wash silver cutlery as soon as possible after it has been used - this prevents food from causing tarnish stains. To clean a lot of silver cutlery quickly, put strips of aluminium foil in a washing-up bowl, and place the silver cutlery on top. Cover the cutlery with boiling water, then add 45 g (3 tbsp) of baking soda, and soak for 10 minutes.

● **Dishwashing silver** Never wash silver and stainless-steel pieces of cutlery together in a dishwasher, since the silver may cause the stainless steel to pit.
● **Decorative handles** Whiten bone handles with a paste of lemon juice and French chalk, applied and left for an hour. Do not immerse bone or mother-of-pearl handles in water, since they may be damaged.

CHROME AND STAINLESS STEEL

It is important not to use abrasive cleaners on chrome, since the plating can be damaged easily. To treat corrosion, use a special chrome cleaner. Although stainless steel is easy to care for, it can become stained by deposits from hard water, grease splashes, and silver cleaner.

CHROME

● **Minor marks** Remove these by wiping over with a little washing-up liquid and water.
● **Shining taps** For a quick shine, rub a handful of plain flour on taps, then polish with a soft cloth. See page 25 for cleaning bathroom taps.

Cleaning chrome
Gently clean chrome with white vinegar. Remove stubborn marks with a solution of bicarbonate of soda and warm water. Rinse.

STAINLESS STEEL

● **General care** Dry stainless steel thoroughly after washing, to prevent a build up of white film. Do not soak stainless steel – it may become pitted. To shine stainless steel, use a commercial cleaner, or one of the methods below.

Buff flour well with a clean, soft cloth

Shining stainless steel
Give stainless-steel pans a good shine by rubbing with flour. Remove heat marks with a scouring pad and lemon juice.

CARING FOR KNIVES

Plunge knife blade in soil

● **Removing smells** If strong fish or garlic smells cling to a knife blade, plunge it into soil. Wash well before use.
● **Keeping knives sharp** Store knives in a wooden knife block, or on a magnetic rack. If you store them with other utensils, the blades will become blunt – and you may cut yourself when reaching in drawers. Alternatively, keep knives in plastic sleeves or in fabric rolls (available from catering-supply shops).

IRON AND PEWTER

Cast iron must always be dried thoroughly after washing, otherwise it will rust. Season it well with cooking oil before use. Pewter should have a soft glow, rather than a shine. Wash it in soapy water, and buff well. Remove grease marks with a little methylated spirit.

CAST IRON

Rub in oil with paper towels

Caring for cast iron
After washing and drying cast-iron pans, rub with vegetable oil. If the pans are rusty, rub them with 15 ml (1 tbsp) citric acid and 600 ml (1 pint) water.

PEWTER

Freezing does not damage metal

Chip wax off with your fingers

Removing wax
To remove wax from pewter candlesticks, place them in the freezer, and the wax will chip off. Use a hairdryer on low to melt away any remaining traces.

TRADITIONAL TIP

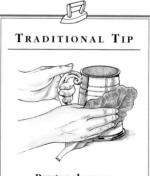

Pewter cleaners
Rub pewter objects with cabbage leaves, or immerse them in leftover water that has been used to boil eggs.

Brass and Copper

Use the same methods to clean brass and copper. Apply a thin layer of lacquer to the surface of these metals to reduce the need for polishing. Use a cardboard template when cleaning brass and copper fittings on furniture, so that no metal polish spills on to the wood.

Cleaning Brass and Copper

● **Removing tarnish** Use a paste of salt and lemon juice, or rub items with half a cut lemon dipped in salt. Rinse.

● **Copper pans** Have copper pans relined when the interior starts to show signs of wear. Copper reacts with food acids.

Salt is dissolved in ammonia

Removing verdigris
If brass or copper turns green, rub with a solution of ammonia and salt. Always wear gloves when using ammonia.

Cleaning ashtrays
After washing a brass or copper ashtray, spray a little wax polish on the inside. In future, you will be able to wipe it out easily.

Caring for Bronze

Shoe polish shines bronze

● **Shining bronze** Wipe bronze objects with a little shoe polish or vegetable oil to maintain a sheen.
● **Cleaning** Dust bronze with a soft cloth. Clean intricate areas with a cotton-wool bud. Apply turpentine to remove any marks.

Other Metals

Some precious metals, such as platinum and gold, appear most commonly in jewellery. Protect gold jewellery by storing it separate from other items. Gold leaf is sometimes used on picture frames and needs to be handled with care to prevent it from coming off.

Caring for Gold
● **Gold chains** Wash in a bowl of soapy water. Use a soft toothbrush to get inside links. Drip dry on a towel; then rub with a chamois leather.

Large Gold Items
● **Cleaning** Clean large gold objects such as goblets and plates with an impregnated cloth for silver cleaning. Buff with a chamois leather.

Apply paint with a soft paint brush

Cleaning Metal
● **Platinum** Clean platinum by immersing it for a few minutes in a jewellery dip. Use a soft toothbrush for intricate areas. Rinse and dry it thoroughly.
● **Lead** Scrub with turpentine or white spirit. Place very dirty objects for five minutes in a solution of one part white vinegar to nine parts water, with a little bicarbonate of soda. Rinse in distilled water.
● **Ormolu** Clean with a solution of 10 ml (2 tsp) ammonia in a cup of warm water. Apply the solution to the object with a cotton-wool bud. Rinse with clear water on a cotton-wool ball, and dry with a soft cloth. Do not use metal polish on ormolu.

Storing gold jewellery
Wrap clean gold jewellery in a chamois leather to maintain brightness. Wash gold jewellery occasionally in soapy water.

Restoring a gilt frame
If a modern gilt frame becomes damaged, use gilt paint, available from art suppliers, to touch up marks. (Gilt paint is poisonous.)

GLASS AND CHINA

GLASS AND CHINA LOOK BEST when sparkling clean. Items that you do not use often should be washed from time to time, or dust will build up and produce a grimy finish. Wipe regularly with a soapy cloth, then a damp one.

CRYSTAL AND GLASSWARE

Wash delicate glasses by hand – using a plastic bowl to prevent breakage – and dry carefully. Never put cut glass or fine crystal in a dishwasher; the strong detergents used will eventually cause a white bloom known as etching, which is impossible to remove.

CLEANING CRYSTAL AND GLASSWARE

Stemmed glasses
When drying stemmed glasses, hold the kitchen cloth steady, and twist the glass around inside it. If you do it the other way around, you may snap the stem.

Making glass shine
Put some lemon skins in the rinsing water after washing glassware. Lemon cuts grease, and the acid released gives shine and brilliance to the glasses.

TRADITIONAL TIP

Polishing glasses
Make a thin paste from baking powder and water, and rub it on to glass. Rinse well, and dry with a soft cloth to create a bright shine. This polish also works well on car windscreens.

CARING FOR GLASS

● **Preventing heat damage** Do not expose glassware to high temperatures, or to extreme changes in temperature – the glassware may break. Gilt and silver decorations on glassware will come off if items are washed or soaked in hot water for too long.
● **Storing glasses** Store wine glasses upright. If you store them upside down, they will develop a musty smell and the rims may be damaged.
● **Removing smells** If bottles or jars smell strongly, wash them, then steep in a solution of 5 g (1 tsp) dry mustard to 1.14 litres (2 pints) warm water overnight. Rinse well.

MAKING REPAIRS TO GLASSWARE

Inner tumbler is filled with ice cubes

Pour hot water into bowl

Hold glass steady

Use a small piece of sandpaper

Unsticking tumblers
If one tumbler becomes stuck in another, stand both in a bowl. Put ice cubes in the top tumbler to make it contract. Pour hot water into the bowl – this will make the outer tumbler expand and release its grip on the inner one.

Treating chips
There is no need to throw away glasses that get chipped. Rub the chip with a piece of extra-fine sandpaper until it is smooth. Then rub the surrounding area of the rim to smoothen it and make the repair less obvious.

SPECIAL GLASS ITEMS

Glass items around the home will attract dust and look dull unless they are cleaned regularly. Do not let dirt build up, or cleaning will become a chore. If you have to carry glassware to another room for cleaning, put it in a wastepaper basket filled with newspaper.

CLEANING AND CARING FOR MIRRORS

Stick strips on back of mirror

Polishing mirrors
Create a sparkling finish on a mirror by applying a few drops of methylated spirit on a damp cloth. Do not allow any liquid to seep under the sides of the frame and behind the glass. Buff with a soft, dry cloth.

Large, heavy mirrors
These can often damage the wallpaper or paint on the wall they hang from. Prevent this by attaching strips of foam rubber or pieces of cork to the back corners of mirrors, using adhesive or double-sided tape.

DECANTERS AND VASES
● **Cleaning** Put a handful of salt and 10 ml (2 tsp) of white vinegar in dull decanters and vases. Shake vigorously, then rinse. Alternatively, use a solution of white vinegar and water, and a little coarse sand. Shake well, then rinse.
● **Stains in crystal vases** To remove stains and grime deposits, fill a vase with water and 30 ml (2 tbsp) ammonia. Leave for several hours, then wash and rinse. Always wear gloves when using ammonia.
● **Stains in decanters** Use a solution of household bleach to remove port stains from decanters. Be sure to rinse thoroughly – until all trace and smell of bleach has gone.
● **Storing decanters** Place a small silica sachet (available from florists) in decanters to absorb any moisture and prevent mustiness.

WATCHES
● **Caring for watches** Get an expert to clean the insides of a watch. Always take a watch off when your hands are in water to prevent the inside workings from rusting.

Use metal polish to buff away scratches

Rub in circular motions

Treating scratches
Remove scratches from watch glass by rubbing firmly for 10 minutes with a piece of cloth wrapped around your finger and dipped in thick metal polish. Polish the face afterwards.

CHANDELIERS
● **Regular dusting** Use a long-handled, fluffy brush to dust a chandelier each time you clean the room. This will reduce the need for frequent thorough cleaning.
● **Cleaning** Turn off the electricity at the mains, and cover each bulb with a plastic bag. Cover the ground below to catch drips. Standing on a ladder, wipe all glass parts with a washing-up liquid solution. Spray cleaners are available for glass beading. Unscrew and clean each bulb, using a metal polish on the metal parts. If you have to dismantle the chandelier, make a diagram, so that you can put it together again.

SPECTACLES
● **Loose screws** If the screws come out of your spectacles easily, dab the ends of the screws with clear nail varnish. Most opticians will also sell tiny screwdrivers.

Dip spectacles in soapy water

Cleaning spectacles
Wash spectacles regularly in a washing-up liquid solution. Rub with neat washing-up liquid to prevent spectacles from clouding over; or polish with eau de cologne or face toner.

CHINA AND CROCKERY

Take good care of your china and crockery, otherwise you could end up with a set of mismatched, chipped items for which you cannot obtain matching replacements. If you break a piece from a set, replace it as soon as possible – some designs go out of production.

CHINA PLATES

● **Storing fine china** When stacking clean china plates, place a paper plate between each one – this prevents the base of a plate from damaging the decorated surface of the one sitting below it.

CASSEROLE DISHES

● **Preventing damage** Before using an unglazed casserole dish, season the outside by rubbing it with a cut onion or garlic cloves. This will give it added strength to withstand high temperatures.

CHINA VASES

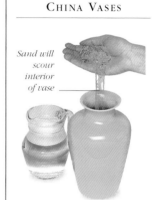

Sand will scour interior of vase

● **Cleaning** Pour a handful of sand or salt into dingy vases. Fill with a washing-up liquid solution, or pour in a little neat vinegar, and shake well. Leave the mixture to soak overnight, then rinse.
● **Deep vases** If a china vase is too deep for cut flowers, simply place some crushed paper towels or newspaper in the bottom of the vase.

CLEANING INTERIORS OF TEAPOTS

Bicarbonate of soda leaves behind no taste or smell

Rub all stained areas firmly until clean

1 Clean a china teapot by dipping a damp cloth in bicarbonate of soda. (Roll up the cloth to clean the spout.)

2 Rub the inside of the teapot with the cloth, then rinse it well. Store it with the lid off. An old glove thumb will protect the spout.

REPAIRING BROKEN CHINA

You can repair minor damage to china yourself, but valuable pieces are best repaired by an expert. Keep all broken pieces in a plastic bag until they can be reassembled. Do not eat or drink from chipped crockery, since the chipped parts may harbour germs.

REPAIRING CHINA

● **Using adhesive** Before you spread glue on broken china, wipe the edges with a piece of non-fluffy material (not cotton, which will leave fluff). Try not to get fingerprints on the edges. Use epoxy resin for repairs – this will allow you to expose the piece to a low heat afterwards.
● **Improvised clamps** When gluing small pieces of china, use modelling clay or clothes pegs to hold the pieces together as the adhesive sets.

MENDING A BROKEN HANDLE

Sand holds mug in position while you work

Check join for surplus adhesive

1 Place the mug in a box of sand, handle-side up, to hold it in place. Apply adhesive to the broken edges of the handle and to the mug.

2 Fix the handle in position. Wipe away any surplus adhesive around the join. Leave the mug in the sand until the glue is dry.

ORNAMENTAL SURFACES

ORNAMENTAL SURFACES NEED MORE CARE than common substances such as wood, metal, and plastic. You cannot always use a basic household cleaner. Surfaces such as marble, alabaster, onyx, and jade each require a special treatment.

STONE SURFACES

Stone can be used for many surfaces, not just walls and floors. Special stone surfaces are often porous, so should not be wetted. They may also stain easily, so it is important to treat spills and marks quickly. Be careful when carrying them – they may be very heavy.

CARING FOR STONE

● **Marble** This is a porous stone, so treat stains at once. For wine, tea, or coffee stains, rub with a solution of one part hydrogen peroxide to four parts water. Wipe off at once, and repeat if necessary. For other stains, see right.

● **Alabaster** This is highly porous. Clean it with a little white spirit or turpentine. Remember not to put water in alabaster vases – they leak.

● **Jade** You can wash jade, but you must dry it at once with paper towels. Never use abrasive cleaners.

REMOVING STAINS FROM MARBLE

Sour milk will keep salt damp

1 Cover stains on marble surfaces with salt. If the stain is not serious, brush off and reapply the salt as the stain is soaked up.

2 If the stain persists, pour sour milk over the salt, and leave it for several days. Then wipe it off with a damp, wrung-out cloth.

BONE AND HORN

In general, bone, horn, and antique ivory should be wiped gently, not washed. Do not immerse bone knife handles when washing-up. Keep bone and horn out of strong sunlight and away from fierce heat. Rinse horn goblets immediately after use, and dry them thoroughly.

CARING FOR BONE

● **Hairbrushes** Clean tortoiseshell hairbrushes with furniture cream, and clean ivory hairbrushes with white spirit. When washing brushes, rinse the bristles without wetting the backs, and dry with the bristles downwards.

● **Bone handles** Wipe bone handles with methylated spirit to clean them. Lay discoloured handles in sunlight, or rub them with a paste of equal parts hydrogen peroxide and whiting (available from ironmongers).

IVORY

Cleaning piano keys
Use toothpaste on a damp cloth to clean piano keys. Rub gently so as not to damage them. Rinse with milk, and buff well.

CARING FOR PIANOS

● **Plastic keys** Dust regularly and wipe occasionally with a solution of warm water and vinegar on a chamois leather.

● **Ivory keys** Leave the piano open on sunny days so that the keys will be bleached and not turn yellow. See left for cleaning. Keys that are badly discoloured must be scraped and polished by a professional cleaner.

● **Casework** Use a vacuum cleaner to blow dust away from the inside casework.

SOFT FURNISHINGS

THE BEST WAY TO CARE FOR SOFT FURNISHINGS is to vacuum them regularly. Do not let furnishings get grimy, or they will never look good again. Wash or dry clean them as necessary. Regular cleaning makes furnishings last longer.

UPHOLSTERED FURNITURE

Upholstery is subject to much wear and tear and needs care, but simple renovation can make furniture look new. A few pieces of camphor down the backs of sofas prevents musty smells and keeps moths away. See pages 32–55 for removing stains on upholstery.

RENOVATIONS
● **Covering seats** Disguise worn-out chairs and sofas by covering them with large sheets of fabric. Alternatively, make replacement loose covers, or dye existing ones.
● **Patching** Patch holes and worn areas as soon as they occur. First expose the new fabric to sunlight, so that it fades to match the old fabric.
● **Tapestry furniture** To revive dull colours and remove dust, rub damp salt into tapestry. Leave for half an hour, then dust off with a soft brush.

REPAIRS TO UPHOLSTERED FURNITURE

Adding slip covers
Arms are the first part of a chair to show signs of wear. Make a slip cover to place over a worn area to protect it from further damage.

Applying a patch
To patch upholstery, cut a piece of matching fabric, and fold or tack the edges under. Sew the patch in place with tiny stitches.

LEATHER FURNITURE

Keep leather furniture out of direct sunlight, otherwise it may dry out and crack. Use hide food once or twice a year to ensure that the leather remains supple. Rub it in well so that it does not come off on clothes. Dust or vacuum regularly, and clean with saddle soap.

REMOVING STAINS

Ballpoint-pen ink
Treat ballpoint-pen ink with milk applied on a soft cloth. Wipe up other ink spills immediately, then sponge the area with tepid water or a little white spirit.

CARING FOR LEATHER
● **Feeding leather** Keep leather upholstery looking new by wiping clean, then rubbing well with a soft cloth dipped in beaten egg white. Polish thoroughly with a clean cloth.
● **Checking for washability** To see if leather is washable, drip a tiny amount of water on to an inconspicuous area. If the water remains as droplets on the surface, then the leather is washable. If the water is absorbed, the leather must not be washed – dust regularly, and wipe over with a barely damp cloth instead.

GREEN TIP

Natural leather polish
Bring 300 ml (½ pint) linseed oil to boil, allow to cool, then add 300 ml (½ pint) vinegar. Apply on a cloth, then buff.

CURTAINS AND HOUSEHOLD LINEN

Take care of curtains and household linen to prolong their useful life. If you move house, curtains can be altered for your new home. Bed linen can be repaired or recycled when it shows signs of wear. See page 68 for moth-proofing household linen in storage.

SOLVING CURTAIN PROBLEMS
● **Rings and rods** Boil rusty curtain rings in vinegar to make them bright again. Rub soap on old curtain rods to make them run smoothly.

● **Sheer curtains** To stop sheer curtains from being snagged when you are replacing them on rods, slip a finger cut from an old glove over the rod end.

Lengthening curtains
Attach a ruffled edge to the bottom in a matching or toning fabric to lengthen a curtain. Use a fabric of the same weight.

Straight hanging
To keep light curtains hanging properly, place coins inside the hem. Distribute the coins evenly, and stitch them in place.

BEDDING AND LINEN

Use all your linen in rotation, rather than saving some for guests. If linen is stored too long, it deteriorates along the folds and attracts moths. See page 61 for laundering linen.

● **Duvets** Shake daily to keep the filling evenly spread. Duvets will last longer if you air them regularly outdoors.
● **Electric blankets** Remove the wires before washing. Return blankets to the retailer or manufacturer for servicing about every three years.
● **Kitchen cloths** These wear out all over. When worn, double them and sew the edges together to make them last for another few months.

LAMPSHADES

Clean lampshades regularly, otherwise they will be difficult, if not impossible, to clean. In most people's homes they are in full view, so they need regular dusting with a vacuum cleaner or feather duster. Always unplug lamps at the mains before cleaning them.

CLEANING TIPS
● **Parchment shades** Dust gently, and remove marks with an india rubber.
● **Plastic and glass shades** Wash in a washing-up liquid solution, then rinse and dry.
● **Silk shades** Have silk shades cleaned professionally before dirt starts to show.
● **Straw shades** Vacuum raffia and straw shades frequently, since they tend to trap dust.
● **Vellum shades** Mix together one part soapflakes, one part warm water, and two parts methylated spirit. Wipe the lampshade with this solution. Rinse with a cloth dipped in methylated spirit, and apply a little wax furniture polish.

PAPER SHADES

Wipe dirt from creases

Regular dusting
Wipe paper shades with a duster, paying special attention to any creases. Do not use water, since it will cause distortion. Paper shades can be relatively cheap – consider replacing shades that become very dirty.

FABRIC SHADES

Vacuum cleaning
Use the upholstery tool on your vacuum cleaner to clean a fabric lampshade. Do not wash the shade – the fabric could shrink, and the metal frame may rust. If the shade is very dirty, have it professionally cleaned.

AROUND THE HOME

T HE MODERN HOME IS FULL OF ITEMS that need regular cleaning and maintenance to keep them functioning properly and looking good. Electronic equipment, books, candlesticks, and pictures in particular all need regular care.

ELECTRONIC EQUIPMENT

D ust is the enemy of electronic equipment, so items should be kept covered or protected in some way when not in use. Make sure such equipment is sited where it cannot sustain damage, and do not attempt any repairs unless you are certain that you know how.

CLEANING TIPS

● **Telephones** Use methylated spirit to clean off marks. Clean the ear- and mouth-piece with an antiseptic fluid, applied on a piece of cotton wool.
● **Portable radios** Dust these regularly. Clean occasionally with methylated spirit applied on a piece of cotton wool.
● **Cameras** Leave cleaning to a professional. Store cameras in their cases between uses.
● **Compact discs** Clean discs and players with special kits available from record shops.
● **Other equipment** See page 26 for caring for kitchen appliances. See page 64 for cleaning and caring for irons.

CARING FOR VIDEO PLAYERS

Prevent dust from getting into your video player by keeping the cover on. If the room suffers from condensation, keep silica sachets (available from florists) on top of the video player to keep it dry.

● **Cleaning tapes** Clean tapes occasionally, using a cleaning tape, to ensure good-quality pictures on playback.
● **Storing tapes** Store video tapes in cardboard or plastic cases. Number each case and keep a log of what you have recorded. Keep a supply of labels for relabelling tapes when you record over them.

TELEVISIONS

Cleaning a television
Keep dust from settling on a television screen by spraying it with an anti-static product. Clean it weekly with methylated spirit or window cleaner and buff it with a paper towel.

COMPUTERS

Cleaning computers
Dust between the keys of your computer with a cotton-wool bud. Clean the key tops with methylated spirit on a cotton-wool bud. Dust the screen and spray with an anti-static product.

TIME-SAVING TIP

Telephone protector
Place a plastic bag near the telephone when you are engaged in messy tasks such as pastry making or painting. Slip the bag over your hand to answer the telephone.

OFFICE EQUIPMENT

● **Safety** Before cleaning any electrical equipment, make sure that it is turned off at the mains and unplugged.
● **Computer care** Site computers out of direct sunlight, which can cause overheating. Sunlight also makes it difficult for the user to see the computer screen.
● **Answering machines** Dust regularly with a fluffy duster, particularly inside the machine. You can use an aerosol cleaner, but make sure that the machine is dry before you replace the tape.
● **Fax machines** Keep these dusted, and occasionally wipe them with methylated spirit.

DECORATIVE OBJECTS AND BOOKS

The objects in your home are what give it a distinctive character. Keep pictures, books, and bookshelves clean and in good repair. Hang acrylic pictures away from open fires; do not smoke near to them. Keep watercolours out of direct sunlight to prevent fading.

PICTURE CARE

● **Cleaning picture glass** Apply methylated spirit or vinegar on a tissue, then wipe off with a dry tissue. Do not use water, since it may seep around the edges and cause damage.

● **Drying damp prints** Place damp prints or drawings between several pieces of blotting paper under an even weight (a piece of board and a few books is ideal). Change the blotting paper nearest to the drawing as necessary.

MISCELLANEOUS ITEMS

● **Clocks** Clean clockfaces with methylated spirit. Cover a valuable mantle clock with a plastic bag when doing your regular house cleaning.

● **Umbrella stands** Cut a piece of thick foam to put in the base of your umbrella stand to catch excess drips.

PICTURE FRAMES

● **Cleaning** Rub furniture polish into wooden frames. Wipe plastic frames with a washing-up liquid solution.

Cleaning gilt frames
Warm a turpentine bottle in hot water, and rub the warm liquid over the frame. Then clean it with 45 ml (3 tbsp) vinegar in 600 ml (1 pint) cold water. Dry and polish with a soft cloth.

CANDLES

● **Securing a candle** Dip the candle end in hot water before placing it in a tight holder. For a loose holder, wrap the candle end in tape.

Wipe candles with methylated spirit

Caring for candles
Wipe decorative candles that become dirty with methylated spirit. Place new candles in the freezer for a few hours – this will help to make them burn longer.

HANGING PICTURES

● **Marking the spot** When you have chosen the spot for your picture, cover it with a cross of sticky tape. This will prevent the plaster from cracking when you hammer in the nail and picture hook.

● **Preventing slips** If a picture keeps slipping to one side, twist sticky tape around the centre of the picture wire to give it a better grip.

CLEANING BOOKS

● **Dusting** Once a year, remove books from shelves and dust the tops of the leaves with a fluffy acrylic duster. Keep the books firmly shut.

Leather-bound books
Clean leather-bound books once a year with a mixture of lanolin and neatsfood oil (available in saddlery shops). Neutral shoe cream is a passable substitute.

CARING FOR BOOKS

● **Storing books** If you have doors on your bookshelves, leave them open from time to time to let the books air and to prevent mildewing. Do not pack books tightly on shelves; keep similar-sized books together. Beware of storing books above a radiator, which may cause the bindings to crack.

● **Preventing mildew** Oil of lavender, eucalyptus, or cloves, sprinkled on to bookshelves, will prevent mildew from developing.

● **Removing mildew** Cover mildew patches on books with cornflour for a few days before brushing off.

● **Grease stains** See page 55 for treating grease on paper.

ACCESSORIES

MOST PEOPLE HAVE VARIOUS ITEMS that they treasure, even if they are not particularly valuable. Keep them clean, and repair them if necessary. Insure valuable objects and take photographs of them in case they are stolen.

CARING FOR JEWELLERY

Costume jewellery needs minimal care, but valuable pieces should be cleaned often. Do not wear rings with stones during cleaning, since you could cause damage to the settings. See pages 74–75 for cleaning silver, and page 77 for cleaning gold and platinum.

PREVENTING DAMAGE
● **Checking jewellery** Check jewellery each time you wear it for any damaged links and faulty clasps. Have rings checked by a jeweller a few times a year for loose stones.
● **Chains** Fasten chains when you are not wearing them to prevent knotting. Do not wear gold chains when you go swimming – the chlorine in pools makes gold brittle.

COSTUME JEWELLERY
● **Cleaning** Cover costume jewellery with baking powder, then brush off gently with a soft toothbrush.

CLEANING VALUABLE JEWELLERY

Place items to soak before brushing them

Lay each piece to dry separately

1 Soak jewellery in a solution of washing-up liquid in a bowl for a few minutes – do not use a sink. Brush items gently with a toothbrush.

2 Rinse the jewellery and lay it on a kitchen cloth. Dry it with a hairdryer on a low setting. Check the water for stones before you discard it.

PRECIOUS STONES

Amber

● **Fragile stones** Amber, coral, and jet are fragile stones. Wash using the method above. Do not use chemicals on them.

Ruby

● **Hard stones** Clean rubies, diamonds, and other hard stones as above, or use a special jewellery solution.

Emerald

● **Emeralds** These are soft and chip easily, allowing water into cracks. It is best to have them cleaned by a professional jeweller.

Jade

● **Jade** This should be washed, then dried immediately. Use a soft cloth – any abrasive surface or grit will scratch it.

Opal

● **Opals and turquoise** These are porous stones, so they should not be washed. Shine them with a chamois leather. Brush fixings with a toothbrush.

Pearl

● **Pearls** The best way to keep these stones clean is to wear them. If you wear yours only infrequently, rub them gently with a chamois leather occasionally.

JEWELLERY REPAIR AND STORAGE

Fit valuable brooches with a safety chain in addition to the clasp. Wrap gold items in tissue and store in separate boxes so that they do not get scratched. If a gold or silver ring is causing skin discolouration, coat it with clear nail varnish – this will not damage the metal.

MAKING MINOR REPAIRS TO JEWELLERY

Restringing a necklace
Place the beads in the correct order along a crease in a piece of paper. Restring using fishing line – it is extremely strong.

Untangling chains
Lay a knotted chain on a piece of waxed paper, and put a drop of baby oil on the knot. Untangle with a pair of needles.

STORING PIECES OF JEWELLERY
● **Necklaces** Prevent necklaces from tangling by hanging them from cup hooks screwed into a wooden clothes hanger.

● **Costume jewellery** Use egg cartons to store jewellery – the bottom for small items, the lid for necklaces and bracelets.

STUCK RINGS

● **Using soap** Loosen a stuck ring by wetting your hands and rubbing soap lather above and below the ring until the ring slides off.
● **Using ice** If a ring is stuck because your finger has swollen in hot weather, put your hand in a bowl of iced water. Soak your hand until the ring can be slipped off.

MISCELLANEOUS ITEMS

Objects such as combs, fountain pens, and handbags need regular attention to keep them in good repair. Clean canvas bags with clear liquid bath cleaner, then rinse well. Rub leather bags with neutral shoe polish. See page 79 for cleaning watches and spectacles.

PERSONAL ITEMS
● **Handbags** To prevent metal handbag frames and clasps from tarnishing, paint them with two coats of clear nail varnish before use. If a handbag handle breaks, replace it with chandelier chain from a hardware store.
● **Combs** Wash combs in cold water with a few drops of ammonia or 10 g (2 tsp) bicarbonate of soda. See page 81 for cleaning brushes.
● **Fluffy toys** To clean non-washable fluffy toys, shake in a plastic bag that contains bicarbonate of soda. Brush well, preferably outdoors.

PLAYING CARDS

Rub mark gently with piece of white bread

Cleaning off marks
Rub playing cards with crustless white bread to remove dirt and grease. Dust with talcum powder occasionally to keep them free from grease and grime.

FOUNTAIN PENS

Cleaning a fountain pen
Occasionally, take fountain pens apart and soak the pieces in vinegar. Leave for an hour, then rinse them in warm water, and leave to dry on a paper towel.

HOME IMPROVEMENTS

QUICK REFERENCE

Household Tools, p. 90

House Painting, p. 92

How to Paint, p. 94

Special Areas, p. 96

Finishing Off, p. 98

Wallpapering, p. 100

Other Techniques, p. 104

K *EEPING YOUR HOME IN good condition maintains it, and may increase its value. You will also save a great deal of money by doing your own decorating and simple home repairs. However, unless you are an expert, do not expect to save time. Make sure you have all the equipment you need before you begin, and plan everything ahead. Begin jobs only when you are sure that you have the time and energy to complete them.*

BASIC HOUSEHOLD TOOL KIT

A good-quality set of household tools will last a lifetime – if you can afford it, invest in the best. Keep tools together in a sturdy box with a handle so that you can find them easily. The items listed below can be used for most DIY jobs in the home.

● **Pliers** These can be used for bending, straightening, or cutting wire; and for gripping nails and tacks for removal.
● **Spanners** Buy spanners in several different sizes. They are useful for tightening and loosening nuts and bolts.
● **Screwdrivers** You will need single-slot and cross-head screwdrivers in different sizes.
● **Claw hammer** This can be used both for knocking in nails and for taking them out.
● **Cutting tools** You will need a pair of sharp scissors and a craft knife with extra blades.
● **Other equipment** Buy sturdy gloves to protect your hands. You will need sandpaper in a variety of strengths; various sizes of nails, screws, and rawlplugs; a tape measure; string; masking tape; and oil for keeping tools free of rust.

Sandpaper (various grades)

Pair of scissors

Single-slot screwdrivers

Cross-head screwdrivers

Claw hammer

Screws

Rawlplugs

Nails

Sturdy gloves

Masking tape

Craft knife

Pliers

Tape measure

Oil

String

Spanners

ADDITIONAL EQUIPMENT

The following equipment is useful if you are going to do a lot of home improvements.

● **Pincers** These are good for pulling out nails and tacks.

● **Extra screwdrivers** A ratchet screwdriver is a good buy, as is a short-bladed screwdriver.

● **Extra spanners** An adjustable spanner and mole wrench are useful, especially for plumbing.

● **Saws** You will need a panel saw and different sizes of hacksaw, depending on the type of job you are doing.

● **Extra hammers** A cross-peen hammer is useful for panel pins. Use a club hammer with a chisel for any masonry work.

● **Chisels** You can use these for woodwork, as well as for various masonry jobs.

● **Other equipment** Use a bradawl to start screw-holes, a pair of goggles to protect your eyes, and a sponge for dirty jobs. An electric drill and bits, a stepladder, and a workbench are other useful additions.

Chisel

Small chisel

Cross-peen hammer

Club hammer

Ratchet screwdriver

Sponge

Goggles

Adjustable spanner

Short-bladed screwdriver

Bradawl

Pincers

Large hacksaw

Small hacksaw

Panel saw

Electric drill

Mole wrench

Masonry drill bits

General-purpose drill bits

Stepladder

Portable workbench

HOUSEHOLD TOOLS

K EEP TOOLS IN GOOD CONDITION for maximum efficiency. Keep cutting tools sharp to avoid cutting yourself by having to press too hard. Wear goggles to avoid getting debris in your eyes, and strong gloves to protect your hands.

CARE AND STORAGE

I mprove the efficiency of your tools by taking good care of them. You can sharpen cutting tools yourself with an oilstone, or take them to a shop to be ground professionally. Clean tools after each use, no matter how tired you are, before putting them away somewhere safe.

CARING FOR CHISELS

Wear gloves to protect hands from steel wool

Oiling chisel blades
To keep a chisel blade sharp and free from rust, rub on oil with wire wool. Protect your hands with gloves. Wipe off the oil with a paper towel before storing.

SANDING SAWS

Wrap sandpaper around block

Smoothing handles
Wrap sandpaper around a sanding block, and use it to rub off any roughness from a saw handle – otherwise your hand may blister or get splinters.

CLEANING HAMMERS

Protect a solid surface with newspaper

Cleaning the head
If you keep mishitting with a hammer, the head may be dirty. Rub it in sand or soil, or use emery paper. Try the hammer on a test piece of wood first.

STORING TOOLS IN CONTAINERS

Use ordinary school chalk

Nail shows exact contents

Using a toolbox
Put a few pieces of chalk in each section of your toolbox. Chalk attracts damp and will prevent any rust from developing.

Labelling storage cans
Make a foolproof label for cans of nails or screws simply by taping an example of what is in each tin on to the outside.

PREVENTING TOOLS FROM RUSTING

● **Small items** Store tools such as hammers, screwdrivers, and chisels indoors in a bucket filled with dry sand to keep them clean and prevent rust.

● **Screws and nails** Use polish tins or cold-cream jars for storing screws and nails. Any remaining grease will help to prevent the nails from rusting.

MAINTAINING TOOLS

● **Removing rust** To remove rust, rub with a rust solvent on wire wool until the metal becomes bright again. Finish by rubbing with a little oil.
● **Waxing blades** Rubbing a little automobile paste wax into tool blades will help to stop them from corroding.
● **Rope and cord** Prevent rope from fraying by applying shellac to the ends. To stop nylon cord and twine from fraying, heat the ends over a flame until the strands have bonded together securely.
● **Using a pegboard** Hang tools on a pegboard using special pegboard hooks. Do not store tools loosely in a drawer, since they are easily damaged or blunted in this way.

USING TOOLS

It is important that you use tools correctly, otherwise you could end up with crooked sawlines, bent nails, or missed screwmarks – or you may injure yourself. Always concentrate when working with tools; only use tools for the purpose for which they were designed.

USEFUL SAWING TECHNIQUES

● **Scoring** For a straight saw line, score the wood with a knife along a steel rule. Cut a small, triangular wedge along the score line and on the waste side of the wood. Then start sawing in the groove.

● **Improvising a sawhorse** If you do not have a workbench, improvise one by turning a wooden stepladder on its side and laying the wood across it. Clamp the wood on both sides of the ladder for safety.

Wrap damp sandpaper around block

● **Using a cork block** Wrap sandpaper around a cork or wood sanding block to give yourself a good grip. When sanding awkward surfaces, use a pack of playing cards instead of a block – the cards will move slightly to fit the surface being sanded.
● **Good sanding sense** Always wear gloves when sanding – otherwise you may roughen and hurt your fingers. Hire an electric sander if you are going to sand large areas.

Tape marks starting point

Using a guide
To make a straight sawcut, place a length of wood over the piece that you want to cut. Clamp the length of wood in position, then use its edge as a cutting guide.

Splinter-free plywood
Stop plywood from splintering as you cut it by putting a piece of masking tape at the start of the sawline. Mark the spot with a pencil before starting to saw.

WORKING WITH NAILS AND SCREWS

● **Tight screws** To undo tight screws, turn the screwdriver slightly in the tightening direction, then immediately in the opposite direction.

Using small nails
If a nail is too small to grasp firmly, push it through a piece of card to hold it in position during hammering. Tear away the piece of card when you have finished.

● **Loose screws** If screws on appliances keep coming loose, apply a little shellac or clear nail varnish under the heads before tightening them.
● **Filling screwholes** If you have made a screwhole in the wrong place and need to drill just beside it, put a matchstick in the first hole to fill it up.
● **Awkward spaces** To start a screw in a hard-to-reach spot, rub some beeswax on the screw head so that the slot is filled with wax – this will give the screwdriver a firmer grip, and help it stay in place until the screw gets started.
● **Nails in plaster** Prevent plaster from chipping as you bang in a nail by putting clear tape over the spot first.

Quick screw finder
Tip screws onto newspaper to find the right size quickly, then funnel the remaining screws back into the can.

HOUSE PAINTING

P AINTING IS ONE OF THE CHEAPEST and quickest ways to give a fresh look to a room. It is best that you decide on fabrics and floor covering – which are considerably more expensive than paint – before choosing the paint itself.

PAINTING EQUIPMENT

Painting is such a large job that you must assemble all your equipment before you start work. Make sure you have enough brushes or rollers of the right size and type for the job you are intending to embark on.

● **Brushes** Natural-bristle brushes are expensive but have a longer life than synthetic ones, and the bristles do not fall out as easily. Buy brushes in several different sizes. A brush with angled bristles makes painting around windows easier.

● **Roller and paint pad** These are suitable for covering a large area quickly. Both are best used to apply water-based paints.

● **Containers** If you are using a roller or pad you will need a paint tray. Pour paint into paint kettles if you are working with brushes – you can also paint straight from the can. Store any leftover paint in a glass jar.

● **Other equipment** Additional useful items include a scraper for removing old paint, a dampened sponge for wiping off fresh paint marks, and masking tape for keeping glass free from paint while painting windows.

Angled-head brush

Small brush

Varnishing brush

Medium brush

Wide brush

Large brush

Roller

Glass jar

Paint kettle

Paint tray

Masking tape

Scraper

Paint pad

Sponge

PROTECTION FROM PAINT

Before you start to paint, cover any furniture that you cannot take out of the room with dust sheets. Cover the floor with newspaper, and wear clothes kept especially for messy jobs. Protect your eyes with safety goggles when painting ceilings.

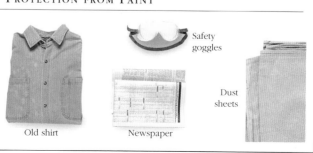

Old shirt

Safety goggles

Newspaper

Dust sheets

PREPARING SURFACES

The quality of a final paint finish depends to some extent on the preparation of the surface before you begin painting. Cleaning surfaces, smoothing them, providing a key for the paint to adhere to, and filling in holes will all help to ensure a professional end result.

TYPES OF SURFACE

Plaster
Make sure plaster is perfectly dry before sealing it with primer prior to painting.

Brick
Remove mould, replace damaged mortar, brush well, and apply a coat of sealer before painting.

Bare wood
First treat knots with "knotting" solution. Apply a wood primer according to wood type.

Painted wood
Sand down the finish if it is uneven. Otherwise, wash with sugar soap, rinse, and let dry.

Distemper
Scrub off distemper with water and a nylon pot scourer. Paint with stabilizing solution.

Emulsion paint
Wash emulsioned walls with sugar soap. Hang lining paper (see p. 102) if wallpapering.

Wallpaper
Paint over paper, or wet it well in sections, and scrape off (see p. 101). Then treat as for plaster.

Ceramic tiles
Clean with an ammonia solution, then sand down to key for paint. Use enamel paint.

REPAIRING SURFACES

Fill any holes or cracks in the surface to be painted with cellulose wall filler, and allow to dry thoroughly. Sand the surface until it is level, then paint. Stuff deep holes and cracks with newspaper before applying wall filler. Make sure that it will not flake off when dry.

REMOVING OLD PAINT

FILLING A HOLE BEFORE PAINTING

Sanding flaky paint
Vacuum away any dust, then sand flaky paint using sandpaper wrapped around a block. Wash the area, and allow to dry.

1 Remove as much dust as possible from the hole with a paint brush. Wet the hole with a damp cloth so that the filler will be held in place.

2 Apply filler with a putty knife, smoothing it as level as possible. Scrape off as much surplus as you can, leave to dry, then sand.

HOW TO PAINT

Bᴇꜰᴏʀᴇ ꜱᴛᴀʀᴛɪɴɢ ᴛᴏ ᴘᴀɪɴᴛ, remove pictures, ornaments, and as much furniture as you can. Big pieces need to be shifted around while you paint the ceiling. After that, they can be grouped in the middle of the room and covered.

WORKING WITH PAINT

Cover the floor with newspaper or dust sheets (do not use plastic sheeting, which is slippery). Put on protective clothing. Try to avoid interruptions – they can cause accidents such as upset paint cans or lines on walls where you have suddenly stopped painting.

PAINT CANS
● **Opening paint** Dust the rim of the can so debris does not fall into the paint. Prise open with the blunt side of a knife.

Keeping rims clean
Stick masking tape around the rim of the paint can to prevent paint from getting into it. The lid will still fit securely when closed.

PAINT KETTLES
● **Dust-free paint** Pour small amounts of paint at a time into the kettle to keep the rest of the paint dirt-free.

Foil keeps paint kettle clean

Lining a paint kettle
To keep a paint kettle clean, line it with foil before you pour in the paint. Discard the foil when you have finished painting.

TYPES OF PAINT

● **Primer** This is used before painting porous surfaces such as bare plaster, wood, and various metals.
● **Undercoat** This is painted over the primer coat before the top coat is applied.
● **Emulsion** This comes in a variety of colours and is easy to apply. It also dries quickly.
● **Gloss** These oil-based paints are hardwearing. They are particularly good for woodwork, but can be more difficult to apply than paints that are water based.
● **Textured paints** These hide cracks and irregularities. They are generally thick and have a rough finish.

PROBLEM SOLVING

Excess paint drips into can

Protect work surface with paper plate

Drip-free painting
To avoid drips down the side of a can, tie a piece of string across the can, and use this to wipe excess paint off a brush. Stand the paint can on a paper plate to protect the floor from drips.

Stocking sieves debris out of paint

Straining lumpy paint
If paint is lumpy or has bits of debris in it, strain it through a "sieve" before using. Use an old stocking, a pair of tights, or a piece of muslin, stretched over a paint kettle, to strain the paint.

BRIGHT IDEA

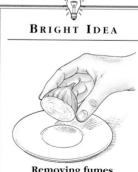

Removing fumes
Cut down on paint smells during decorating by leaving half an onion, cut-side up, on a plate in the room. Replace the onion daily until the smell of paint disappears.

BASIC TECHNIQUES

Rollers and paint pads are ideal for covering large areas, but they can be messy to use. Painting with brushes will give the best finish, although the task may take longer. Remove dust particles from clean paint brushes by lightly brushing them against your hand.

BRUSHES

Avoiding brush marks
Work your brush both vertically and horizontally over the area to avoid brush marks showing in a particular direction. Overlap sections until the wall is evenly covered with paint.

ROLLERS

Covering a large area
Rollers cover an area quickly. Tip the paint into a tray, and dip the roller in it, rolling along the ridged part to spread the paint evenly. Roll paint diagonally on the wall in the shape of a W.

PAINT PADS

Working in all directions
Paint pads are cheap, disposable, and come in different sizes. Starting near a corner, carefully smooth the pad over the wall in all directions without lifting it. Work in wide bands of colour.

PAINTING ROOMS

Painting a room in the correct order helps minimize the risk of splashing paint onto newly painted surfaces. Work on small sections at a time. If you stop for a break, paint up to a corner of a wall first – stopping in the middle for any length of time will leave a line.

ORDER OF PAINTING AROUND A ROOM

1 Ceiling
Paint first, starting across from a window

2 Walls
Paint after ceiling, starting at top right corner of wall

3 Door
Paint after walls
(see p. 97)

4 Windows
Paint after doors
(see p. 97)

5 Skirting boards
Paint last, first masking any surrounding paint *(see p. 96)*

The best sequence
Work downwards from the top of the room to the bottom. Start with the ceiling, followed by the walls, and finally paint all of the woodwork, including doors, window frames, and skirting boards.

ESTIMATING PAINT QUANTITIES

To estimate the quantity of paint you will need, visualize the walls as a series of rectangles. Multiply the heights of the rectangles by the widths, and add the total. Treat any windows with mouldings as a whole rectangle. Calculate the area of a flat door as above. If the door is panelled, work out the area and add 25 per cent.

PAINT GUIDELINES

Primer: 1 litre (0.22 gal) covers 12 sq m (130 sq ft).

Undercoat: 1 litre (0.22 gal) covers 16 sq m (170 sq ft).

Emulsion: 1 litre (0.22 gal) covers 12 sq m (130 sq ft).

Gloss: 1 litre (0.22 gal) covers 14 sq m (150 sq ft).

Special Areas

S OME AREAS OF THE HOME require more effort than others when painting. These include ceilings, skirting boards, doors, and floors, as well as behind pipes. It is worthwhile taking time and care to paint these areas properly.

Ceilings

T he general rule when painting ceilings is to paint away from the window. However, if you are covering white paint with more white paint, work towards the window so that you get the benefit of the light showing what has already been done. Paint ceilings in strips.

REACHING THE CEILING

Plank must protrude well beyond step

Steps must be identical in height

Ladder feet must be securely placed

CEILING BRUSH

Making a platform
If you cannot afford scaffolding to reach a ceiling, fix a plank securely between two ladders.

Do not be tempted to stand on a table or chair, since they will be unsafe and may fall over.

Avoiding drips
When painting a ceiling, stop paint running back down the brush handle by pushing the handle through a paper plate.

Awkward Spaces

T here are several tricks you can employ to make it easier to paint awkward areas. For example, paint alternate stairs, and wait until they are dry before painting the others. Cover taps and handles with plastic bags secured with rubber bands to keep them paint-free.

PAINTING WOODWORK

Skirting boards
Hold a piece of thick card above a skirting board as you paint to protect the surface of the wall. Paint the skirting boards on one side of a room at a time.

PAINTING METALWORK

Painting pipes
When painting pipes, hold card behind them to protect the wall. Use oil-based paint on indoor pipes, and anti-climb paint on outside pipes to deter burglars.

DIFFICULT AREAS
● **Radiator** Make a pad for painting behind a radiator by winding fabric around an unpicked wire coat hanger.
● **Bricks** Take care when painting near bare brickwork, since it will be impossible to remove splashes of paint.
● **Guttering** Instead of painting metal outdoor pipes and guttering, consider replacing them with plastic ones. Plastic pipes last much longer and do not need painting. If you need to paint the wall underneath them, unclip and remove them first.

DOORS AND WINDOWS

These need to be rubbed down really well before you paint or varnish them. When painting window frames, protect the glass first by rubbing it with soap or sticking masking tape around the edges – otherwise you will spend hours cleaning the glass afterwards.

PAINTING DOORS AND FRAMES

● **Door edges** Do not forget to paint the edge of a door. Shut it while painting the face, then wedge it open until dry.

● **Hinges** Rub petroleum jelly on door knobs and hinges before painting the door. Paint smears will wipe off easily.

Flat door   *Paint door frames last*   Panelled door

Painting doors
Follow the numbered sequences, left, when painting flat doors and those with panels. Start at the top, and paint downwards in narrow, horizontal bands. Paint mouldings on panelled doors with a small brush.

PAINTING WINDOWS

● **Start early** Open windows and paint them early in the day so that they will be dry by night and you can close them without fear of them sticking.

● **Wet paint** If you need to close a window and the paint is not completely dry, rub talc along the contact area.

MONEY-SAVING TIP

Filling woodwork
Fill cracks in woodwork with a mixture of flour and the paint you are using. When it hardens it will match.

Taping windows
When painting window frames, stick masking tape around the edges of the glass so that you do not get paint on it. Remove the tape when the paint is dry.

VARNISHING WOODWORK

Bare wood is easily stained and will show marks unless sealed with varnish. This finish is also easier to clean than bare wood. Polyurethane and Danish oil are the best types of varnish to use, since they resist stains, water, and heat. For wooden areas that get a lot of use, use a hardwearing marine varnish.

1 Apply knotting to seal any knots. Then wrap a cloth around your forefinger, and rub varnish into the wood in the direction of the grain.

2 When the varnish is dry, rub it down well with extra-fine sandpaper to give a smooth finish. If a knot still leaks resin, apply more knotting to it.

3 Dust the surface well, then apply a second coat of varnish. Work in line with the grain. Sand down the finish before applying the final coat.

FINISHING OFF

I**T IS VITAL TO CLEAN YOUR TOOLS** at the end of every painting session. If you do not, skin will form on top of the paint, and brushes and rollers will harden and become difficult to clean. You may then have to throw them away.

CLEANING EQUIPMENT

White spirit or warm water and detergent will clean off most paint. Some paints need special solvents – read the instructions on the paint can carefully. When brushes and rollers are clean, shake them to remove excess water, and wipe dry with a lint-free cloth.

CLEANING BASICS
● **Avoid fumes** Ventilate the room well when cleaning painting equipment with white spirit or solvents, since these chemicals may release unpleasant fumes. Do not smoke in the cleaning area.
● **Emulsion** Water-based paints can be washed off in warm water and detergent.
● **Oil-based paint** Clean brushes by wiping thoroughly on newspaper. Swirl the brushes in white spirit, and rinse in warm, soapy water followed by clean water.

ROLLERS AND BRUSHES

Cleaning a roller
Run the roller over several sheets of old newspaper to remove as much paint as possible. Then wash the roller in warm water and detergent.

Nail keeps brush suspended

Bristles are not bent

Soaking a brush
To soak a brush in solvent, drill a hole in the handle, and push a long nail through it. Balance the nail across a jar. This will keep the bristles from bending.

STORING EQUIPMENT

When storing brushes for a long time, make sure that the bristles are straight, then wrap the brushes in foil or heavy paper, or hang them up. To replace the lid on a paint can, lay a piece of wood across the rim and gently tap it all around with a hammer.

TEMPORARY MEASURES

Protecting brushes
When taking a break, wrap brushes in foil or clingfilm to keep them moist. Alternatively, place the bristles in a plastic bag and immerse the bag in water.

PAINT STORAGE

Colour code paint can

Upside-down cans
Store paint cans upside down to prevent a skin from forming on the paint. Dab paint on the base of the can so that you can find the right colour next time.

BRUSH STORAGE

Hanging brushes
Drill a hole in the handles of new brushes to hang them up. Never store brushes standing on their bristles, since resulting kinks are difficult to remove.

AFTER PAINTING

Once you have finished cleaning your equipment, make sure that it is ready for your next painting session. Soften old brushes that have hardened, update your decorating log book (see below), and put equipment away where you can easily find it again.

KEEPING BRUSHES IN GOOD REPAIR

● **Softening brushes** If a paint brush has become stiff through not being cleaned properly, simmer it in vinegar until it is soft. Scrape off the old paint with a wire brush.

● **Oiling brushes** Work a few drops of oil into clean, dry brush bristles to keep them soft and ready for the next use. Wipe off excess oil before hanging up for storage.

CLEANING UP SPILLS

● **Paint stains** See page 46 for removing paint stains from clothes and furnishings. To remove dried paint from hair, rub with a little white spirit, applied on a paper towel.

CLEANING HANDS

Rub oil well into hands

Use ordinary cooking oil

Natural paint remover
Rub vegetable oil into your hands to remove dried paint from the skin. Wipe them dry with a paper towel. The vegetable oil will not dry out your hands as white spirit does.

TOUCHING UP

Pour leftover paint from kettle into jar

Storing sample paint
Pour a little paint into a clean, dry, screwtop jar for touching up paintwork. This is especially important if the colour is not ready mixed – producing an exact match will be difficult.

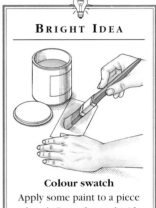

BRIGHT IDEA

Colour swatch
Apply some paint to a piece of card. Carry the card with you as a colour swatch when shopping for furnishings that are to match the paintwork.

KEEPING A HOME-DECORATING LOG

It will be of enormous help when you come to redecorate or sell your home if you have kept a separate log book of the materials you have used, as well as the quantities. Make notes while you are decorating. You can then refer to your log book in the future, and all the details will be at your fingertips.

● **Format** Use an exercise book, or create a decorating section in your home log book (see p. 9).
● **Recording details** Note the quantity, colour, code number, type and cost of wallpaper or paint, and where you bought it. If you make a paint colour swatch, store it in this section.
● **Flooring** Use a colour picture cut from the manufacturer's literature to record new floor coverings. Samples will be too bulky to put in the log book.
● **Shopping** When you redecorate, take the log book with you to shops. You can then be certain that whatever you buy will match what you have.

● **Fabric samples** Stick fabric samples in your log book. Note details such as the manufacturer, the fabric's name, and the code number. For curtains, note the heading used and the curtain maker's name. For blinds, note the brand of blind stiffener.

Hanging Wallpaper

Using a wall covering, whether paper or vinyl, allows you to decorate walls in a variety of patterns and a mixture of shades and colours. Hanging wallpaper is trickier than painting, so it is best to begin with a small room.

Wallpapering Equipment

These are the basic items you will need for hanging wallpaper. You may prefer to hire some of the bulkier items if you do not have adequate storage space for them in your home.

● **Equipment quality** Use tools of good quality: blunt scissors will tear paper, and a cheap pasting brush will shed bristles.
● **Plumbline** There is no need to buy a plumbline – you can make your own (see p. 103).
● **Extras** Use a clean broom for holding up pasted paper when working near the ceiling.

Sponge

Paper hanging brush

Pasting brush

Wooden dowelling

Wallpaper scissors

Wallpaper trough

Seam roller

Pasting table

Bucket with handle

Steam stripper

Types of Wallpaper

Different types of wallpaper serve different functions. Make sure the wallpaper you choose is suited to the condition of the walls and the use of the room.

● **Quantity** Always buy one more roll than you think you need. Mistakes happen and there can be colour changes from one batch to another.
● **Thick paper** Buy thick or textured paper if you want to cover rough or cracked walls. These will not stretch or tear as easily as thin paper would.

LINING
This is good for covering slightly uneven walls before hanging decorative paper.

VINYL
A wipe-clean surface makes this good for kitchens bathrooms, and children's rooms.

TEXTURED
This is ideal for uneven walls. It must be painted and may be hard to remove.

DECORATED
A wide range of decorative colours and patterns is available. Try a sample at home.

BEFORE YOU START

Remove all old wallpaper before applying new. If working on a previously painted surface, first wash it well, and allow it to dry. Make sure bare plaster is dry before painting with size so that wallpaper paste will stick. Wear overalls or old clothes for protection.

REMOVING OLD WALLPAPER

By hand
Using a sponge, thoroughly soak a small area of wallpaper with water. Make a few random slits in the area with the corner of a scraper, and begin scraping off the paper, working upwards.

Using a steamer
A steamer will dissolve the paste behind the old wallpaper with blasts of steam. You can work on a larger area than by hand, but you still need to scrape the paper off afterwards.

Peeling off vinyl
Starting at the bottom, peel off vinyl with care – you should find walls lined with backing paper underneath. This backing can either be removed or covered with fresh wallpaper.

PREPARATION

Make sure any painting has been done in the room first, since wallpaper paste can easily be wiped off painted surfaces. Get all your equipment ready, and cut several lengths of paper to the correct size, allowing at least 10 cm (4 in) more than the height of the wall.

STARTING WORK
● **Ceilings** Always paper the ceiling before starting on the walls so that paste will not drip on to the new paper.

WALLPAPER PASTE
● **Using a roller** Consider using a roller rather than a sponge to apply paste to paper more quickly.

Applying size
If you first apply a coat of size to the walls, it allows you to slide the paper around for a perfect pattern match. Size also reduces the absorbency of the surface.

Mixing paste
Follow the manufacturer's instructions for mixing together the powder and water. Mix well with a piece of dowel, and leave until the bubbles subside.

BRIGHT IDEA

Covering grease spots
Paint any grease spots on the walls with emulsion before wallpapering. This will prevent the grease from soaking through the paper.

USING LINING PAPER

Lining paper provides a smooth surface for the top layer of wallpaper. It is sold in several thicknesses. Leave to dry for 48 hours before wallpapering. Hanging lining paper will also give you practice in fitting paper around awkward areas such as light switches.

ON CEILINGS

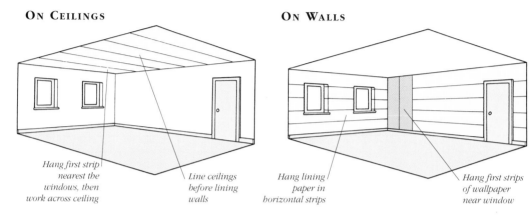

Hang first strip nearest the windows, then work across ceiling

Line ceilings before lining walls

ON WALLS

Hang lining paper in horizontal strips

Hang first strips of wallpaper near window

ORDER OF WORK

Begin on the most important wall. With a dominant pattern, start by hanging the central piece above the focal point – probably a fireplace. Otherwise, start to the left of a window. Finish at a corner nearest to the door so that any minor mismatches will not be seen.

The right order
Begin papering near a window or at the focal point of a room. Work away from the starting point in both directions, and finish off in a corner near a door.

FINISHING WORK
● **Trimming edges** Press the paper into the corner of the wall and ceiling at the top, and the wall and floor or skirting board at the bottom. Pull the paper away and trim along the crease with scissors.

Start papering at focal point

If room has no focal point, start papering here

Finish papering at a corner

PAPER FOR CEILINGS	
Perimeter of room	Number of rolls
9–12 m (30–40 ft)	2
13–15 m (42–50 ft)	3
16–18 m (55–60 ft)	4
19–21 m (65–70 ft)	6
22–24 m (75–80 ft)	7
25–27 m (85–90 ft)	9
28–30 m (95–100 ft)	10

PAPER FOR WALLS									
	Number of rolls according to perimeter of room								
Wall height	9 m (30 ft)	12 m (38 ft)	14 m (46 ft)	16 m (52 ft)	18 m (59 ft)	21 m (69 ft)	23 m (75 ft)	26 m (85 ft)	28 m (92 ft)
2.14 m (7 ft)	4	5	6	7	8	9	10	12	13
2.45 m (8 ft)	5	6	7	9	10	11	12	14	15
2.75 m (9 ft)	6	7	8	9	10	12	13	14	15
3 m (10 ft)	6	8	9	10	12	13	15	16	18

USEFUL TECHNIQUES

When you have finished wallpapering the room, record the amount of paper that you used in your decorating log (see p. 99), or write it somewhere inconspicuous, for example behind a light switch. This saves having to recalculate quantities when next you decorate.

WALLPAPERING AIDS

● **Screwholes** To locate screwholes for fixtures when repapering, place a matchstick in the rawlplug, protruding about 3 mm (⅛ in). Brush the wallpaper over it, so you will see where to put the screws.

● **Protecting paper** If you need to protect wallpaper, paint a commercial protective sealant over it once the wallpaper paste is dry.

● **Excess paste** Tie a piece of string across the paste bucket so that you can remove surplus paste from the brush.

LIGHT SWITCHES

Cutting to fit
When papering around a light switch, cut a diagonal cross in the paper. Peel back the paper triangles, and trim flush.

MONEY-SAVING TIP

Homemade plumbline
Tie a pair of scissors to a string to make your own plumbline in an instant.

WALLPAPERING FAULTS

Careful preparation of walls and wallpaper will help minimize most common wallpapering problems. Minor faults, such as bubbles, shiny patches, and uneven edges, can be corrected relatively easily. However, if you have spoiled a length of wallpaper, it is best to start again, using a fresh sheet.

1 To remove bubbles of air, use a craft knife and carefully slit a small cross in the paper at the centre of the air bubble.

2 Gently fold back the flaps and, using a small, narrow brush, carefully insert fresh wallpaper paste into the slits.

3 Replace the flaps and smooth the edges together with a paperhanging brush. Wipe with a damp sponge.

Lifting Seams
If seams have come loose, lift edges with a craft knife. Apply paste, and sponge in place.

Shiny Patches
These are due to paste drying on the surface. Use a ball of soft white bread to remove them.

OTHER FAULTS

● **Uneven edges** It is easy to cut an uneven edge, particularly at the junction of the wall and ceiling. An uneven edge can be disguised by a thin border.

● **Creases** These can be caused by applying paper to an uneven wall. Cut along the crease, and repaste the paper. Sponge it flat.

● **Damp patches** Damp patches and stains cannot be remedied. Strip the paper and start again.

OTHER TECHNIQUES

Most homes contain woodwork, tiling, and shelving, as well as different types of flooring. These will need repairing or replacing at some stage if you want to redecorate your home properly. Call an expert if you are unsure.

━━ WOODWORK ━━

Good-quality, bare wood can just be sealed or stained, rather than painted. Always sand down well and use knotting to seal any knots before you apply the paint or varnish. Cover wood to be painted in primer, then with undercoat before applying a top coat of paint.

WOODWORK BASICS
● **Woodworm** Be alert for tiny holes in wood with particles of sawdust coming out of them – these usually indicate woodworm infestation. If a large area of woodwork has been infected, professional treatment is essential. This should carry a guarantee covering it for several years.
● **Painting wood** Before painting wood, wipe over it with a cloth soaked in white spirit. This will provide a key for the paint. Apply several coats of oil-based paint.

STRIPPING WOOD

Use fine sawdust

Applying wood stripper
When stripping vertical surfaces, sprinkle sawdust on to the wood stripper – this makes it drip off slowly and gives it time to work.

TRADITIONAL TIP

Reviving scent
Restore natural scent to cedar chests or wardrobes by sanding the interiors.

━━ TILING ━━

Tiles enhance decor by providing a different type of surface from either paint or paper. Mirror tiles will help make a room look bigger. Tiles are ideal in the kitchen and bathroom, since they can withstand heat, grease, and moisture better than paint or wallpaper.

BEFORE TILING
● **Choosing tiles** Buy self-adhesive tiles if you can afford them. They are not as messy to lay as ordinary tiles that need adhesive. For large areas, buy mosaics of tiles already joined together.
● **Sound surfaces** Make sure that the surface to be tiled is firm, dry, and undamaged. Do not lay tiles over wallpaper – it may tear, causing the tiles to fall off and break. Make sure that paint on a painted wall is not flaking. You can lay new tiles over old ones if the old tiles are not cracked or loose.

LAYING TILES
● **Preparing walls** Rub down the surface of the wall with coarse-grade sandpaper to provide a rough key to help the tiling adhesive to stick.
● **Fixing accessories** To fix accessories on tiled walls, you will have to drill holes in the tiles. First scrape a small hole in the required spot with a sharp tool. Then put masking tape in a cross over the hole to prevent the drill bit from slipping and breaking the tile. Do not use a hammer and nail to make a hole in a tile – the tile will probably shatter.

REPAIRS TO TILES

Replacing tiles
If a tile is cracked, you do not need to retile the whole wall. Chip out the damaged tile, using a cold chisel and mallet, and replace it with a new one.

FLOORING

Most types of flooring can be laid by an amateur. However, poor laying can spoil the look of flooring, and of the whole room, so if you are not confident about doing a good job, leave it to an expert. See pages 14–17 for caring for different types of floor surface.

VINYL FLOORING
● **Laying vinyl** Begin in front of a window and lay the vinyl running away from it. Lay it at right angles to floorboards, or on a sheet of hardboard.

Laying around fittings
Trim vinyl flooring to fit around awkward shapes by first tracing the shape onto newspaper with a thick pen. Cut out and use as a template for a perfect fit.

LAYING CARPET
● **Carpet tiles** Hammer several small nails through a piece of wood and use to grip the carpet with the nails when pushing the tiles together.

Stair carpeting
Leave a little extra carpet at the top and bottom of the stairs. This way, you can move the carpet each year to even out wear along the step edges.

OTHER FLOORING
● **Cork** This type of floor is easy to lay, but take care to get the grain running in the right direction unless you want it to look random. Cork is a good insulator, muffles noise, and is warm to walk on. Use PVC-coated cork in areas subject to heavy wear.
● **Linoleum** When laying linoleum, allow for the fact that it tends to stretch. Lay it out flat first and leave it for a while before cutting it to size.
● **Quarry tiles** These must be laid professionally, on a solid base. See page 16 for treating the white patches that may appear on newly laid floors.
● **Wood tiles** Allow wood tiles to acclimatize to the room for several days before laying.

SHELVES

When fitting shelves, it is important to consider what you will store on them. Books in particular are heavy and need to be supported at regular intervals, so that the shelves do not bow in the centre. Choose a style that will match the decor of the room.

CHOOSING SHELVES
● **Using bricks** Construct a cheap shelf unit using piles of bricks with planks of planed wood laid between them at appropriate intervals.
● **Using glass** Glass shelves should be made from plate glass with a bevelled front edge so that you cannot cut yourself on them. Use double-sided adhesive pads between glass and supports to prevent the glass from slipping.
● **Brackets** Use strong shelf brackets to support heavy equipment such as a music system or a television. Make sure that the walls are strong enough to support the weight.

PUTTING UP SHELVES

On partition walls
Fix shelf brackets to the load-bearing points of partition walls (timber uprights, called studs). To locate the studs, tap the wall gently with a hammer until the quality of the sound changes.

ADAPTING SHELVES

Displaying plates
Nail quadrant beading along a shelf that will be used to display items, such as plates, upright. The beading prevents the plates from slipping off. Varnish or paint it to match the shelf.

HOME MAINTENANCE

QUICK REFERENCE
Plumbing, p. 107
Electricity & Fuel, p. 111
Heating & Cooling, p. 114
General Repairs, p. 116
Home Security, p. 118

KEEPING YOUR HOME *in good repair means that all fittings and equipment work properly, and that long-term problems are avoided. Good repair maintains the value of your home if you own it, and helps to safeguard your deposit if you rent it. Treat any problems as soon as you spot them, either yourself or by calling in professional help.*

A WELL-MAINTAINED HOME

Make time to look at your home with an outsider's eye. It is only too easy to accept that a tap drips or a light bulb needs replacing, and to live with the problem. Failure to put things right immediately can cause inconvenience – and sometimes even danger.

Windows are an obvious access point for thieves (see p. 118)

Keep fire extinguishers accessible – in a fire, every second counts

Fit smoke detectors on each floor

Ensure stairs are always in good repair and have adequate lighting (see p. 112)

Lighting accounts for 10 per cent of electricity bills – see p. 113 for tips on reducing your bill

The bathroom uses the most water in the house – see p. 107 for keeping plumbing in good repair

Running too many appliances at once can overload your system (see p. 12)

Most household fires start in the kitchen – fit a fire blanket close to the cooker

Place floor mats inside exterior doors to keep floors clean

Keep floors well insulated, and use a smooth, easy-to-clean surface in kitchens – see p. 116 for floor repairs

Running an efficient home
This costs extra time and money, but forestalls disasters such as burglaries, fires, and floods. Install smoke alarms, fire extinguishers, and burglar alarms, and place secure locks on doors and windows. Always make repairs immediately.

PLUMBING

DRIPS AND LEAKS MAY SEEM minor irritations but can, if left unrepaired, cause flooding and damage to woodwork and plaster. Leaks are also dangerous near electrical fittings. Call in a plumber if you cannot fix such faults yourself.

BASIC PLUMBING KIT

Be prepared for plumbing problems by keeping a tool kit for routine maintenance and emergencies. Buy the very best tools you can afford, since they will be easier to use than cheap ones, and will last longer. Make sure you know how to use them safely and effectively. Store your tools where you can easily find them in an emergency.

Mole wrench

Resin

Insulating tape

Sink plunger

Adjustable spanner

DRIPPING TAPS

Drips are annoying and also extremely wasteful – particularly if they come from a hot-water tap. Drips also create a build up of limescale on sinks or baths. A dripping tap may just need a new washer, or may indicate a major problem, such as a cracked pipe.

REPLACING WASHERS

1 Turn off the water supply feeding the tap. Use an adjustable spanner to unscrew the tap cover, inserting a soft cloth between the tap and the spanner to avoid scratching the metallic finish.

2 Unscrew the large nut inside with an open-ended spanner. Remove the valve mechanism, lift out the old washer, and replace it with a new one. Reassemble the tap.

PLUMBING BASICS
● **Water supply** Make sure you know where to turn off the water in your home. Turn it off and on from time to time so that you can easily shut it off in an emergency.
● **Timing jobs** It is always best to start plumbing jobs early in the morning. This way, if you have to make a trip to the shops for any missing parts, you will not find them closed.
● **Buying washers** When buying a replacement washer, get several spares at once. Store where you can find them easily, for example near the main shut-off valve.

STEMMING LEAKING TAP HANDLES
● **Old taps** Leaking handles indicate that the gland, which prevents water coming past the spindle when the tap is on, is worn and needs replacing.

BRIGHT IDEA

Silencing drips
Tie a piece of string to the spout of a dripping tap. The water will flow noiselessly down the string and into the sink instead of dripping.

● **Modern taps** These have O-ring seals instead of glands. If an O-ring needs replacing, you need to know the make of the tap to buy a new one.

DRIPPING PIPES

Burst and dripping pipes can cause floods that ruin furnishings and even bring down ceilings. Therefore, you must act quickly when you find that there is damage to a pipe. Before attempting any repairs, turn off the water at the mains. You may have to call in a plumber.

TEMPORARY REPAIRS

● **Copper pipes** Enclose the cracked pipe in a piece of garden hose split along its length. Secure with hose clips.

Lead and plastic pipes
Squeeze petroleum jelly into the crack. Wrap a rag or waterproof tape around the pipe until you can get it fixed properly.

> ### WARNING
> If a pipe is leaking near electrical fittings, turn off the mains supply immediately.

PERMANENT REPAIRS

1 Rub the pipe with abrasive paper so that epoxy resin adhesive will stick to it. Smear the adhesive over the crack.

2 Bind fibreglass tape or plumber's waterproof tape around the damaged area at least twice. Smear more resin over the newly taped surface.

3 Leave the adhesive to set hard before you turn on the water. Leave all the taps on until water comes through to prevent airlocks forming in the pipes (see below).

WHAT TO DO WHEN A PIPE BURSTS

1 Turn off the main water supply and open all the taps to drain the system.

2 Turn off the water heater to prevent the metal of the pipes from overheating and cracking.

3 If water is running through light fittings, switch off the lights, and take the appropriate fuse out of the main fuse box.

4 Try to find the source of the leak. Bind the crack with a cloth or waterproof tape. Keep a bucket under it, and contact a plumber.

5 Meanwhile, if ceiling plaster is bulging, move furniture and carpets away, and place a bucket under the area. Pierce the bulge to let the accumulated water out. This will limit the damage to one area.

NOISY PIPES

Most pipe noises are caused by pipes vibrating against each other because they are not supported properly. If the pipes are not secure, put foam rubber between them and the walls, or secure them to a wooden batten. If this fails, you may have an airlock.

CAUSES OF NOISE

● **Airlocks** Air may get into pipes if a lot of water is suddenly drawn off the system. Try tapping along the pipes with a mallet wrapped in cloth to shift the air.
● **Other causes** The main storage cistern may need a larger ball float. You could also try installing a special equilibrium ball valve in place of a standard one. This will move less under mains pressure, so will be quieter.

CURING AN AIRLOCK IN A PIPE

1 Turn all taps on full to run water through the pipes.
If this fails, connect a piece of garden hose between a mains tap and the one that is faulty.

2 Turn on the faulty tap, then the clear one. The pressure of the mains water should push the air out of the pipe and back into the tank.

3 Turn off the taps when the noise in the pipe stops. Remove the hose from the mains tap, and drain it before disconnecting the other end. Reduce the pressure of the mains water supply to prevent the airlock from recurring.

FROZEN PIPES

Frozen pipes should be thawed out as soon as possible to prevent them from cracking. Thaw U-bends under a sink by wrapping them in cloths wrung out in hot water. You can thaw frozen outdoor pipes by pouring boiling water around the area of the pipe that is frozen.

THAWING A FROZEN INDOOR PIPE

1 Turn off the mains. Turn on taps fed from the frozen pipe to let the water out. Feel all the way along the pipe to locate the frozen area.

2 Hold a hairdryer on a warm setting close to the frozen part of the pipe. Do not put it too near plastic pipes, or they may melt.

PREVENTING FREEZES

● **Keeping cold air out** Keep bath and basin plugs in place to prevent waste pipes and drains from freezing.
● **Keeping water moving** For pipes that tend to freeze regularly, leave cold taps on slightly overnight during cold spells in the winter.
● **Traditional cure** Put a handful of cooking salt down drains last thing at night to prevent pipes from freezing.
● **Insulating pipes** Insulate pipes using foam secured in place with lagging tape.

BLOCKED DRAINS AND SINKS

Sinks and drains often become blocked because grease, food scraps, or other solid waste has been poured down them. Keep drains clear with a mixture of salt, baking soda, and cream of tartar. Do not use caustic soda – it will combine with fat to form a hard plug.

REMOVING BLOCKAGES FROM PIPES

● **Sinks and baths** Bale out water in a blocked sink into a bucket. Pour a cupful of washing soda followed by boiling water down the drain. Repeat if necessary.

● **Outside drains** Use the treatments described left to remove blockages outdoors. For serious blockages, you may have to use drain rods or call in a plumber.

SMELLY DRAINS

● **Keeping drains fresh** Flush washing soda down a drain with hot water to stop smells.

Using a plunger
If the treatment above fails, use a plunger. Smear the rim with petroleum jelly, place it over the plughole, and run water until the cup is covered. Pump the handle in an up-and-down movement.

U-bend blockages
If the blockage is in the U-bend, it will not respond to a plunger. Place a bucket underneath the bend, and unscrew the U-bend. Carefully poke a piece of wire up the pipe until you free it.

TIME-SAVING TIP

Unscrewing U-bends
Before replacing a U-bend, smear petroleum jelly around the threads of the screw before doing it up. Next time, it will come off easily.

TOILETS AND APPLIANCES

Blocked toilets usually occur if something unsuitable has been flushed away. You will know a toilet is blocked if water rises to the rim and drains slowly. Overflowing from cisterns and appliances can cause major flooding if not fixed immediately.

UNBLOCKING TOILETS

1 If your toilet is blocked, stop flushing and let the water drain away as close to its usual level as possible.

2 Throw a bucket of water into the bowl, all at once. If the blockage remains, push a toilet plunger to the bottom of the bowl, and pump up and down vigorously.

OVERFLOWING CISTERNS

● **Causes** Overflows may be caused by a damaged ball float, the float arm being at the wrong angle, or a worn washer in the inlet valve.

Stopping an overflow
If a cistern is overflowing, raise the ball float arm. Tie it to a wooden spoon to hold it in a raised position until you can get a new float arm fixed.

OVERFLOWING APPLIANCES

● **Soap problems** Some washing machines and dishwashers may overflow if you use the wrong detergent, or too much. Turn the dial until the machine begins to empty. Run a rinse cycle with the machine empty before rinsing clothes or crockery to get rid of the excess soap.
● **Machine faults** If the detergent is not a problem, check that the filter and soap compartment have been put in properly. If you cannot see a reason for the overflow, empty the machine, unplug it, and call a plumber. Turn off electricity if the water is near switches or sockets.

SAVING WATER

Simple measures around the home will help you conserve water and save money on your household bills. Bathing uses up over 25 per cent of all household water, so shower instead if possible. Never leave the bathroom tap running while you clean your teeth.

KITCHEN

● **Washing dishes** Dishwashers are only economical if you have a full load of dishes. Wash up small loads by hand.

Leftover water
Use water left in jugs and kettles to water indoor plants. Washing-up water can be used to water outdoor plants if you do not use harsh washing-up detergents.

LAUNDRY

● **Washing machines** When buying a new washing machine, remember front-loading machines use less water than top-loading ones. Save water by washing full loads only (unless your machine has a half-load or short-cycle option).

OUTDOORS

● **Car washing** Use a bucket to wash your car, and use a hose only for rinsing. Leaving the hose to run idly wastes hundreds of litres of water.
● **Cleaning driveways** Sweep driveways and garden paths with a stiff broom instead of hosing them down.

BATHROOM

● **Wasted water** Dripping taps waste hundreds of litres of water each year. Drips from hot-water taps waste energy as well as water.

Vegetable dye stains water

Test for leaks
Your cistern may be leaking and wasting water. To test for leaks, drip vegetable dye in it. The dye will appear in the toilet if there is a leak. If so, call a plumber.

ELECTRICITY AND FUEL

ELECTRICITY CAN KILL, so it is vital to treat it with respect. Before working on anything electrical, turn off the mains switch and remove the fuse that protects the circuit on which you are working. Check that the circuit is dead.

BASIC ELECTRICAL EQUIPMENT

Keep your electrical repair tools together in a box, so that in the event of a power cut you will know where to find everything. A torch is vital in a power cut, so keep one especially for this emergency and check regularly that its batteries are still in working order. Make sure that you know how to use the repair tools safely and correctly.

Torch

Pliers

Electrical screwdriver with protected handle

Insulating tape

Wire strippers

SAFETY WITH ELECTRICITY

Check all plugs and flexes regularly for damage. Fix loose connections straight away, otherwise they may become dangerous. Never run flexes under carpets, since they may become worn and the wires may be exposed. Do not hammer nails into walls near sockets.

BASIC SAFETY
● **Dry hands** Do not touch electrical equipment with wet hands, feet, or cloths. Water conducts electricity, and you may get a shock.
● **Avoid overloading** Do not use an adaptor to plug in more appliances than a circuit can safely accommodate. You could overload the system.

Wrap tape tightly around damaged area

Repairing flexes
If a flex has become worn, wrap it tightly in insulating tape to make it safe. Replace it with a new flex as soon as possible.

APPLIANCES
● **Earthing** Ensure that all metal appliances are earthed to prevent electric shocks.
● **Plugs** Appliances should have plugs with double insulation. Replace cracked or broken plugs before moisture can get into them. Use strong rubber plugs for frequently used portable appliances.

Electrical fires
Use a special fire extinguisher on electrical fires. Never use water – it will cause a short circuit and electrical shocks.

DANGER SIGNALS

It is best to call an expert to deal with electrical wiring problems, for example if the wiring looks dangerous, or if an appliance is not working and you cannot diagnose the fault. Be aware of the warning signs of electrical problems given below, and familiarize yourself with the emergency treatment for electrical shock given on pages 167 and 171.

● A "fishy" or burning smell This can indicate that an appliance plug is overheating and starting to melt. Switch off the appliance and remove the plug from the socket.
● **Warm plugs** If a plug feels warm, switch it off, and take it out of the wall. Turn off the mains, and remove the fuse for that circuit. Check the wiring in the plug and socket. A fault in either, if left, may cause a fire.

LIGHTS AND APPLIANCES

Good lighting is essential in the home. Turn off lights in empty rooms, and put timer switches on lights in halls and outside so that they come on when the house is empty. Keep appliances in good repair – faulty items can cause fires, power failure, or electrical shock.

LIGHT CARE
● **Correct bulbs** Always use the recommended strength bulb for each lampshade. Clean lamps regularly.

Keep bulbs clean
Dust can reduce the light given out by a bulb by as much as 50 per cent. Use a feather duster to clean ceiling bulbs and light fittings. See also page 20.

LIGHTING YOUR HOME
● **Lighting plans** Take time to make a lighting plan before you decorate a home. Use the right strength bulb for each area – dim lighting may suit eating areas, while kitchen, bathroom, and reading areas require bright lighting.
● **Light switches** Put luminous paint or stickers on all light switches so that you can find them easily in the dark.
● **Lighting and safety** In a home with small children, fit childproof safety sockets, and use plugs with sheathed pins. Use a nightlight for children afraid of the dark. Illuminate hazards such as outdoor steps at night with low-level lights.

APPLIANCE PROBLEMS
● **Fuses and sockets** If an appliance stops working, check the manufacturer's handbook. You may have to replace the fuse in the plug (see below). If it still fails, plug in an appliance that you know is working to see if there is a fault in the socket.
● **Overloading** Do not plug too many lights and appliances into the same socket – you may overload it and cause a fire.
● **Dangerous appliances** If an appliance gives you a shock, the plug or flex may be poorly insulated. Do not use the appliance until an electrician has repaired it.

POWER FAILURE

If you lose electricity, it may mean that a fuse needs replacing, or that there is a widespread power cut. If you have advance warning of a power cut, switch refrigerator and freezer controls to maximum, and put candles and matches where you can easily find them.

CIRCUIT FAILURE
1 If several appliances or lights in one area fail at once, a circuit fuse in the mains fuse box has probably blown. Switch off everything on that particular circuit.

2 Replace the blown fuse. If the fuses are not labelled, look for scorch marks. Check for and repair broken wires.

3 Check for and repair any visible damage to plugs and flexes used on the circuit.

4 Switch on appliances and lights one at a time. If the fuse blows again, the circuit may be overloaded or an appliance may be faulty.

POWER CUTS
● **When power returns** Reset electric clocks and timer switches. Do not open the freezer for at least six hours.

During a power cut
Turn off all your appliances and lights – apart from one bulb, and the refrigerator and freezer. A power surge when electricity is restored could blow a fuse.

BRIGHT IDEA

Emergency candles
Keep a pair of candles in the refrigerator or freezer at all times, so that you are sure to find them in a power failure.

OTHER FUEL SOURCES

Fuels such as gas and coal can be hazardous and should be treated with caution. If you smell gas or burning, investigate immediately. A gas leak could lead to an explosion, while an uncontrolled fire in a fireplace can burn down a building. Both can be fatal.

EMERGENCY ACTION FOR GAS LEAKS

1 If there is a strong smell of gas, extinguish cigarettes, candles, and gas cooker flames. Switch off any machines that might produce sparks, such as a vacuum cleaner. Leave lights on or off.

2 Cut off the supply of gas entering the house by turning off the tap beside the gas meter. Turn the handle of the tap until it is at a right angle to the pipe.

3 Open as many windows as possible to let in fresh air to dissipate the gas fumes. Evacuate the whole building, and warn neighbours. Take anyone unconscious outside for treatment (see p. 168).

4 Call the gas company's emergency line. On no account enter a room to investigate the smell of gas yourself – the fumes may quickly overpower you.

OPEN FIRES

● **Safety** If an open fire goes out of control, pour water on it to put it out. If the chimney is alight, call the fire brigade. Have your chimneys swept regularly to prevent soot from building up.
● **Slow fires** Draw a slow fire by holding an open newspaper across the fireplace. Leave a 3–5 cm (1–2 in) gap at the bottom for air to reach the fire.

SAVING FUEL

Using fuel economically can save quite a bit of money. Even simple ideas, such as turning down the thermostat on the hot-water cylinder, can save fuel. Major tasks, such as insulating the loft or lagging your pipes, will make a considerable difference in the long run.

KETTLES

Use a mug as a measure

Boiling water
Boil only as much water as you require, using a mug or cup to measure the right amount. If you are heating water in an electric kettle, make sure that the heating element is always completely covered over.

ELECTRONICS
● **Televisions** Do not leave the television on remote control overnight. Switch it off properly to save money.
● **Choosing appliances** Buy energy-efficient appliances, and choose the best you can afford – they will last longest.

IN THE KITCHEN
● **Appliances** Buy energy-saving small appliances such as electric frying pans, slow cookers, and deep fryers. They use considerably less energy than ovens and stoves.
● **Ovens** When using a standard oven, make sure you benefit from its capacity. Rather than baking a single pizza, for example, cook several items at once.
● **Stoves** Keeping stoves clean will maximize reflective heat.
● **Microwave ovens** Use a microwave whenever possible. It uses far less energy than standard cookers.
● **Freezers** Open the freezer as infrequently as possible. Every time you let cold air out, it has to work harder to regain its temperature.
● **Pots and pans** Make sure saucepan lids fit tightly. Use pots the same size or slightly larger than cooking elements.

MONEY-SAVING TIP

Paying for energy
Keep a money jar by main light switches, and fine family members each time a light is left on in an empty room.

LIGHTING
● **Reflecting light** Place lamps in corners of rooms to reflect light. Pale walls in a room will require less lighting than those with dark walls.

HEATING AND COOLING

INSULATING YOUR HOME WILL KEEP it warm in winter and cool in summer, and will also save you money on your heating and cooling bills. The initial expenditure on insulation could easily be recouped in just a couple of years.

A COOL HOME

A WARM HOME

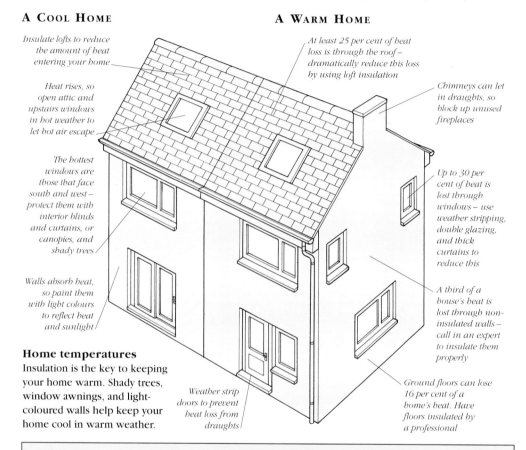

Insulate lofts to reduce the amount of heat entering your home

Heat rises, so open attic and upstairs windows in hot weather to let hot air escape

The hottest windows are those that face south and west – protect them with interior blinds and curtains, or canopies, and shady trees

Walls absorb heat, so paint them with light colours to reflect heat and sunlight

At least 25 per cent of heat loss is through the roof – dramatically reduce this loss by using loft insulation

Chimneys can let in draughts, so block up unused fireplaces

Up to 30 per cent of heat is lost through windows – use weather stripping, double glazing, and thick curtains to reduce this

A third of a house's heat is lost through non-insulated walls – call in an expert to insulate them properly

Weather strip doors to prevent heat loss from draughts

Ground floors can lose 16 per cent of a home's heat. Have floors insulated by a professional

Home temperatures

Insulation is the key to keeping your home warm. Shady trees, window awnings, and light-coloured walls help keep your home cool in warm weather.

REDUCING COOLING AND HEATING BILLS

COOLING BILLS

● **Windows** Fit outdoor canopies over sunny windows to shade them, or plant shady trees and trellises to protect them.
● **Fans** Install a whole-house fan to pull heat out of the house. A low-speed ceiling fan in the kitchen will be more efficient than a high-speed one.
● **Air conditioners** Fit air conditioners on the shadier side of the house, or put up a canopy over it. Make sure you clean a conditioner's air filter regularly.

HEATING BILLS

● **Thermostats** Turn down your central heating and hot water thermostats by a couple of degrees to save 10 per cent off your electricity bills.
● **Lagging** The heat-saving benefits of lagging hot-water pipes and cylinders will be obvious almost immediately.
● **Double glazing** This is initially expensive but will pay for itself in the long run. Fit temporary double glazing as a cheap alternative (see opposite).

● **Floor insulation** Fill in cracks in floorboards, and insulate floors with carpets. Call an expert to insulate under the floor – it will be worth the cost in the long run.
● **Loft insulation** A quarter of a home's heat is lost through the roof. Prevent this by insulating the loft or attic with fibreglass or mineral wool.
● **Weather stripping** Buy adhesive insulation strips for draughty doors and windows.

KEEPING WARM

The cost of keeping warm in winter does not need to be high. Wear more or warmer clothes. Keep doors to heated rooms closed, and shut off unused rooms so that you do not have to heat them. Fit a draught-excluding flap to the letter box.

RADIATORS
● **Stop heat rising** Fit a shelf directly above a radiator to make heat flow into the room rather than rising away.

DRAUGHTS
● **Draught finder** Close doors and windows, and walk around with a candle. Where it flickers, you have a draught.

DOUBLE GLAZING
● **Temporary measures** Use sheets of plexiglass or heavy plastic as double glazing, secured with strong tape.

Heat reflector
Make radiators more efficient by taping aluminium foil to card behind them, shiny side in. The foil will reflect heat into the room and not through the walls.

Draught excluder
Stuff an old jacket sleeve with wadding, and sew it up to make a draught excluder for a door. Use a bright colour so that no will one trip over it.

Using plastic sheeting
Clear plastic sheeting, fixed to windows with tape, provides instant double glazing. Shrink it to fit with a hair dryer, and peel it off in the summer.

KEEPING COOL

Insulating your home properly will help keep it cool as well as warm. Wear loose clothing around the house in hot weather, and avoid using the oven or cooker in the heat of the day. Open attic or top-floor windows, and try to circulate air with cross-ventilation.

NATURAL SOLUTIONS
● **Avoid artifical light** Light bulbs give out more heat than you might imagine. Use natural daylight as long as possible, and do not switch lights on until it is essential.
● **Landscaping for shade** Plant trees outside to shade your home. Deciduous trees will provide shade in summer and allow light in when their branches are bare in winter.

REDUCING HUMIDITY
● **Showering** Steam can dramatically increase the level of humidity in your home. When showering, open the windows to let as much moisture escape as possible.

KEEPING HEAT OUT
● **Draw curtains** Draw blinds and curtains during the hottest part of the day to shade rooms from the rays of the sun.

Reflect solar radiation
Staple or tape aluminium foil inside the roof space to reflect the sun's heat outwards. Heat passing into the house will be reduced by at least 20 per cent.

GREEN TIP

Reduce humidity
Keep lids on saucepans to reduce the humidity caused by steam. You will also use less energy to cook foods and so save money. Close internal kitchen doors while cooking to keep other rooms cool.

GENERAL REPAIRS

Y OU CAN SAVE A LOT OF MONEY by doing simple repairs around the home yourself. Minor problems with floors, doors, windows, and stairs can be fixed without much expense. More complex jobs may require a professional.

FLOORS

C reaks and gaps in wooden floorboards cause irritation and draughts, but can be easily fixed. Concrete floors may sometimes be uneven, so bumps should be chipped away with a chisel and club hammer. Lift damaged vinyl tiles with a hot iron over aluminium foil.

WOODEN FLOORS
● **Square-edged boards** If a board is cracked or split, find the joists by locating the nails at each end. Drill close to the joists and cut out the board with a padsaw. Replace with a new piece of wood.
● **Tongue-and-groove boards** Saw out a damaged tongue-and-groove board along the edge. It cannot be replaced, so substitute it with an ordinary floorboard, supported at each end by a block of wood screwed to each joist.

QUICK INSULATION

Using homemade filler
Fill spaces between floorboards with papier mâché made from newspaper and wallpaper paste. Sand smooth when dry.

SQUEAKY FLOORS

Using talcum powder
To silence squeaks, shake talcum powder between floorboards. Refix loose boards to the joists with long nails at an angle.

DOORS

T o prevent a door from slamming, fit a sprung-door closer or use a doorstop. Stop a door from rattling by moving the lock catch, or fix a draught excluder inside the frame. Lift a sagging door by tightening or moving the hinges. Repair rotten parts of wood quickly.

STICKING DOORS

Finding the problem
Rub chalk down the edge of the door, then close it. The chalk will leave a mark on the frame at the contact point. Plane the area. If sliding doors stick, apply floor polish to the tracks.

STICKING HINGES

Lubricating a hinge
Treat a sticking hinge by rubbing pencil lead along the spine. Alternatively, smear a little light oil along the hinge with a cloth, working the hinge back and forth until it moves freely.

BRIGHT IDEA

Oiling sticking locks
To loosen a sticking lock, put a little oil on the key. Put the key in the lock, and give it a few turns to loosen the lock.

STAIRS

The best way to deal with creaking stairs is from below. If you cannot get underneath, take up any carpet and firmly screw the front of the tread to the top of the riser. Make sure that stairs are well lit and that any carpeting is securely laid so that no one can trip over it.

THREE WAYS TO REPAIR CREAKING STAIRS

Gluing a riser
Push a screwdriver between the tread and the riser and insert a piece of card covered in wood-work adhesive. Leave it there. Repeat until squeak has gone.

Adding a wood block
A persistent squeak may need tackling from under the stairs. Glue a triangular block of wood into the corner of the tread and riser. Secure it with screws.

Replacing wedges
With old stairs, you may have to replace the stair wedges to fix a squeak. Clean off the old glue, reapply, then hammer the new wedges back into place.

WINDOWS

If a window has broken and you cannot repair it or get a glazier at once, board it up with chipboard. Always wear heavy gloves when dealing with glass. Cover small cracks temporarily with polythene and masking tape. Make sure window panes are sealed properly.

BROKEN WINDOWS
● **Handling broken glass** Wear thick gardening gloves when handling broken glass, and use goggles if you have to break any glass. Dispose of broken glass in newspaper.

Removing glass
Carefully criss-cross pieces of masking tape over a broken window pane. Cover the glass with a heavy cloth, then tap gently with a hammer to break away the pieces from the window without splintering.

REPLACING PANES
1 Buy a pane of glass that is 1.5 mm (¹⁄₁₆ in) smaller than the window opening on all sides. Chip out any old putty. Clean out the recess, and paint it with primer.

2 Lay a bed of fresh putty in the rebate in the window frame. Press the new piece of glass into position around the edges – not in the centre, where it could break. Insert glazing brads or clips to keep the pane of glass in place.

WINDOW PROBLEMS

● **Damaged putty** As putty hardens, it may crack and fall out. Chip it out with a chisel, and replace all the putty – not just the damaged section.
● **Sticking windows** A build up of paint may cause a wooden window to stick. Strip paint off the edge, and plane it to fit the frame. Repaint the wood.
● **Condensation** Install secondary double glazing to prevent condensation on metal window frames.

HOME SECURITY

MAKING YOUR HOME SECURE will help to deter any opportunist intruders. Install security locks on doors and windows, a good-quality burglar alarm, and outdoor lights. Join the Neighbourhood Watch if one exists in your area.

VULNERABLE AREAS OF THE HOME

Skylights can be a security risk – fit them with iron bars if your roof is easily accessible

Skylights can be reached via a drainpipe – paint drainpipe with anti-climb paint

Keep hedges low to avoid screening burglars

Windows near a roof or drainpipe are easy to reach – never leave them unlocked

Keep access to the back of your house locked

Secure sliding doors with special locks

A well-secured home

Locks and alarms deter burglars, but you must also be sure not to "invite" them into your home. Make sure your home always appears occupied – even while you are away. Poor outside lighting and dense shrubbery provide a cover for burglars while they break in.

Back windows or those hidden by shrubs are often targeted by burglars

Fit locks to the back door as well as the front – most burglars gain access at the backs of houses

---

MAKING YOUR HOME MORE SECURE

● **Alarms** Install a house alarm system, and make sure it is easily visible in order to deter any casual intruders.
● **Doors** Fit good-quality, solid-wood exterior doors. Flimsy doors can be easily kicked in. Fit secure locks to exit doors, and a chain or spyhole so that you can inspect any visitors.
● **Windows** Fit locks to every window, especially windows close to drainpipes, ground-floor windows, and French windows. Lock them each time you go out.

● **Rear entrances** Make the rear of your home as inaccessible as possible. Most burglars break in at the backs of houses.
● **Garage** Secure the door leading from the garage to the house, as well as the garage doors. A burglar could work unseen in the garage.
● **Hedges** Keep hedges trimmed as low as possible so that anyone trying to break in can be easily seen. Prickly hedges and shrubs will also act as a deterrent to intruders.

● **Drainpipes** Put anti-climb paint on drainpipes. It never dries, so is impossible to climb and leaves marks on clothes.
● **Sheds** Padlock sheds so that your tools cannot be used to break into the house. Put shed door hinges on the inside so that they cannot be removed to take the door off.
● **Ladders** Lock away ladders or padlock them horizontally to walls so that burglers cannot use them to break into the house through the upper floors.

INSIDE YOUR HOME

Locks, bolts, and alarms are only as good as the fabric of the home they are protecting. Make it more difficult for thieves to get in by having good-quality doors and windows that are always kept locked. Always change the locks when you move into a new house.

SECURING DOORS AND WINDOWS

● **Internal doors** Do not lock internal doors. Burglars will think you are hiding valuables and may break them down.

● **Exterior doors** Fit special bolts into the hinge sides of exterior doors to make them harder to break through.

Casement windows
Sink a long screw into a casement window beside the handle to prevent it from being opened. Fit permanent locks to windows as soon as possible.

Sash windows
Install locks on sash windows, or put a long wood screw through the meeting rails. Do not permanently screw down windows, in case of a fire.

DRAWING CURTAINS

● **Daytime** Open curtains during the day. Drawn curtains show you are out, and also enable burglars to work inside without being seen.
● **Evening** Draw your curtains at night when you have lights on, so that no one can see any valuable possessions.

POSSESSIONS

● **Marking** Print your name and postcode on valuables in invisible ink so you can prove ownership to the police. Record all serial numbers.
● **Photographing** Take a picture of all your valuable objects so you can prove they are yours if they are stolen.

IN A BURGLARY

● **Confronting a burglar** If you interrupt a burglary, do not provoke the burglar. Co-operate if necessary, then call the police. If you return to find a burglar in your house, telephone the police from a neighbour's house.

HOLIDAY SECURITY PRECAUTIONS

● **Luggage labels** Labelling your luggage by sticking the address to the outside announces that your house is unoccupied. Place labels inside cases instead.

● **Deliveries** Cancel deliveries such as milk and newspapers.
● **Mail** Arrange for a neighbour to push mail right through the letter box. In a glazed porch, the neighbour should pick it up and put it out of sight. Otherwise, hang a curtain over the glass to hide any mail you receive.
● **Timer switches** Install several timer switches to turn on lights and the television at night.
● **Garage door** Close the garage door so that no one can see if your car is not there.

● **Car** On a short holiday, leave your car outside your home. Ask a neighbour to brush snow or ice off the car if you are going to be away for a long time.
● **Indicate occupation** Ask a neighbour to mow the lawn, sweep up leaves, and leave signs of occupation, such as footprints in snow on the path.
● **Protection** Put any valuables in a bank before you go away. Tell the police that your house will be empty so that they can keep an eye on it for you.

FOOD & DRINK

QUICK REFERENCE

Fruit & Vegetables, p. 122

Meat, Dairy, & Eggs, p. 126

Bread, Pasta, & Rice, p. 130

All the Extras, p. 132

Baking & Sweets, p. 136

Beverages, p. 140

GOOD FOOD DEPENDS *more on choosing the best ingredients and preparing them well than it does on using fancy recipes and complicated techniques. Assemble ingredients and equipment before you start cooking, and always allow yourself ample time and space in the kitchen – this will help to prevent accidents such as burns and fires, as well as avoiding ruined dishes and frayed tempers.*

EQUIPMENT AND INGREDIENTS

Keep your kitchen well organized – it is difficult to work in a room cluttered with hardly used gadgets and items put back in the wrong places. See pages 26–30 for cleaning kitchens and equipment, and use the tips below to solve common kitchen problems.

SOLVING COMMON PROBLEMS

Keep cap on tube

Flatten tube before you start pressing

Cork has been screwed into position

Push straw to bottom of bottle

Introducing air through straw will release stuck sauce

Emptying paste tubes
To get the last bit of paste out of a tube, use a rolling pin to push the contents up to the top.

Replacing a pan knob
If a saucepan lid loses its knob, replace it with an ordinary cork, which will be heat-resistant.

Making sauce flow
If thick sauce is stuck in a bottle, insert a straw to introduce air into it; then remove the straw.

HOW TO UNSCREW A TIGHT JAR

There are a number of ways to make unscrewing tight jars easier:

- **Finding a grip** Wear a rubber glove on one hand to grip the tight lid firmly, then twist. Use a pair of nutcrackers to grip small lids.
- **Using heat** Hold the lid under hot, running water to expand the metal.
- **Loosening the lid** Tap all around the lid at an angle with a spoon.

BURNS AND FIRES

- **Avoiding burns** Turn saucepan handles inwards during cooking; this prevents pans from being knocked over and causing scalds.
- **Oil fires** If you do not have a kitchen blanket, smother flames with a lid, or throw salt, earth, washing soda, or bath salts on the flames. Do not use water on oil fires.

KITCHEN BASICS

When using an oven, fill it with as many items as possible to save energy – and remember that dishes on the top shelf will cook faster than those at the bottom. Cover saucepans when cooking – the food will heat more quickly with the lid on than with it off.

KITCHEN ITEMS

● **Kitchen containers** Measure the volumes of all your dishes and basins. Write the volume on the bottom of each one in nail varnish. This will make it easy for you to locate the right item when in a hurry.

● **Heating plates** Putting plates in the oven can cause discolouration or cracking. Heat plates by holding them under hot, running water for several minutes instead.

● **Cookbooks** Keep a series of exercise books for your recipes, and index each one for ease of reference. Cover much-used cookbooks with aluminium foil so that you can wipe them clean easily.

SEASONING FOOD

When to add salt
Add salt to soups or stews early to enhance flavour. Add salt to roasted meat near the end – the meat becomes tough otherwise. Cook vegetables in salted water.

BRIGHT IDEA

Clean cookbooks
To prevent a cookbook from being soiled when you refer to it during cooking, open it to the required page and slip it into a clear plastic bag before you start cooking. The book will remain clean, no matter how messy the task.

RECTIFYING MISTAKES

If food does not turn out as intended, do not panic. Lumpy sauces can be liquidized to a smooth consistency. Add potato or yoghurt to dishes with too many hot chillies. Use potato to thicken thin soups; add a little flour made into a paste with milk to thicken thin sauces.

EXCESS FAT

● **In cooked dishes** Place the dish in the refrigerator and allow it to cool until the fat hardens on the top. Lift all the fat off with a spoon.

Ice cubes will cause fat around them to congeal

During preparation
Drop ice cubes into the food – fat will cling to them. Remove at once. Alternatively, brush a lettuce leaf over the surface.

BURNED FOOD

● **Stews** Tip the stew into a new saucepan – the burned stew will stay behind. Add water to the unburned stew, and chilli powder or pepper to disguise any burned taste.

● **Chops** Grill vegetables such as tomatoes and mushrooms, cut up the burned chops, and serve on skewers as kebabs.

BOIL OVERS

● **Preventing** Stop milk from boiling over by rinsing the pan in cold water first. Grease the rims of pans to prevent other liquids from boiling over.

● **Rescuing** If milk is about to boil over, remove it from the heat and bump the saucepan sharply as you put it down.

OVER-SALTED FOOD

● **Vegetables** Pour boiling water on boiled vegetables. Mash boiled potatoes with milk and a beaten egg.

Soups and stews
Add raw potato to soup or stew, boil, then throw out the potato. Alternatively, make a new batch without salt, and add to the first.

FRUIT AND VEGETABLES

BUY FRUIT AND VEGETABLES FRESH in small quantities, so that you do not have to store them for too long. Check fruit bowls and vegetable containers regularly, and throw out damaged items so that any rot does not spread.

STORAGE

Store highly perishable salad vegetables and soft fruit in the refrigerator. You can buy bags containing a gas that makes them last longer. If fruit such as bananas are becoming over-ripe, liquidize them, and store in the freezer for use in baking cakes or bread.

FRUIT STORAGE
● **Apples** Store unblemished apples on trays or racks, not touching each other. Remove any that are not perfect.
● **Lemons** These will keep for a month in the refrigerator if stored in a jar of cold water.

VEGETABLE STORAGE
● **Fresh mushrooms** Cover mushrooms with damp paper towels and refrigerate. They will keep for several days.
● **Tomatoes and cucumbers** These taste best when stored at room temperature, rather than being refrigerated.

POTATOES

Preserving a glut
If you have too many potatoes, stop them from sprouting by storing a few apples with them. If you have peeled too many potatoes, cover them with water and store in the refrigerator.

WATER STORAGE

Make sure stems are covered in water

Keeping food crisp
Certain vegetables are best stored in water. Stand spring onions and celery in a tumbler of water in the refrigerator. Store watercress and olives in a bowl of water in the refrigerator.

RIPENING FRUIT

Many fruits will continue to ripen after they have been picked, but it is still useful to know the best methods for ripening different varieties. Refrigerating fruit will slow down the ripening process, while storing already-ripe fruit in a dark place tends to hasten ripening.

TOMATOES

Avoiding sunlight
Ripen tomatoes by storing them out of direct sunlight – a drawer is ideal. Exposure to sunlight merely softens tomatoes; it does not ripen them more quickly.

APPLES AND PEARS

Add ripe apple to bag

Hastening ripening
Ripen apples and pears by placing them in a brown paper bag with an already-ripe apple. Pierce a few holes in the bag, and store in a cool, dark place.

RIPENING TIPS
● **Green fruit** Ripen green fruit in a perforated plastic bag. The holes let in air but retain ethylene – the odourless gas that promotes ripening.
● **Avocados** Ripen avocados by placing them in a warm airing cupboard, or in a plastic bag with a piece of banana peel, or by burying them in a bowl of flour. Refrigeration will stop them from ripening.
● **Bananas** To stop bananas from ripening, refrigerate them – the skins may darken but the flesh will stay firm.

SALAD VEGETABLES

Keep a small, dry sponge in the vegetable compartment of your refrigerator – it will absorb moisture, and help prevent mildew and food spoilage. To give salad a mild flavour of garlic, rub half a peeled garlic clove around the salad bowl before you put the salad into it.

PREPARING MIXED SALADS

Push food with back of knife to avoid dulling blade

Saucer creates a false bottom – water collects underneath

Draining a salad
Place a saucer upside down in a salad bowl before adding the salad. Water from the washed lettuce leaves will then collect beneath the saucer, and not make the salad soggy.

REVIVING LETTUCE
● **Soggy lettuce** Soak soggy lettuce for an hour in a bowl of water combined with 10 ml (2 tsp) of lemon juice in the refrigerator. To keep a head of lettuce crisp, store it in a plastic bag in the refrigerator.
● **Wilted lettuce** Sprinkle the lettuce with cool water, wrap it in a kitchen cloth, then refrigerate it for an hour.

PREPARING LETTUCE
● **Cutting leaves** Cut crisp-headed lettuces and Chinese leaves across the root into strips. Hold the root end and chop from the top, discarding any brown bits.

Tearing lettuce
To prepare soft-leaf lettuces, tear with your fingers - cutting will make the edges turn brown. For buffet eating, make sure you tear the lettuce into bite-sized pieces that do not need further cutting.

PREPARING VEGETABLES

To prevent vitamin loss and reduce the risk of spoiling, prepare vegetables as near to their cooking time as possible. Peel vegetables with a sharp knife or vegetable peeler to avoid removing too much skin. Alternatively, scrub vegetables clean, using a scouring pad.

AUBERGINES

Sprinkle salt over cut slices

Drawing out juices
Slice aubergines, sprinkle both sides with salt, and leave to drain for 30 minutes, turning once to release the bitter juices. Rinse and dry with paper towels.

OTHER VEGETABLES
● **Peeling peppers** To skin a pepper, hold it on a skewer over a naked flame until it is charred all over. Rub the skin off with a paper towel.
● **Peeling tomatoes** Plunge tomatoes into boiling water, leave for one or two minutes, then immerse them in cold water. The skins will split, so that you can peel them easily.
● **Preparing corn** To remove silk from corn cobs, remove the husks, then rub the ears with a damp paper towel.
● **Slicing onion** Grate onion if a recipe calls for it to be finely chopped. Leave the stem on to hold the onion together.

TRADITIONAL TIP

Tearless onions
Cut off the root end of an onion last to prevent tears. Peeling under cold, running water also helps. Breathe through your mouth.

COOKING VEGETABLES

Cook vegetables for as short a time as possible. Cut them into small pieces for cooking, and use the minimum amount of water. Reserve the water in which vegetables have been boiled, and use it for making soups, stocks, and sauces – it is full of vitamins.

BOILED VEGETABLES

- **Frozen vegetables** Restore freshness to frozen vegetables by pouring boiling water over them before cooking.
- **Cabbage** Add a pinch of bicarbonate of soda to boiling cabbage to eliminate odour and keep the cabbage green. Alternatively, place an end of bread on top of the cabbage while it is being cooked. Remove before serving.
- **Cauliflower** To keep boiled cauliflower from becoming yellow, add 30 ml (2 tbsp) of milk to the cooking water.

ROASTING PEPPERS

Apply oil with a pastry brush

Protecting the skins

Coat peppers with olive oil before stuffing and baking them. They will keep their colour, and the skins will not split.

BOILING CORN

Add fresh or bottled lemon juice

Perfect sweetcorn

Add 5 ml (1 tsp) of lemon juice to sweetcorn to keep it yellow. Do not add salt to the cooking water – it will toughen the corn.

PREPARING BROCCOLI

Cutting the stems

Make cross-shaped incisions in the ends of broccoli stems, so that the stems cook in the same amount of time as the florets.

CARROT SWEETENER

In tomato sauce

If your tomato-based sauce is acidic, add some grated carrot to sweeten it. The carrot will also help to thicken the sauce.

OTHER VEGETABLES

- **Pulses** Adding a pinch of bicarbonate of soda to the cooking water will prevent pulses from going soft.
- **Mushrooms** Fry mushrooms quickly over a high heat to prevent them from going hard.
- **Spinach** After cooking fresh spinach, drain it well and press it between two plates to remove excess moisture. Toss in hot, seasoned butter.
- **Beetroot** Cook whole to retain juices. Simmer for two hours – the skins will slip off.

PREPARING POTATOES

Putting a metal skewer through a potato speeds up the baking time. Alternatively, parboil potatoes for 15 minutes – this cuts the baking time in half.

- **Mashed potatoes** Adding 5 g (1 tsp) of baking powder to mashed potatoes will create a light, fluffy texture. If mashed potatoes become soggy after you have added milk (this usually occurs if the potatoes have been overcooked), make them fluffy by adding powdered milk.
- **Leftover baked potatoes** These can be rebaked if you dip them in water and bake in a 150°C (300°F) oven for 20 minutes.

- **Crisp roast potatoes** After scrubbing potatoes, rub the surfaces with a little salt – this will help to produce a crisp skin. Scratch a criss-cross pattern on potatoes with a fork, and roast in hot fat in a high oven.
- **Old potatoes** To improve the flavour of old potatoes, add a little sugar to the water in which they are boiled. Add 5 ml (1 tsp) of white vinegar to prevent the potatoes from going dark.

PREPARING FRUIT

If you need to delay cooking peeled apples, place them in salted water to prevent them from going brown; rinse the apples before use.

A pinch of salt adds flavour to cooked apples. To reduce the amount of sugar used in stewing fruit, add the sugar after the fruit is cooked.

STONING AND SKINNING
● **Seeds and stones** Remove seeds from grapes with the small end of a paper clip. Use the tip of a vegetable peeler to remove stones from cherries.

Pour enough water to cover the fruit

Skinning fruit
Place thin-skinned fruits such as peaches in a bowl, and pour boiling water over them. After one minute, pour away the water, then peel the fruit.

PRESERVING FRESHNESS
● **Strawberries** Rinse and drain fresh strawberries well before hulling. Washing them after hulling lets water into the fruit, so that they become soggy.

Keeping bananas yellow
Add a little sherry to sliced bananas to prevent them from turning brown. Alternatively, sprinkle pineapple or lemon juice on to the banana slices.

MELONS
● **Storing** Wrap melons that are stored in the refrigerator – the flavour and scent will stay inside the fruit and not be transferred to other foods.

Cut a small slice from each side

Serving melon
To serve a melon on a plate, cut a slice off the side so that the fruit will sit flat. This is useful if you want to use the melon itself as a bowl to hold a fruit salad.

CITRUS FRUIT

Storing citrus fruit at room temperature will double the amount of juice you can extract from it. Alternatively, submerge the fruit in hot water for 15 minutes before squeezing. Use dried citrus peel for a pleasant scent in rooms, or scatter it in drawers to keep clothes fresh.

EXTRACTING JUICE

Piercing a hole
Extract a small amount of lemon juice through a hole made with a skewer. Then wrap the lemon in aluminium foil, and refrigerate.

ORANGES AND LEMONS
● **Citrus juice** Oranges and lemons will yield maximum juice if you heat them in a microwave before squeezing.
● **Peeling oranges** Before you peel an orange, place it in a bowl of boiling water for about five minutes. The peel will then lift off easily.
● **Storing lemons** A cut lemon will not dry out if you smear the surface with egg white. Lemons freeze well, so you can store any unused portions in the freezer. If you use only small pieces of lemon (or lime) at a time, cut the fruit in quarters and keep in the freezer in a plastic bag.

MONEY-SAVING TIP

Homemade citrus peel
Grate leftover citrus peel, add a little sugar, and store this homemade peel in an airtight jar in the refrigerator.

MEAT, DAIRY, AND EGGS

THESE ARE THE PROTEIN STAPLES of most people's diets and can be prepared in hundreds of ways to suit all tastes. Meat and fish are expensive and should not be wasted – add leftovers to stews, and use bones to make soup stock.

PREPARING AND COOKING MEAT

Cook meat over high heat initially to seal in the juices. Turn meat with tongs rather than a fork, to avoid making holes that let juices out. Do not sprinkle salt on meat before cooking – this encourages juices to escape. Add salt just before you serve the meat.

SAUSAGES

● **Strings** To prevent meat from spilling out of a string of sausages, separate them only when they are nearly cooked.

Shrinkless sausages
Roll sausages in flour before you fry them. This will prevent them from shrinking and breaking up in the pan. Alternatively, boil them first for eight minutes.

TECHNIQUES FOR FRYING MEAT

● **Oil-free frying** When frying hamburgers, sprinkle the pan lightly with salt instead of using cooking oil. The patties will fry in their juices, without sticking to the pan.

Quick-frying technique
To cook hamburgers quickly and evenly all over, make holes in the centres when shaping the patties. The holes will disappear as the meat cooks and swells.

SEASONING MEAT

Coat one piece of meat at a time

Applying a coating
To coat meat quickly and with a minimum of mess, put seasoned flour in a plastic bag and add the meat. Shake the bag until the meat is thoroughly coated.

● **Bacon** To stop bacon from curling, prick the frying pieces with a fork, or dip the strips in cold water before frying them.

Preventing spattering
Inverting a metal colander over a frying pan prevents fat from spattering the surrounding area, while allowing steam to escape. Use oven gloves to remove it.

GRILLING MEAT

● **Quick grilling** Speed up grilling by preheating the grill and its grid for 10 minutes.

Reducing fire risk
Put slices of bread under the grid in a grill pan to soak up dripping fat and prevent it from smoking. This will reduce the chance of the fat catching fire.

LAMB, PORK, AND HAM

● **Serving lamb** To prevent lamb's fat from congealing unattractively, use very hot plates for serving the meat.
● **Pork crackling** Score the rind of a pork joint deeply in a criss-cross pattern. Rub with oil, then with salt, and roast.
● **Ham** Soak over-salty ham in milk for half an hour. For juicy boiled ham, allow the ham to cool in the cooking water.

TOUGH MEAT

● **Marinading** Use vinegar to tenderize tough meat. Mix vinegar with equal parts of warm stock or cooking oil, and marinade meat in this for one hour before cooking.

POULTRY AND FISH

Poultry must be thawed and thoroughly cooked, otherwise it may produce food poisoning. If you need to skin a fresh fish, the job will be easiest if you freeze the fish first. After using a pan for cooking fish, wash it with vinegar to remove the fishy odour.

POULTRY
● **Roasting chicken** When roasting an unstuffed chicken, season the cavity as well as the skin. Place half a lemon in the cavity to flavour the flesh.
● **Roasting duck and goose** Prick duck flesh before roasting so that fat escapes. Do not prick goose – losing fat will make the flesh dry.

FISH
● **Slippery fish** To handle slippery fish, wet your hands, then dip them in salt; or rub vinegar on to the fish.
● **Poached fish** Adding 15 ml (1 tbsp) of vinegar to the cooking water will prevent poached fish from crumbling.

SOAKING FISH

Reserve liquid from thawing fish for sauce

Using milk
Thaw frozen fish in milk to give the fish a fresh taste; use the milk to make the accompanying sauce. Soak anchovies for half an hour in milk to reduce saltiness.

REDUCING FISH SMELLS
● **Fried fish** Adding lemon juice to the fat used to fry fish reduces the smoke and odour.

Fish smells on hands
Rub your hands with vinegar, lemon juice, or salt, then rinse them in tepid water before washing them. You will prevent the fishy smell from setting.

SOUPS, STEWS, AND CASSEROLES

Soups and stews are best made in advance, so that the flavours have time to mingle. Add tea, beer, or wine to stews to tenderize any tough meat. Add a little instant potato to thicken thin soups. See page 121 for removing excess fat from soups and stews.

CLARIFYING STOCK

Add eggshells

Using eggshells
Add eggshells to cloudy stock – any impurities will cling to the insides of the shells. Remove the shells when the stock is clear.

SOUP STOCK
● **Fish stock** Use the bones and clean heads from filleted fish to make fish stock. Do not simmer fish stock for longer than 20 minutes, otherwise it tends to become bitter.
● **Storing stock** Freeze soup stock in ice-cube trays, then store the cubes in a plastic bag in the freezer until needed.

STEWS AND CASSEROLES
● **Broken casserole dishes** Use a piece of aluminium foil to cover a casserole dish if you have broken the lid.
● **Bouquet garnis** Make your own bouquet garni for stews by tying two sprigs of parsley, one bay leaf, and a sprig of thyme in a piece of muslin.

TIME-SAVING TIP

Opening soup cans
Before opening a can of soup, shake it well, then open it at the bottom end. All the soup will slide out neatly, without sticking to the can.

DAIRY FOODS

Dairy products perish quickly, and should be kept refrigerated. Take butter out of the refrigerator about half an hour before you intend using it – softened butter spreads easily. When cooking with cream, be careful not to allow it to boil, which will make it curdle.

FRYING WITH BUTTER

Add oil as butter begins to melt

Adding cooking oil
Before sautéeing vegetables or meat in butter, add a little olive or vegetable oil to the pan. This will lower the point at which butter would burn, and leave the food a rich, golden colour.

SOFTENING BUTTER

Place warm bowl over butter

Quick solution
To soften butter for spreading, invert a small, heated bowl over the butter. Heat the bowl by rinsing it with hot water, or by filling it with cold water and heating it in a microwave.

USING DAIRY FOODS
● **Butter stretcher** Beat a little milk into butter to soften it and make it go further when making lots of sandwiches.
● **Yoghurt** Use yoghurt as a low-fat substitute for sour cream. Buy plain yoghurt and flavour it yourself instead of buying flavoured yoghurt.
● **Ice cream** Prevent crystals from forming on opened ice cream by placing waxed paper over the ice cream before you replace the lid.
● **Milk** Prevent milk from boiling over by adding a clean marble to the pan – this stirs the contents. Alternatively, use the method on page 121.

TECHNIQUES FOR WHIPPING CREAM
● **Perfect whipped cream** When whipping cream, use half single and half double, with a little caster sugar. If you overwhip cream, add a little milk or yoghurt to restore the correct consistency.

Foil prevents splashing

Preventing splashes
Avoid splattering cream when whipping it with an electric mixer by pushing the beater shafts through a circle of foil. Cover the bowl with the foil so that no cream splashes out.

● **Cream substitute** Should you run out of cream for whipping, you can substitute evaporated milk instead. If you add the juice of half a lemon to a small can of milk, the milk will whip stiff.

Cream that will not whip
If you have difficulty getting cream to whip, add one egg white, chill thoroughly, then whip the cream again. A few drops of lemon juice added to cream will also help.

TIPS FOR CHEESE

● **Storing cheese** Butter the cut edge of a block of cheese to prevent it from drying out. Wrap cheese in a moist paper towel, then in clingfilm, and store in the refrigerator.
● **Grating cheese** Put cheese in the freezer for 15 minutes to make it grate easily.
● **Stale cheese** Grate stale cheese and mix it with onion to make a sandwich filling.
● **Cottage cheese** Make a sour cream substitute by running cottage cheese through a blender. Always store cottage cheese containers upside down.

EGGS

Brown and white eggs are no different in quality. Eggs will keep longest if stored thin-end down. If they are to be beaten, store them at room temperature. To test whether an egg is fresh, put it in a bowl of cold water – if the egg rises to the top, it is not fresh.

SEPARATING EGGS

● **Removing yolk** Use a piece of eggshell to remove any bits of yolk from egg whites. The thin end of the shell is ideal for picking up the yolk.

Glass keeps yolk separate from white

Separating an egg
To separate an egg easily, break it on to a saucer and place a small tumbler over the yolk. Holding the glass and saucer together firmly, pour the egg white off into a container.

BOILED EGGS

● **Cutting hardboiled eggs** To slice hardboiled eggs cleanly, first dip your knife in boiling water. For chopped eggs, cut first along the length, then along the width.

Preventing cracking
Pierce the end of an egg before boiling it, using a pin. This will allow air to escape from the shell, and will prevent the shell from cracking. Add vinegar to the water to seal cracked eggs.

BEATING EGGS

● **Clean bowls** Rinse a bowl with cold water before you beat egg yolks in it – the yolks will slide out without sticking to the sides of the bowl.

Small quantities of salt and vinegar will stiffen whites

Beating egg whites
Add 5 ml (1 tsp) white vinegar and a pinch of salt to egg whites if they will not stiffen when you are beating them. Any bits of yolk present in the whites will make them difficult to beat.

EGGS FOR GARNISH

Stir gently to avoid breaking eggs

Centring the yolks
When boiling eggs for garnish, stir them gently but continually with a wooden spoon, so that the yolks do not settle on one side. Immerse them in cold water after boiling, then peel.

TRADITIONAL TIP

Preventing tarnish
Egg yolk tarnishes silver. Use plastic or stainless-steel cutlery when eating boiled eggs to save polishing silver.

COOKING TIPS

● **Poached eggs** Add a few drops of white vinegar to the pan to stop poached eggs from losing their shape. For perfect poached eggs, stir the water as it boils, and drop each egg into the well created by the movement of the water.
● **Scrambled eggs** To make scrambled eggs stretch, add 15 g (1 tbsp) of breadcrumbs to every three eggs.

STORING EGGS

● **Yolks** Egg yolks will remain fresh for several days if they are submerged in cold water and stored in the refrigerator.
● **Freezing** Egg whites can be frozen. Store them in a clearly labelled, plastic container.

MAYONNAISE

● **Homemade** When making mayonnaise, add the oil one drop at a time to prevent curdling. Try not to pause during the making process.

BREAD, PASTA, AND RICE

THESE ARE DIET ESSENTIALS that provide fibre and energy. Bread only lasts a few days if stored at room temperature – but stale bread has its own uses. Store dry pasta and rice in airtight containers. Fresh pasta should be refrigerated.

BREAD

Keep sliced bread in the refrigerator. Bread and breadcrumbs freeze well, but should not be kept in the freezer for any longer than a couple of months. When slicing fresh bread, dip the bread knife into boiling water first – it will then cut through the bread easily.

TOAST
● **Thin bread slices** When making toast with thin slices of bread, place two pieces in each side of the toaster – this will prevent the bread from curling or breaking.

BREADCRUMBS
● **Stale bread** When making breadcrumbs from stale bread, put the bread in a plastic bag and roll with a rolling pin.
● **Breadcrumb substitute** If you run out of breadcrumbs, use cornflakes or any other dry cereal instead, crushed in a food processor or blender.

FRESH BREAD

Keeping bread fresh
Put a slice of apple or potato in a bread bin to prevent bread from drying out. Clean a bread bin weekly to prevent mildew from forming (see p. 29).

Grating for breadcrumbs
Fresh bread does not crumble into breadcrumbs easily. If you must make crumbs using fresh bread, freeze the loaf first, then grate it to make it into crumbs.

STORING AND MAKING SANDWICHES
● **Freezing** Make sandwiches in advance and freeze them. Remove them from the freezer several hours before serving.

Cut loaf into sandwiches after fillings have been added

Preserving sandwiches
If you have to make sandwiches the night before but want to keep them moist and fresh, wrap them up in a few lettuce leaves, then in aluminium foil, and refrigerate them overnight.

Layer sandwiches
Make layer sandwiches quickly and easily by slicing a loaf of bread horizontally, and applying the chosen filling to each layer. Reassemble the loaf, then cut into individual vertical slices.

HOMEMADE BREAD

● **Adding salt** Make sure you use exactly the right amount of salt in bread making – too much salt will kill the yeast; too little salt will cause the dough to rise too fast.
● **Covering dough** Bread dough must be covered in order to rise well. A damp cloth is the traditional way, but clingfilm works just as well, and can be discarded.
● **Quick bread** Warm the flour used in bread making in a low oven for a few minutes before you mix the dough – this will help the bread to bake quickly.
● **Crisp bread** For a crisp crust on homemade bread, brush the loaf with oil before you put it in the oven.

LEFTOVER BREAD

Stale bread need not be thrown away – it can be freshened up as shown below, or made into breadcrumbs (see opposite). Fry leftover toast to make fried bread. Sandwiches that are left over from a party can be dipped in egg, then fried and served as a breakfast dish.

REVIVING BREAD, BUNS, AND BISCUITS

Use a pastry brush

Biscuits should not overlap

Moistening bread
To freshen stale bread, brush water over the bread, then wrap it in a sheet of aluminium foil. Heat the bread in a medium oven for around 10 minutes, or until the bread feels springy.

Dipping buns in milk
Buns can become stale quickly, but if you have some left over, dip them into a bowl of milk, then put them in a hot oven for a few minutes. They will freshen up and the tops will crispen.

Crisping biscuits
Soggy biscuits can be crisped up on a baking sheet in the oven for a few minutes. Alternatively, place them in a microwave on high for 30 seconds. These methods also revive stale cereal.

PASTA AND RICE

Pasta can be added to soup to make the soup go further. If pasta sticks together, toss it in a clean pan with a little olive oil to separate the strands. To keep cooked rice hot, stand the container over a pan of simmering water, and cover it with a kitchen towel.

BASIC TECHNIQUES FOR COOKING PASTA

● **Fresh pasta** To cook fresh pasta, drop it into a large pan of rapidly boiling, salted water. Cook for five minutes, or until the pasta rises to the surface. Serve very hot.

● **Preventing sticking** When pasta is just cooked, add 15 ml (1 tbsp) of cold water to the pan before draining.

PREPARING RICE

● **Overcooked rice** Rinse rice that has been overcooked in cold water, then drain it well. Spread the rice on greaseproof paper, and heat it in a warm oven for about 30 minutes.

Add oil before pasta starts to boil

Protect your hands from hot metal

Add pure or bottled lemon juice

Preventing boil overs
A small amount of oil or butter added to the water when cooking pasta prevents it from boiling over or sticking together.

Small portions
Cook a small portion of pasta in a metal colander set in a pan full of water. Lift out the colander when the pasta is cooked.

Perfect rice
Add a little lemon juice to white rice while it is cooking to keep it white and fluffy. Add butter to prevent it from boiling over.

ALL THE EXTRAS

SSENTIAL INGREDIENTS IN every kitchen are those which – like flavourings, nuts, and oils – add flavour and interest to dishes. Preserving foods in season and making perfect sauces are skills that will stand every cook in good stead.

NUTS

Store nuts in a dark, dry, and cool place. Warmth turns the fat in nuts rancid, so that they shrivel in their shells. Heating nuts briefly in an oven or a microwave will make them easy to crack. To chop nuts easily, put them in a plastic bag and crush with a rolling pin.

WALNUTS

Soaking in salted water
Soak walnuts in a bowl of salted water overnight. They will be easy to crack afterwards, and the flesh will remain whole.

PEANUT BUTTER

Use liquid honey to moisten peanut butter

Preventing dryness
If peanut butter goes dry, adding a spoonful of liquid honey will make the peanut butter moist again. Stir the honey in well.

USING NUTS

● **Chestnuts** To prepare, cut a slit in the flat side of each shell. Cover with water and boil for 10 minutes. Remove the shells with a paring knife.
● **Coconuts** Pierce the eyes of a coconut with an ice pick, and drain out the juice. Using a hammer, crack open the coconut to get at the flesh.
● **Brazil nuts** Store Brazil nuts in the freezer – they will shell easily, and will not break up.
● **Walnuts** If walnuts taste old, cover with boiling water, drain, then heat on a shallow pan in a medium oven for 20 minutes.

OILS

Heating a frying pan before you add butter or oil will prevent foods from sticking. Sprinkle a pinch of salt into frying pans to stop oil from spattering. Adding 15 ml (1 tbsp) of vinegar to fat before deep frying will prevent food from absorbing too much fat.

REUSING OIL

Straining impurities
Clean oil that has been used for deep frying by straining it through a fine metal sieve. Store the oil in a sealed container.

CHOOSING OILS

● **Types of oil** Use oils that contain polyunsaturated fats for cooking: corn, sesame, olive, cottonseed, peanut, safflower, sunflower, and soya bean. Avoid coconut and palm oils, which contain saturated fat. Peanut oil is good for frying at high temperatures.

DEEP FRYING

● **Removing flavours** Oil can be reused until it turns brown. If it takes on food flavours, fry sliced potato in the oil until crisp to remove the flavours.

TRADITIONAL TIP

"Non-stick" pan
To season a new frying pan, boil some vinegar in it. This will prevent food from sticking to the pan when frying in the future.

HERBS AND SEASONINGS

Dried herbs are stronger than fresh herbs – 15 g (1 tbsp) of dried herbs equals 30 g (2 tbsp) of fresh herbs. To make your own herb vinegar, steep a handful of fresh herbs in 600 ml (1 pint) of vinegar for two weeks. Shake daily. Strain into a lidded container.

PREPARING HERBS

Simple cutting
Instead of cutting fresh herbs on a chopping board with a knife, it is quicker and more efficient to use a pair of food scissors to snip the herbs directly into a bowl.

TIPS ON USE
● **Salt** Put a few grains of rice in a salt shaker to prevent salt from clogging. If you double a recipe, you only need to use one-and-a-half times as much salt. See page 121 for when to add salt to dishes.
● **Parsley** Add parsley to dishes just before they have finished cooking – cooked parsley has a bitter flavour. Chew parsley to get rid of garlic breath.
● **Tarragon** Before using, soak dried tarragon in warm water to bring out the flavour.

GARLIC

Immerse cloves completely in oil

Storing in oil
Peel garlic cloves and place them in a bottle of olive or vegetable oil to preserve them. You can use the flavoured oil at a later date to make salad dressings.

SWEET FLAVOURINGS

Put a few crackers in your sugar cannister to prevent sugar from caking. Store brown sugar in the freezer to stop it from going hard. If a recipe calls for caster sugar and you do not have any, grind granulated sugar in a blender and use this as a substitute instead.

HARD BROWN SUGAR
● **Softening** Hardened brown sugar will soften in two days if you add a slice of bread or apple to the container.

Quick solution
If brown sugar has hardened and you need a little in a hurry, grate off the amount required, using the fine end of a grater.

MEASURING SYRUP
● **By subtraction** To measure syrup, place the container on scales, and remove spoonfuls of syrup until the container's weight diminishes by the required amount.

Preventing sticking
Before measuring syrup, grease the measuring cup - the syrup will slide out. Heat measuring spoons in hot water before use.

QUICK RESCUES
● **Brown sugar substitute** Use white sugar and molasses in baking if you run out of brown sugar. Add 15 ml (1 tbsp) of molasses to each 225 g (8 oz) of white sugar.

Restoring honey
If honey (or jam) crystallizes, stand the jar in a bowl of boiling water for a few minutes until it becomes runny again.

SAUCES AND SOUFFLÉS

Leftover sauces can be reheated and used as toppings for vegetables, added to pie fillings, or used in pasta sauces. If a sauce goes lumpy, beat it in an electric blender until it is smooth. A can of soup can be used as a quick substitute for sauce in an emergency.

PREVENTING PROBLEMS
● **Greasy sauces** Add a small amount of baking soda to greasy sauces to absorb fat. Alternatively, see page 121.
● **Lumpy sauces** If beating a sauce in a blender fails to remove lumps, strain the sauce through a sieve.

Preventing "skins"
Spread a thin layer of melted butter or cream over sauces after cooking to prevent a skin from forming. When you are ready to use the sauce, stir in the butter or cream to add flavour.

TIME-SAVING TIP

Heating liquids
If you need a small amount of melted butter, boiling water, or hot milk, use a metal ladle to heat it directly over the ring. The long handle prevents burned fingers.

MAKING GRAVY
● **Quick recipe** To make gravy for roasted meat, sprinkle a little flour into the juices left in the roasting pan. Then add water, stock, or wine to create the required consistency.
● **Thickening gravy** Mix water and flour into a paste, then add gradually to the gravy while bringing it to the boil. Alternatively, thicken gravy by adding instant potato flakes.

VARIOUS SAUCES
● **Cheese sauce** Use a pinch of cayenne pepper or a dash of lemon juice or mustard to add interest to a cheese sauce.
● **Apple sauce** A pinch of salt added to apple sauce will bring out the flavour and allow you to use less sugar.
● **Hollandaise sauce** If this begins to curdle, beat in a small amount of hot water.

MAKING AND RESCUING SOUFFLÉS
● **Light soufflés** Add a pinch of cream of tartar to egg whites during whisking – this makes soufflés light and fluffy.

● **Collapsed soufflé** If a sweet soufflé collapses, spoon it into a glass dish and decorate with whipped cream or biscuits.

WHITE SAUCE
● **Reheating** White sauce will keep in the refrigerator for a week. Reheat the sauce over a pan of simmering water, rather than using direct heat.

Combine all ingredients, then simmer together

Instant white sauce
There is no need to make white sauce in stages. Put the butter, flour, milk, and any seasonings in a pan. Heat them all up together, stirring all the time to prevent lumps from forming.

MAKING PANCAKES

● **Useful tips** When making pancakes, heat the frying pan before you add the oil or butter to prevent pancakes from sticking. Use heated plates to serve pancakes.
● **Pouring batter** Make your pancake batter in a jug instead of a bowl – this way you can pour the batter neatly into the frying pan.
● **Preventing burning** Rub raw potato over the griddle before frying pancakes to prevent them from sticking.

● **Pancake additions** A dash of soda water added to the batter for pancakes makes them light and fluffy. Adding 5 ml (1 tsp) of honey to the pancake batter will make pancakes moist.
● **Storing pancakes** Stack leftover pancakes on a plate with waxed paper between each one to prevent them from sticking together. Wrap them in clingfilm, and store in the refrigerator for a few days, or in the freezer. Reheat them in an oven or a microwave.

PRESERVING

Save used jars and their lids in a safe place, and recycle them when you make jams or other preserves. When potting jam, stand the warmed jars on a cloth or wooden board. Always warm a thermometer in water before putting it in hot jam – otherwise it may crack.

PREPARING JAM JARS

Nail varnish provides protective coating

Tempering jars
Wash jars thoroughly, then place them upside down on a baking tray in a cold oven. Switch the oven on low, and leave the jars for 10 minutes. They will now be tempered, and will not crack when you pour hot jam in.

Labelling and decorating
Paint clear nail varnish over jam-jar labels to prevent the writing from smudging. Wait until jam has cooled before labelling jars, otherwise the labels will not stick. Decorate jam to be given as a gift with fabric and ribbon.

REDUCING SCUM
● **Using butter** Reduce scum by stirring in a lump of butter when the jam is ready to set, or by rubbing butter inside a jam kettle before you use it.
● **In jars** Prevent scum in jars by add 30 ml (2 tbsp) of vinegar to the water you use when sterilizing the jars.

SETTING JAM
● **If jam will not set** Add 15 ml (1 tbsp) of pure lemon juice to every 450 g (1 lb) of fruit. (Remove the pan from the heat while testing for setting.)
● **Potted jam not setting** Stand the jars in a baking tin full of hot water and place in a low oven for a few minutes.

AVOIDING PROBLEMS
● **Time-saver** Heat the sugar used in jam-making in a bowl in a moderate oven while you cook the fruit. This speeds up the dissolving process when you combine the ingredients.
● **Using jam kettles** Do not fill jam kettles more than halfway, since the jam may boil over.

HOME FREEZING

Line freezer baskets with net so that small items do not fall through. A full, tightly packed freezer runs economically.

● **Freezer log** Keep a log of what is stored in a deep freezer, along with the date that each item went in.
● **Ice cubes** Use plastic egg boxes to make extra ice cubes for drinks parties.
● **Stock** Freeze excess stock in ice-cube trays for later use. Degrease stock before freezing it (see p. 121).
● **Non-stick storage** Freeze soft fruit, vegetables, and pulses spread out on trays. Bag up when frozen hard.

● **Soups and stews** Line a container with a plastic bag and pour soup or stew into it. Remove the plastic bag when the contents are frozen solid, to free the container for other uses.
● **Cake** Freeze odd pieces of cake until you have enough to make a trifle.
● **Herbs** Pack chopped parsley and mint in ice-cube moulds, cover with water, and freeze. Reserve for adding to sauces.

BAKING AND SWEETS

HOMEMADE CAKES AND BISCUITS ARE, in general, much nicer than shop-bought ones. Many cake mixtures freeze well, and it is worth doubling up recipes so that you can later bake treats quickly, with no time-consuming preparation.

CAKE MAKING

Place a shallow tray of water in the bottom of the oven while cakes are baking to prevent them from burning. Avoid opening the oven door during baking; if you have to in order to check a cake, close the door gently afterwards – otherwise the cake may collapse.

GENERAL TIPS

● **Greasing tins** Use wax-paper butter wrappers to line cake tins instead of parchment. Save foil butter wrappers and use them to grease cake tins.
● **Unsticking cakes** If a cake sticks to the tin, stand the tin on a damp cloth for a few minutes, then try removing the cake from the tin again.
● **Dried fruit** Soak dried fruit such as raisins and currants in tea overnight to improve the flavour. Roll dried fruit in flour before stirring into cake batter; this prevents the fruit from sinking to the bottom.

MISSING INGREDIENTS

Useful substitutes
Replace a missing egg with 5 ml (1 tsp) of white vinegar. To make your own self-raising flour, add 10 g (2 tsp) of baking powder to 225 g (8 oz) plain flour.

PREVENTING STICKING

Pull foil to unstick cake

Using aluminium foil
Place a strip of foil across a cake tin before you put in the cake mixture. This keeps the centre – the part most likely to stick – out of contact with the cake tin.

SLICING A SANDWICH CAKE IN HALF

Place thread around circumference of
Cross ends of thread
Cotton thread produces perfect cut

1 Use strong cotton thread to cut a sponge cake into two layers. Line the thread up around the cake carefully, then cross the two ends.

2 Pull the two ends firmly so that the thread slices evenly through the cake, then lift off the top layer. This method produces a clean cut.

PREVENTING CAKE TINS FROM RUSTING

● **New tins** Grease new cake tins and heat in the oven for 15 minutes to prevent them from rusting in the future.

● **Used tins** To make sure that tins are thoroughly dry after washing, put them in a hot oven for a few minutes.

PROBLEM SOLVING

● **Sunken centre** If the centre of a cake sinks, cut out the middle with a glass tumbler, and discard it. Make a ring cake from the remainder.
● **Dry cake** If a fruit cake seems dry, prick the top all over with a darning needle and sprinkle with whisky or brandy. Leave it to soak in.
● **Burned cake** If a cake has burned, cut off the worst bits, turn the cake upside down, and ice the base.
● **Cracked cake** If a cake has cracked, you may have used too much raising agent. Cut off the top layer, reverse it, and sandwich with cream.
● **Leftover batter** Store excess batter in the refrigerator, and use it to make pancakes.

DECORATING CAKES

Improvise a piping bag for icing either by cutting off the corner of a strong plastic bag, or by rolling sheets of greaseproof paper into a cone shape. Use fancily shaped biscuit cutters to mark out patterns to ice on a cake; or mark out your own design with pin pricks.

ICING AND TOPPINGS

● **Before icing** To keep icing from running off a cake, dust a little icing sugar on to the cake before you ice it.

● **Royal icing** Adding 2.5 ml (½ tsp) glycerine to royal icing will prevent it from becoming too brittle when it hardens.

● **Coloured sugar** To make coloured sugar for decorating cakes, put a couple of drops of food colouring into a small plastic bag with 10 g (2 tsp) of white sugar. Tie the bag, and work the sugar and the colouring together with your fingers for a few minutes.

● **Icing sugar** If you need to make icing sugar stretch, add a little plain flour to it.

USING CHOCOLATE

Making shapes

Use a vegetable peeler to make chocolate curls and shavings. Chill the chocolate first in the refrigerator or freezer. For flat shapes, pour melted chocolate on to greaseproof paper. Chill, then cut out the shapes.

BRIGHT IDEA

Making candied flowers
To use real flowers as cake decorations, dip the flowers in beaten egg white, then in caster sugar. Arrange them on the tops of cakes. Candied flowers will keep for a few days in an airtight container.

STORING AND SERVING

Fruit cakes have good keeping qualities, and the flavour improves if they are stored, well wrapped, for several months. Lighter cakes such as sponges and Madeira are best eaten fresh. Dust serving plates with white sugar to prevent cakes from sticking to them.

STORING CAKES IN TINS

Place apple half among cakes

Keeping cakes fresh

Put half an apple in the cake tin to keep cakes fresh and moist. Alternatively, cover the cut portion of a cake with a slice of bread, held in place with toothpicks - this will prevent the cake from drying out.

Lift tin away from lid

Upside-down storage

Store an iced cake on the lid of a cake tin - this makes it easy to remove the cake for serving without damaging the icing each time. Remember that the cake tin is supposed to be upside down before you open it.

PRESERVING FRESHNESS

● **Slicing cake** When slicing only a few pieces from a fresh cake, take the slices from the centre, then slide the two halves together. The cake will stay fresh longer.

● **Cake mix** If you use cake mixes, do not keep them for longer than six months, since they will deteriorate.

FREEZING CAKES

● **Small portions** For packed lunches, cut a cake into slices and wrap and freeze the slices individually. Remove from the freezer in the morning.

● **Spice cake** Leave cloves out of a spice cake if you plan to freeze it. Cloves get stronger when they are frozen.

PREPARING PASTRY

The secret of successful pastry making is to keep everything cool – your hands, the fat, the water, and the rolling surface should all be as cold as possible. Chill pastry in the refrigerator for at least half an hour before rolling, so that it will not shrink while baking.

ROLLING PASTRY
● **Flouring equipment** Sprinkle flour on to the pastry board and the rolling pin – never directly on to the pastry.

Improvised rolling pin
A straight-sided wine bottle filled with chilled water makes an ideal rolling pin because it keeps the pastry cool. Always roll pastry in the same direction.

ADDING FAT

Grating chilled fat
Small pieces of fat are easier to rub into flour than large ones. Cool fat for pastry making in the refrigerator, then grate it on the coarse end of a grater.

PERFECT PASTRY
● **Handle with care** Keep pastry light by using the tips of your fingers to rub the fat into the flour. Be careful not to overwork the pastry.
● **Crisp pastry** For extra crisp pie crusts, substitute 15 ml (1 tbsp) of white vinegar for the same amount of water.
● **Flaky pastry** Replace 15 ml (1 tbsp) of water with the same amount of orange or lemon juice for flaky pastry.
● **Storing pastry** Shortcrust pastry can be stored – without the water or salt added – for two weeks in the refrigerator. Add the missing ingredients before you use the pastry.

BAKING PASTRY

Glaze pies with egg or milk before baking. When reheating pies, place a small dish of water in the oven to keep the pastry moist. Two-crust pies should be baked on the bottom shelf of an oven so that the bottom crust bakes thoroughly, without the top crust burning.

PREVENTING SOGGINESS
● **Glass ovenware** If you bake pastry in a glass dish, place the dish on a metal baking tray in the oven – the bottom crust will cook thoroughly.

SPECIAL TECHNIQUES
● **Pie funnels** Insert pieces of drinking straws in pie centres as improvised pie funnels.

Use dried beans as a substitute for baking beads

Applying coatings
Brush a pastry shell with egg white before adding the filling to prevent it from becoming soggy. Brush uncooked pastry with melted butter before freezing.

Baking pastry blind
Place dried pulses or rice on foil inside a pastry case and bake for fifteen minutes. Remove the foil and pulses, then bake the pastry for a further five minutes.

PASTRY-MAKING PROBLEMS

● **Hard pastry** This is caused by adding too much water, and adding flour will not solve the problem. Always use exact measures – do not try to estimate quantities.
● **Crumbly pastry** This is caused by adding insufficient water, resulting in a pastry that will break and cause fillings to leak. Always check the consistency of the dough with your hands, and add more cold water if necessary.
● **Thin pastry** If pastry rises through a flan filling during baking, the pastry is not heavy enough to stay in place. Baking pastry blind before adding fillings will prevent this from happening.

BISCUITS

Keep a batch of prepared biscuit mix in the refrigerator so that you can make biscuits in minutes. Store biscuits in airtight containers, but do not mix different types since their moisture contents may vary. A piece of bread in the container keeps biscuits moist.

AFTER BAKING

Loosen biscuits while hot

Damp kitchen cloth

Preventing sticking
Placing a tray of biscuits on a damp kitchen cloth makes the biscuits easy to remove. Lift them off the tray while they are still warm.

ADDITIONAL TIPS
● **Preventing spreading** Chill baking trays before you place biscuit dough on them – this will prevent the dough from spreading during baking.
● **Fragile biscuits** Line the baking tin with non-stick silicone paper when baking biscuits that are fragile and likely to break easily.
● **Biscuit crumbs** To crush biscuits for making pudding and cheesecake bases, put them in a plastic bag and crush them with a rolling pin.
● **Sprinkling sugar** Use an empty salt or spice container to sprinkle sugar on biscuits.

CUTTING BISCUITS
● **Time-savers** Dip biscuit cutters in flour to make them cut cleanly. To cut biscuits quickly, roll the dough into a sausage shape and slice it.

BAKING BISCUITS
● **Testing batches** Always test bake one biscuit first, since the moisture content of flour varies. This saves ruining a whole tray of biscuits.

SWEETS AND TREATS

When making boiled sweets, add a small amount of vinegar or a pinch of salt to the ingredients before cooking to cut down on the sweetness. If you use gelatine in a dessert, be sure to dissolve the gelatine thoroughly in water before adding it to the other ingredients.

CHOCOLATE
● **Melting chocolate** Butter the pan before melting chocolate so that it will pour out easily. Alternatively, line a pan with foil when melting chocolate; discard the foil afterwards.
● **Improvised chocolate** If you run out of cooking chocolate, add 60 g (4 tbsp) of cocoa powder to 5 g (1 tsp) of butter and use this as a substitute.

OTHER SWEETS
● **Pie fillings** Add 5 ml (1 tsp) of vinegar to pecan or maple syrup pie filling to cut down on the sugary sweetness.
● **Jelly** Wet the inside of a jelly mould before pouring in the jelly so that it will be easy to turn out. Alternatively, dip the mould briefly in hot water before unmoulding the jelly.

MERINGUES
● **Handling** To lift meringues from an oven tray without breakage, place the tray on a wet cloth as soon as it is taken from the oven.

Making crisp meringue
To make your meringue crisp every time, add 5 ml (1 tsp) of white vinegar to every three egg whites. Alternatively, add a pinch of cream of tartar.

BRIGHT IDEA

Saving marshmallows
Store marshmallows in the freezer to prevent them from drying out. When ready to use for decoration or grilling, cut them apart with sharp kitchen scissors. Dipping the scissors in hot water first will make the job easier.

BEVERAGES

BASIC HOT DRINKS SUCH AS coffee and tea can be much enhanced in flavour with the addition of extra ingredients. It is best to use purified water in drinks, particularly in areas where the tap water has a distinctive taste.

HOT DRINKS

Keep ground coffee in a tightly covered container in the refrigerator. Using purified water in a coffee maker prolongs the life of the machine and improves the taste of the coffee. To enhance the flavour of tea, place a piece of dried orange peel inside your tea tin.

MAKING HOT DRINKS

- **Coffee machines** Place coins under the pot in drip coffee makers – this will prevent a scum from forming and will keep the coffee from burning.
- **Best instant coffee** Add cold milk to the coffee powder or granules first, then add boiling water, and stir thoroughly.
- **Leftover coffee** Freeze in ice-cube trays and add to milk eggnog, or to too-hot coffee.
- **Adding flavours** Dissolve lemon drops or mint candy in tea in place of sugar. Add flavour to coffee by putting vanilla or almond extract into the water as the coffee brews.

COFFEE

Perfect fresh coffee
Add a pinch of salt to coffee before brewing to help reduce bitterness. To preserve a fresh taste, remove the filter basket as soon as the coffee is brewed.

LEFTOVER TEA

Using leftover tea
Soaking dried fruit that will be used in baking – such as prunes, raisins, and sultanas – in leftover tea will make the fruit plump and improve their flavour.

THERMOS FLASKS

Sugar lumps prevent mustiness

Storage and care
Put a couple of sugar lumps in thermos flasks to keep them fresh. Store with the lids off. To clean a thermos flask, fill it with hot water and bicarbonate of soda, and leave overnight. Never immerse thermos flasks in water.

HOT CHOCOLATE

Beat hot chocolate with balloon whisk

Preventing problems
Whisk hot chocolate in a pan until frothy to prevent a scum from forming. Alternatively, put it in a blender and whisk at high speed before serving. Rinse the pan in cold water before adding the hot chocolate (see p. 121).

TRADITIONAL TIP

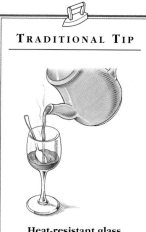

Heat-resistant glass
Put a metal spoon into a glass before pouring in any hot liquid – this will prevent the glass from cracking.

SOFT DRINKS

To be truly refreshing, soft drinks should be chilled. If your refrigerator is too full to chill drinks for a party, buy extra ice and chill the drinks in plastic buckets. Wrap adhesive tape around the caps of opened bottled drinks to prevent them from losing their fizz.

MAKING JUICE AND OTHER COLD DRINKS

● **Using fruit** Grate the peel from oranges, lemons, or limes, and mix the peel with a little sugar and enough boiling water to cover. When cool, strain and add the fruit juices, plus enough cold water to give a refreshing flavour.

● **Powdered drinks** When making cool drinks using a flavoured mix, dissolve the sugar first in a little hot water before adding it to the mix.

● **Decorative glasses** To make decorative drinking glasses for children's parties, dip the rims in egg white, then in a dish of hundreds-and-thousands or coloured sugar (see p. 137).

● **Decorating punch** Freeze clusters of grapes and add them to punches as a garnish.

● **Iced tea** To prevent iced tea from becoming foamy, add the water to the jug or the glass before you add the tea.

Squeezing citrus fruit
To get the maximum amount of juice from citrus fruit, roll the fruit on a flat surface before squeezing. Vitamin C in citrus juice is destroyed by exposure to air, so cover juice when storing.

CHILLING PUNCH

● **Decorative ice cubes** Freeze twists of lemon, orange, or cucumber in ice cubes and add these to cocktails.

Serving cold punch
When serving a cold punch, freeze some of the punch in ice-cube trays beforehand. Add these cubes to chill the punch – when they melt they will not dilute the punch as ice would.

ALCOHOLIC DRINKS

Store spirits upright, but bottles of wine on their sides. If a wine cork has swollen and you cannot get it back in, soak it in boiling water to make it pliable. See page 161 for estimating drink quantities for parties; see pages 39–40 for removing alcohol stains.

STORING WINE

Ideal conditions
Store wine bottles on their sides so that the wine stays in contact with the cork - this prevents the cork from drying out. Ideally, wine should be stored at a cool, constant temperature.

LEFTOVER WINE

Freeze leftover wine in ice-cube trays

Saving wine for cooking
Pour leftover wine into ice-cube trays, and freeze it. The cubes can be added to gravy, soups, and stews. Add white wine that has become sour to vinegar, or use it for marinading meat.

SERVING WINE

● **Filling glasses** Wine glasses should only be half filled, to preserve the bouquet – but fill champagne glasses to the top to make the bubbles last.

● **Champagne** When opening a champagne bottle, hold it at a 45 degree angle, and turn the bottle, not the cork.

CIDER

● **Heating drinks** Serve hot cider from a cooker on a low setting when entertaining. You can heat small quantities of cider in a microwave.

● **Wine substitute** Dry cider can be used as a substitute for wine in savoury dishes.

HOUSEKEEPING

QUICK REFERENCE
House Plants, p. 144
Sewing, p. 148
Children & Pets, p. 150
Health & Beauty, p. 154
Cars & Garages, p. 158
Entertaining, p. 160
Moving House, p. 162

*R*UNNING A HOME *well does not mean that you should have to put all your effort into doing so. There are short cuts that you can take to make various household tasks quick and simple. If you organize your home, you will not have to spend time constantly cleaning or tidying up, and will have more time for relaxing and enjoying your home. Use your talents to create an environment that reflects your taste and suits your needs.*

STORING AND SAVING

Keep things in the rooms in which they are used, and make sure everyone gets into the habit of returning them to their proper places. Organize your cupboards so that you can reach everyday objects easily. Reuse items as often as possible to save money and time.

USING SCREWTOP JARS

Under-shelf storage
Save screwtop jars, and attach their lids securely underneath shelves with screws. Use them to store sugar or dry beans; in a toolroom they can be used for storing nails and screws.

EXTENSION LEADS

Tube holds lead together

Storing extension leads
Use wide cardboard tubes from posters and toilet paper to keep extension leads in storage. Carefully coil the leads so that they will not tangle or trail over a drawer or cupboard.

STORING MISCELLANEOUS ITEMS

● **Tablecloths** Sprinkle clean plastic tablecloths with a little talcum powder before putting them away. This will prevent stickiness and mildew.
● **Clingfilm** Store clingfilm in the refrigerator – this makes it less likely to stick to itself.

● **Newspapers** Keep old newspapers in a box with a slot at the bottom – each time you need one, you can pull it from the bottom of the pile.
● **Accessories** Store these in boxes in the unused spaces at the bottoms of cupboards.

SAVING AND PRESERVING

● **Boxes** Save small, lidded boxes and store buttons and pins in them. Use large boxes for storing postcards and photographs. Label each box with the contents.
● **Hot-water bottles** Cut the top off an old hot-water bottle, stuff it with old tights, and seal the end with sticky tape. Use it as a kneeling pad for scrubbing or gardening.
● **Labels and stamps** Do not throw away postage stamps, or gummed labels that have stuck together. Place a piece of thin paper over them, and press with a warm iron until they come apart again.
● **Newspaper clippings** To preserve a newspaper clipping, soak it in a solution of 1.14 litres (2 pints) of soda water and one milk of magnesia tablet for an hour. Remove the clipping, lay it on a towel, and pat dry.

WRAPPING AND PACKING

Many a packet has gone astray in the post because of being inadequately wrapped. Wrapping materials such as brown paper and string can be reused several times with a little care. Use foam freezer cartons as gift boxes and old greetings cards as gift tags.

TIPS FOR GIFT WRAPPING ITEMS

Heat melts adhesive on tape

TIME-SAVING TIP

Tape-end finder
Stick a small button at the end of a roll of adhesive tape. When you use the tape, the end will be easy to find, and the button can be removed.

Reusing paper
Do not throw out old wrapping paper. A warm iron will smooth out creases and wrinkles, and will remove adhesive tape so that you can use the paper again.

Measuring gifts
Cut wrapping paper to the correct length by measuring the gift first with a piece of string. Use the string to measure out enough paper to wrap the gift.

PROTECTING DELICATE OBJECTS

● **China** Wrap pieces of fine china to be sent in the post in several layers of damp paper. When the paper dries, it will shrink to protect the china.

● **Fragile items** If you have no bubble wrap for packing fragile items, use egg cartons or stale popcorn to line the box and prevent breakage.

● **Documents** Wrap items you do not want to fold, such as documents or silk scarves, around a cardboard tube. Secure with masking tape.

SENDING ITEMS BY POST

Make sure that anything you have wrapped up is securely fastened and that it carries the recipient's name in large letters. Print your own name in small letters, so that the package will be returned to you if for some reason it cannot be delivered.

SENDING SAFELY

● **Valuable items** Use the registered and recorded mailing services for valuable items that must be insured.
● **Get-well cards** If you send a card to a hospital, write the patient's home address as the return address on the envelope. If the patient has been discharged, they will receive the card at home.
● **Postcards** When you go on holiday, make sticky address labels for everyone to whom you intend to send postcards. That way, you can leave your address book at home.

USING STRING

Pull end of string through lid

Storing string
To prevent string from tangling, store it in a screwtop jar. Punch a hole in the lid, and pull the end of the string through this.

Tying a parcel
Before tying up a parcel, wet the string. It will not slip when it is being tied, and when it dries it will shrink and stay in position.

HOUSE PLANTS AND FLOWERS

P LANTS AND FRESH FLOWERS ENHANCE a home. The secret to making indoor plants thrive is to match their native growing conditions to their positions in your house as closely as possible, and to feed and water them carefully. •

CARING FOR PLANTS

S ome house plants thrive on neglect; others need a lot of care. Trial and error – or a good book – will tell you how often to water different types and what kind of shade or sun they like. If you have a garden, put them outside in summer, and they should thrive.

PLANT-CARE BASICS
● **Choosing soil** Do not use garden soil for potting house plants. It is not sterile and will produce bacteria that thrive inside the house. Buy the appropriate mix for indoor plants from a garden shop.
● **Raising humidity** Central heating dries out the air. To raise the humidity for indoor plants, mist them with a fine spray of water once a week.
● **Cleaning plants** Dust plants regularly. Clean shiny-leaved plants with glycerine – this creates a shine but does not attract dust. A solution of half milk and half water is also effective for shining leaves.

Mix plants of different shapes and sizes for best effects

Make sure plants are free of diseases before adding to groups

Grouping plants
House plants thrive best when grouped together, particularly in a dry room. Make sure that all the plants have the same light, temperature, and humidity needs.

FEEDING PLANTS

Place homemade fertilizer in plant pot

Using kitchen leftovers
Mix a little cold tea, used tea leaves, or coffee grounds with plant soil to aerate it and feed the plants. This mixture is good for ferns. The water from boiling eggs is also nutritious for plants.

POTTING PLANTS

Creating good drainage
Place a layer of broken clay pots, tiles, or stones in the bottom of a pot before you add any soil. This allows water to drain properly, and keeps the plant's roots from becoming waterlogged.

PLANTS BY WINDOWS
● **Windowboxes** Cover the soil in windowboxes with gravel to prevent rain from splashing it on to windows.
● **Winter care** Move plants that are near windows into the room on winter nights to protect them from cold. Keep them away from hot radiators.

NEW PLANTS
● **Plant quarantine** Keep new plants away from others for a few weeks until you are sure that they are disease-free.
● **Repotted plants** Do not feed newly repotted plants for two or three months – if you do, the roots of the plants may not spread to the new soil.

WATERING PLANTS

Use room-temperature water on plants; water that is too cold or hot may damage plants. Allow the water to stand overnight before use to permit harmful chemicals to evaporate or settle. To test if a plant needs watering, check the soil with your fingers.

HOLIDAY WATERING

● **Using a bath** When you go away on holiday, place house plants in the bath on thickly folded towels in a few centimetres of water, and they should look after themselves.

● **Using string** To water plants while you are away, place one end of a piece of string in a bucket of water, and the other in the soil of the plants. The bucket must be positioned higher than the plant. The string will soak up the water.

USING TEA

An occasional feeding
Water plants with cool, leftover tea occasionally to give them a boost. Do not do this too often, however – the caffeine in the tea may be too strong for them.

HANGING BASKETS

Ice-cube watering
To avoid drips when watering hanging baskets, use ice cubes, placing a few on the soil. Only use them infrequently as they are too cold for regular use.

GROWING PROBLEMS

Watch your house plants for signs of infestation or failure to flourish. House plants thrive best if you rotate them regularly by a quarter of a turn – this evenly distributes their exposure to sunlight. Good ventilation is important to plants, but avoid draughts.

REMEDIAL ACTIONS

● **Pests** Treat disease by wrapping the plant in a plastic bag together with a pest strip. Leave it for a few days.

Wrap tape tightly around break

Fixing a broken stem
To support and mend a broken stem, make a splint using two toothpicks and a piece of adhesive tape. Inspect the join from time to time to make sure that the area is mending itself.

SPECIAL EFFECTS

● **Supports** Support tall plants with adjustable brass-effect curtain rods. Use brass wire to tie the plants to the rods.

Bend hanger into shape

Making a trellis
Make your own trellis for ivy from a wire coat hanger. Snip off the hook, and bend the hanger into the desired shape - perhaps a diamond, a heart, or a star. Push the two ends into the pot.

SPECIAL CARE

● **African violets** Feed African violets with tomato fertilizer to encourage blooming. These plants are happiest in small pots, so do not be tempted to pot them on. Display them on a sunny windowsill.

● **Bulbs** Always water bulbous plants from the saucer, so the soil absorbs the water. Be careful not to allow water to fall on to the leaves. Store bulbs in plastic net bags and hang them up so that they are well ventilated.

● **Succulents** Cacti and some other succulent house plants originate from the desert, and need infrequent watering only. Watch your fingers when handling spiky types. Use tongs if you need to repot cacti and succulents.

CUT FLOWERS

Cut flowers can be made to last much longer than usual if you take certain steps to preserve them – so do not rush home or in from the garden and expect to arrange them at once. Shop-bought flowers will need greater attention than home-grown ones.

PREPARING CUT FLOWERS FOR ARRANGEMENTS

Cut at an angle

Asprin may help flowers last longer

1 Use a pair of scissors, secateurs, or a sharp knife to cut each flower stem at a slanted angle. Split the ends of thick stems before starting to arrange them in the vase, so that they have the best chance of taking in moisture.

2 Remove from the stem all the leaves that would be beneath the waterline in the vase. Otherwise, they will decay and poison the water, causing the flowers to die quickly, and the water to become brown and brackish.

3 Add two aspirins to the water in vases to prolong the life of the flowers. If you are using a clear vase, add 15 ml (1 tbsp) of liquid bleach to each 1.14 litres (2 pints) of water – this prevents the water from becoming cloudy.

ARRANGING FLOWERS

Some people have a greater knack for flower arranging than others. If your skills are limited, use straight-sided vases in which the flowers will virtually arrange themselves. Otherwise, make sure you have plenty of holding ballast in the base of the vase.

OVERCOMING COMMON PROBLEMS

AIDS TO ARRANGING

● **Tall vase** If a vase is too deep for displaying your flowers, place crushed paper napkins, paper towels, or newspaper in the base.
● **Positioning blooms** Plastic hair rollers attached together with sticky tape and placed in the vase will help to keep flowers in position.
● **Centre flowers** Crumpled chicken wire is particularly good in wide-based vases where flowers in the centre of an arrangement need to be held securely in position.
● **Containers** You can use unconventional containers such as old teapots, wine goblets, and milk jugs for arranging cut flowers.

Lengthening short stems
To make short-stemmed flowers appear longer, slip the stems into plastic drinking straws before you arrange them in the water. Make sure that there is enough water to reach up to the stems.

Reviving wilted flowers
Snip off the ends of the stems of wilting flowers, and stand the flowers in a little boiling water for a few seconds. Then stand them up to their necks in cold water for several hours.

PREPARING SPECIFIC FLOWER TYPES

Check the treatment that is best for different types of flower, and remember to vary it in a mixed arrangement. Fill the hollow stems of dahlias and lupins with water and plug them with cotton wool before arranging them. Cut off any shrubby twigs with closed buds.

PREPARING ROSES

Petals and stems
Strip away damaged petals and cut thorns from the stems with a sharp knife. Split the stems or crush them with a hammer. Christmas roses will wilt quickly unless the stems are crushed all the way up, almost to the top.

TULIP STEMS

Treat fresh tulips to prevent them from drooping

Keeping stems straight
To prevent tulip stems from curving, wrap them tightly in wet newspaper and stand in 5 cm (2 in) of water for at least an hour. Then push a short pin through each stem, just below each flower head, to let in air.

PREPARING LILIES

Lily anthers cause staining

Anthers and stems
Cut off the anthers of flowers such as lilies to prevent the pollen from staining the petals, as well as wall coverings and clothes. Cut the stems at an angle, and stand the flowers up to their necks in water.

DRIED AND ARTIFICIAL FLOWERS

Dried flowers can look just as attractive as fresh ones, particularly if they have been dried naturally after being picked. However, their colours fade in sunlight, and they therefore need to be replaced regularly. Silk flowers can look attractive for years with care.

DRIED FLOWERS
● **Choosing** Good blooms include delphiniums, larkspur, and African violets. Pick them when they are just open.

How to dry flowers
Tie small flower bunches with string, and hang them upside down in a dry, cool, dark place. Leave for a few days – until all the moisture has evaporated.

SILK FLOWERS
● **Cleaning** Put silk flowers in a plastic bag with 30 g (2 tbsp) salt. Shake it well so that the dust clings to the salt.

Dusting silk flowers
Remove dust from silk and dried flower arrangements using a hairdryer on a warm setting. Be careful where you do this – you may blow dust on to the wall.

TRADITIONAL TIP

Colouring flowers
Change the colour of cut flowers by adding a little food colouring to warm water and placing stems in the solution. Use pale-coloured blooms and not too much colouring.

147

SEWING

Making your own repairs to clothes and soft furnishings can save you money as well as time. You do not need to be an expert to carry out basic repairs – many techniques require no more than a little common sense.

SEWING BASICS

Keep an emergency sewing kit to hand in a workbox. This kit should contain several needles of different sizes, thread in various colours, buttons, straight pins, safety pins, and sharp scissors. This selection of items should enable you to do running repairs quickly.

THREAD

Trouble-free sewing
When using double thread, knot each strand separately, so that it does not become tangled. Spray hairspray on your fingers to make threading needles easy.

EXTRA TOOLS
● **Removing threads** Use a pair of eyebrow tweezers to remove tacking or stitching from a loose button.
● **Using thimbles** Wet your finger to create suction before putting on your thimble.

SEWING FABRICS
● **Thick material** To make sewing thick fabric seams easier, rub the material with a damp bar of hard soap.
● **Pile fabrics** When sewing pile fabric such as velvet on a sewing machine, put tissue paper over the pile to stop the fabric from sliding around.
● **Flimsy fabric** Before cutting a delicate fabric, run the pair of scissors in hot water, then dry them thoroughly. They will cut the fabric cleanly.

PIN CUSHIONS

Deterring rust
Make a pin cushion from a fabric bag filled with dry, used coffee grounds. These prevent the pins from rusting. Alternatively, stick the pins in a bar of soap.

CARING FOR PINS
● **Picking up pins** Keep a magnet handy for picking up spilled pins. Use a flashlight to locate pins that drop on the floor.

Make a loop out of pipe cleaner

Storing safety pins
Keep safety pins together by threading them on to a pipe cleaner. Twist the ends together, and store them in your workbox so that you can find them easily.

SEWING MACHINES
● **Sharpening needles** Stitch through a piece of canvas or fine sandpaper to sharpen sewing-machine needles.
● **Oiling machines** When oiling your machine or taking it apart, put a desk blotter underneath to stop it from soiling fabric, thread, and the surface underneath. When you have finished, stitch several rows on a piece of blotting paper to remove all traces of oil.
● **Steadying machines** If your sewing machine tends to slip around, stand it on a foam-backed carpet tile to grip.
● **Creeping foot** Glue a piece of foam rubber to the underside of the machine's foot control to stop it from creeping when pressed.
● **Removing lint** Use a small paint brush or brush for an electric razor to remove lint from around the bobbin.

THREADS
● **Basic thread** Keep clear or neutral-coloured thread in your sewing kit, and use this as a substitute when you do not have the right colour.
● **Untangling** If thread tangles while you are hand sewing, rub it over a bar of hard soap.
● **Storing synthetic thread** Keep synthetic threads in the refrigerator – this will prevent static electricity when sewing.

ZIPS AND BUTTONS

The right buttons can make even cheap garments look expensive. Cut buttons off of worn-out garments and save them for later use. When buying specialty buttons, buy at least one extra button – this saves having to replace the whole set if one button falls off.

BUTTONS
● **Storing buttons** After you remove buttons from outfits, stitch the buttons together, or string them on a safety pin.

Removing tight buttons
If it is difficult to snip off a tight button, slide a comb underneath it to lift it away from the fabric, and slice it off carefully with a sharp knife or a razor blade. Be careful not to cut the fabric.

ZIPS
● **Recycling** Give new life to an old zip by spraying it with starch. This will make the fabric stiff and easy to sew.

Repairing zips
If a zip is damaged near the base, pull the slide below the broken teeth and cut them off. Pull the slide over the missing teeth, and stitch directly above them – this creates a new base for the zip.

SEWING BUTTONS
● **Leaving a space** Place a hairgrip, matchstick, or pin under a button when sewing it on, so that it is not fixed too tightly against the fabric and the buttonhole can fit over it.
● **Four-hole buttons** Sew four-hole buttons by stitching two holes at a time, then finish off the thread before doing the other two holes. This way, the buttons will not fall off, even if they become loose.

SPECIAL BUTTONS
● **Children's buttons** When sewing buttons on children's clothes, use dental floss or elastic thread; the buttons will stay attached longer.
● **Small buttons** Store extra-small buttons in plastic pill containers with snap-on lids.

SEWING TECHNIQUES

All your mending and sewing will be in vain if you do not start and finish off each job correctly, whether by hand or by machine. Make sure that thread is correctly anchored at both ends. Press seams with a hot iron over a damp cloth to keep them neat and flat.

BUTTONHOLES

Cutting thick fabric
To cut straight buttonholes in heavy fabric easily, place the area to be cut over a bar of household soap. Use a sharp craft knife or a safety razor blade to make the incisions.

TIME-SAVERS
● **Sewing badges** Secure fabric badges on clothes with a dab of latex glue on the back; then stitch the edges in place.
● **Replacement elastic** Pin new elastic to the end of the old piece. Pull the old elastic out to pull the new one in.

KNITTING
● **Knitted clothes** Place the torn part of a garment over a hairbrush to prevent it from stretching while you mend it.
● **Rescuing stitches** Keep a pipecleaner in your knitting bag to hold dropped stitches until you can pick them up.

BRIGHT IDEA

Keeping colours separate
When knitting with more than one colour, place the balls of wool in a net plastic vegetable bag. Pull each colour through a different hole to prevent tangles.

CHILD AND PET CARE

KEEP CHILDREN SAFE in the home by taking basic precautions to prevent accidents, and teaching them how to avoid possible dangers. Pets too are a serious responsibility, but make rewarding companions if well looked after.

CHILD SAFETY

Take babies and very young children with you into shops and up and down stairs. Put them in a safe playpen when you answer the door or telephone or do housework. A small baby can be carried about in a backpack, suitably padded to support its head.

PREVENTING ACCIDENTS
- **Glass doors** Stick coloured labels at child's height on glass doors, so that there is no risk of children walking into them.
- **Pianos** Stick a cork at each end of the piano keyboard so that if the lid falls down, a child's fingers are not hurt.
- **Sockets** Plug socket outlets with covers. They will prevent crawling children from poking their fingers in the sockets.
- **Electric kettles** Use a curly flex – it will not trail over counters for children to pull.

DOORS

A warning bell
Fasten a small bell to a back-door handle, so that you will hear if a child has opened the door. Keep your front door securely locked.

FURNITURE

Securing trailing flexes
Tape electrical flexes firmly to furniture legs with adhesive tape; this prevents children from pulling items on to themselves.

CARING FOR BABIES

It is vital that the mother of a baby looks after her own health, and makes life as easy for herself as possible. When bringing a new baby home, try to put off any visitors for a week or two while you acquaint yourself with the new arrival and recover from the birth.

BABY BOTTLES

Refrigerator organizer
Use an empty cardboard drinks carton to store a baby's bottles upright in the refrigerator. The bottles can be easily removed and will remain in one place, where you can find them easily.

NAPPIES

Using fastenings
If nappy pins become blunt, stick them into a bar of soap – this will also help prevent them from rusting. Use masking tape if the adhesive tape on a disposable nappy will not stick.

FEEDING AND COMFORT
- **Solid food** To make solid food for babies, purée fresh vegetables, store in ice-cube trays, and heat when needed.
- **Night feeds** When feeding a baby, put a hot-water bottle on the mattress so that it is still warm when you put the baby back into the cot.
- **Cleaning bottles** Place a few marbles into the sterilizer when cleaning bottles to draw any scale from the water.
- **Washing hair** Smear a line of petroleum jelly on a baby's forehead above the eyebrows to prevent shampoo from running into the eyes.

TODDLERS

Toddlers usually want to be independent faster than they are able. Make things as easy as possible for them, so that they do not have to learn the hard way – with bruises. Save yourself money by making toys from everyday household items, rather than buying them.

EATING AIDS
● **Securing plates** Use a soap saver with suction pads on both sides to help keep a child's plate steady on a table.

Drinking glasses
Place two rubber bands around a tumbler, about 2.5 cm (1 in) apart, to enable a child to grip it securely. Serve drinks to a child who is ill in bed in a jar with a straw through a hole in the lid.

ILLNESS AND FEAR
● **Taking pills** Get a reluctant child to take a pill by hiding it in a spoonful of jam or honey.
● **Splinters** Before removing a splinter in a child's skin, soak the area in cooking oil to soften the skin, then apply an ice cube to deaden the pain.
● **Removing plasters** Remove an adhesive plaster painlessly by rubbing a piece of cotton wool saturated in baby oil over the surface first.
● **Bedtime** When a child is old enough to move from a cot to a bed, place the cot mattress on the floor beside the bed – this way if the child falls out of the bed during the night, he or she will not be harmed.

BRIGHT IDEA

Long-lasting artworks
Apply a coating of hairspray to a child's drawing – this acts as a fixative and prevents the colours from fading and rubbing off. Hairspray also strengthens the paper.

CHILDREN'S CLOTHES

Unless you are aiming for designer perfection, secondhand clothes make sense for small children. These may be handed down from friends and relatives, or sought out in thrift shops and at jumble sales. Improvise playclothes from old overalls and coats.

KEEPING CLOTHES
● **Children's boots** To avoid losing boots at school, cut two matching shapes from coloured tape and stick them on the backs of the heels – the boots will stand out among others in a group.
● **Altering coats** To lengthen the life of a winter jacket, sew ready-made knitted cuffs to the sleeves.
● **Attaching gloves** To prevent a child's gloves from being lost, sew tape between them, and run the tape through the sleeves of the child's coat.
● **Girls' dresses** Turn dresses inside out if you dry them outdoors. When the hem is let down, the colour will already have faded to match the dress.

SHOES AND BOOTS
● **Laces** Run shoelaces over beeswax or soap before lacing shoes or boots to make the knots last longer. Tie a knot in each end of the laces.

Children's shoes
To teach a child how to put its shoes on correctly, put tape or a mark inside the right shoe so that it is clearly visible. Show the child that this shoe should always be put on the right foot.

PLAYCLOTHES
● **Protecting clothes** Spray knees, cuffs, and collars with fabric protector to keep playclothes clean.

Fixing cross straps
To stop cross straps on rompers and dungarees from continually falling down, sew on a snap fastener at the point where the straps cross over at the back. The snap can be easily undone.

FEEDING PETS

Find out from a vet, or from a book on pet care, how to provide your pet with the nutrition it needs for good health. Feed your pet regularly, and remember that it too likes variety in its diet. A supply of clean water should always be available for it to drink.

HEALTHY PETS

● **Teeth** Give dogs and cats marrow bones to keep their teeth in good shape. Never give chicken or fish bones.

Coat conditioner
Adding a raw egg or 30–45 ml (2–3 tbsp) of melted animal fat or cod-liver oil to a dog's diet each day helps to produce a shiny coat. Vegetable oil does not have the same effect.

FEEDING CATS

● **Large cans** Keep a large can of cat food fresh by dividing it into separate small portions and placing each portion in a plastic sandwich bag. Seal the bag and freeze until needed.
● **The correct food** Do not feed cats with dog food – it does not have enough protein and vitamins for cats' needs.

FEEDING DOGS

● **Dog-food dishes** Keep disposable foam meat dishes from supermarkets to use as dog-food dishes – simply throw them away after use.
● **Tuna oil** Save the oil from a can of tuna and pour it over a dog's dinner for extra taste.

GREEN TIP

Healthy food additions
Save the water from cooked vegetables to add extra flavour and vitamins to your pet's dry food. Allow the water to cool down before adding it to the food.

GROOMING AND CARE

Regular grooming and exercise are the main care elements needed by cats and dogs. They also need to eat grass occasionally, so grow some in a pot if you do not have a garden. Train a puppy to allow its teeth to be cleaned to prevent bad breath.

PREVENTING ODOURS

● **Using vinegar** Place a small dish of vinegar in the room where a dog sleeps, or near a cat-litter tray to absorb odours.

Measure laundry borax

Deodorizing litter trays
Add one part of laundry borax to six parts of cat litter, or 225 g (8 oz) of bicarbonate of soda to a tray of litter, to absorb odours.

TACKLING PARASITES

● **Flea deterrent** If you have no flea collar or powder, rub citrus oil from an orange on an animal's fur to discourage fleas and ticks. Pennyroyal oil under a collar also works.
● **Flea collar** A homemade flea collar can be constructed from a roll of strong fabric stuffed with tansy and catnip.
● **Tick removal** Remove ticks by dabbing them with white spirit so that they back out. Do not pull them – they may leave their heads in the pet's skin and cause infection.
● **Killing lice eggs** To kill lice eggs (called "nits"), wash your pet once every two weeks in a five per cent solution of white vinegar and water.

CLEANING PETS

● **Bathing dogs** Put an old tea strainer in the sink or bath drain to prevent it from becoming clogged with hair.
● **Rinsing soap** When bathing dogs, add vinegar or lemon juice to the rinse water to eliminate any soap smell.
● **Dry bath** Instead of bathing a dog in water, rub bicarbonate of soda into its coat, then brush it out. The bicarbonate of soda acts as a deodorant and a dry cleaner.
● **Matted fur** Remove mats in fur by shampooing, then using conditioner. When the fur is dry, rub talcum powder into the mats and tease them apart. Large mats may have to be cut out by a vet.

PET PROBLEMS

Training your pet to obey house rules may take time and trouble but will pay off in the end. Ask the breeder or a vet for the best methods to use. Start training when the animal is young, before it has a chance to develop habits that may be difficult to correct later.

PROTECTING FURNITURE

● **Keeping pets off** Sprinkle pepper on upholstered surfaces to keep a pet off them. Vacuum it up later.

Preventing chewing
Wipe oil of cloves (from pharmacists) on furniture legs to prevent a new puppy from chewing them. Dogs dislike the smell and the bitter taste.

DOG BEHAVIOUR

● **Acclimatizing a puppy** Help a puppy to adjust to sleeping without its mother by putting a hot-water bottle wrapped up in a towel in its bed. A ticking clock in the bed will simulate its mother's heartbeat.
● **Wetting** If a puppy wets in the house, clean the spot with vinegar and water, then blot with plenty of ammonia. This will take away the smell, and prevent it from happening in that particular area again.
● **Loneliness** If you have to leave a pet alone for a short period, give it something of yours to keep it company, such as a slipper. Soft radio music may provide comfort.

PETS AND SAFETY

● **Night safety** Fix reflective tape to your pet's collar to reduce the risk of it being struck by a car at night.
● **Balconies** Keep pets away from balconies and windows if you do not live on the ground floor. Even a cat can fall from a high-rise window.
● **Flexes** Make sure that electric flexes, cleaning substances, and valuable items are out of a puppy's reach until it has grown up beyond the chewing stage.
● **Car travel** Never let pets sit unrestrained in a car. Use a pet carrier for cats; keep dogs behind a grille, or tie their leads to a rear seatbelt.

SMALL ANIMALS

Small animals that live in hutches or cages, such as rabbits and guinea pigs, can make good pets. They grow up very quickly, and are easy to handle. Small animals may be less expensive to feed than large pets, but they still require your commitment and care.

SMALL ANIMAL CARE

● **Choosing numbers** Find out from your vet whether your pet species likes company or prefers to be alone. Hamsters like to be solitary, and two male mice or rats may fight. Guinea pigs and rabbits like to have companions.
● **Pet toys** To stimulate small animals, give them household objects, such as cotton reels, to play with. Make sure the objects do not have any sharp edges and are not toxic.
● **Chickens** To prevent free-range chickens from eating a favourite plant, cover it with a wire cage. Allow some shoots to push through the cage. The birds can eat these while the plant continues growing.

RABBITS

● **Safe cages** Suspend an outdoor rabbit hutch from a beam to prevent rodents from entering the cage at night.

Natural bedding
Save dry autumn leaves and dried grass cuttings to provide free bedding for rabbits and other small pets. Store the surplus away from anywhere damp to keep the supply going.

WILD BIRDS

● **Bird cake** Mix a winter cake for wild birds from seeds and bacon rinds in melted fat. Put outside in a coconut shell.

Attracting birds
A bird table or bird-feeding net outside the window of anyone housebound or ill will provide entertainment. Replace the food as it is eaten or the birds will find a food source elsewhere.

HEALTH AND BEAUTY

WHILE YOU CAN PAY A FORTUNE for cosmetics that claim to do all manner of things for your skin, hair, and body, the foundations for feeling and looking good can be laid with a balanced diet and a few home treatments.

COSMETICS

There is no need to throw out cosmetics just because they have dried up – they are usually too expensive to waste. Most bottles and jars can be recycled, while their contents can often be mixed with water or oil to rehydrate them and prolong their use.

NAIL VARNISH

Softening nail varnish
Stand hardened nail varnish in a bowl of hot water to return it to its original consistency. Repeat as often as necessary. Keep your nail varnish in the refrigerator to prevent it from thickening.

LIPSTICK

● **Empty tubes** Use a lip brush to get at the ends of a lipstick. Clean empty lipstick tubes out with hot water, and use them for storing kirby grips.

Hold broken end over flame

Repairs to lipstick
To mend a broken lipstick, heat the two ends over a flame until they melt enough to be stuck together again, then cool the lipstick in the refrigerator.

MASCARA

Reviving dried mascara
Use a pipette to pour a couple of drops of hot water into a tube of mascara that is almost finished. Swivel the brush around to mix it well. This will soften dried-out mascara that can then be used.

PERFUME

● **Buying** Buy a trial size of new perfume to see if it suits you before purchasing a standard-sized bottle.
● **Storage** Store perfume in a dark, cool place. Constant exposure to light and heat will cause it to deteriorate.
● **Applying perfume** Oily skin holds perfume better than dry skin, so rub a little petroleum jelly into your skin before applying perfume.
● **Scenting drawers** Cut an old chamois leather into small pieces, and sprinkle it with perfume for your lingerie drawer. The chamois leather will hold the scent of the perfume longer than pieces of cotton wool would.

COSMETIC CARE

● **Storage** To stop bottles from falling over in drawers, cut circles in the lids of small cardboard boxes and place the bottles in the holes.
● **Stuck stoppers** If a stopper on a glass bottle is stuck, pour a little vegetable oil on to it. Hold the bottle near to warm heat, and tap gently all around the stopper until it loosens.
● **Brushes** To keep make-up brushes soft, wash them in hair conditioner occasionally.
● **Pencils** Put eyebrow pencils in the refrigerator for a while before sharpening them. They will be less likely to break.

TRADITIONAL TIP

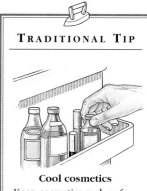

Cool cosmetics
Keep cosmetics such as face toner and moisturizing cream in the refrigerator if the weather is hot. They will be refreshing to use, and those that contain natural ingredients will remain fresh for as long as possible.

NATURAL BEAUTY

Y ou can create natural beauty treatments yourself using fruit and vegetables. These homemade mixtures will be cheaper than manufactured products, contain no artificial additives, and are often kinder on your skin than store-bought cosmetics with chemicals.

SCENTING A BATH

Lemon fresh
Fill a net bag with fresh lemon skins and let water run through it as you fill the bath. The oils in the lemons will be good for your skin, and the fragrance will give the water a delicious scent.

NATURAL INGREDIENTS
● **Puffy eyes** Treat tired, puffy eyes by holding peeled, grated raw potato against them in a clean handkerchief. Alternatively, use cucumber slices or cold, wet teabags.
● **Thick eyelashes** Encourage eyelash growth by dabbing castor oil on your eyes at night. Avoid allowing the oil to run into your eyes.
● **White teeth** Instead of tooth powder, use bicarbonate of soda for whiter teeth.
● **Fresh breath** To sweeten breath, chew parsley.
● **Eliminating foot odour** Baking soda helps to get rid of unpleasant odours from shoes and feet. Dust it over feet and sprinkle in shoes.

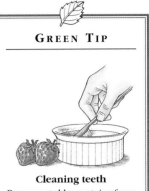

GREEN TIP

Cleaning teeth
Remove stubborn stains from teeth – such as those from tobacco – by dipping your toothbrush in mashed strawberries. Brush your teeth thoroughly, then rinse your mouth with a little salt dissolved in warm water.

HANDS AND NAILS

W ear rubber gloves for rough household tasks – they will help protect your hands and nails from becoming dry and damaged. When applying nail varnish, place your fingers in a bowl of iced water between applications to make each layer of varnish dry quickly.

NAIL CARE
● **Strong nails** Strengthen nails by soaking fingertips in warm water and bicarbonate of soda for 10 minutes once a week.

Softening cuticles
Soak cuticles in a bowl of warm olive oil to soften them. Push them gently back with a cotton-wool bud. Use a little vitamin-E cream to regularly coat cuticles.

CLEANING HANDS
● **Grimy hands** Hands that are very grimy can be cleaned by massaging in a thick paste of oatmeal and water.

Removing stains on skin
Use the cut half of a lemon, or lemon juice, for removing stains from hands and then whitening them. Use vinegar to remove strong food odours, such as fish.

SOFT SKIN
● **Hand lotion** Make your own hand lotion from two parts glycerine to one part lemon juice. Massage a little into the hands after washing them.
● **Soft skin** Soften rough feet and hands by rubbing them in equal proportions of cooking oil and granulated sugar.

VARNISHING NAILS
● **Making varnish stick** Wipe nails with vinegar before you apply nail varnish – this will help the varnish to adhere.
● **Loosening bottle caps** To prevent a nail-varnish bottle cap from sticking to the bottle, rub a little petroleum jelly in the grooves of the cap.

SKINCARE

Keep your skin scrupulously clean if you want to avoid spots and blemishes. To remove blackheads, steam your face over a bowl of warm water. Clean skin often if you live or work in a highly polluted area. Best of all, take care of your skin from the inside out.

SUNBURN

● **Reducing heat** Pat skin that has been sunburned with a cold, wet teabag, or dab the area with cider vinegar.

Natural remedy
Apply a thin coating of plain, natural yoghurt to sunburned areas to take away the pain. Adding 300 ml (½ pint) cider vinegar to a tepid bath will also soothe sunburned skin.

CLEANSING

Sprinkle sugar on cleanser

Making a cleansing scrub
Add 5 g (1 tsp) of granulated sugar to your regular cream cleanser or to lather from toilet soap. This makes an economical homemade scrub that will exfoliate rough areas of skin.

GENERAL SKINCARE

● **Body lotion** Make up a body lotion of equal proportions of glycerine and rosewater and smooth over the skin in the evening before going to bed.
● **Skin softener** Put a handful of oatmeal in the bath water to smooth and soften skin. It will not produce the scum left by many bath oils.
● **Elbows** Rest your elbows in the skin of an avocado for a few minutes to soften them. The avocado pit will also lubricate dry skin. Rest your elbows in lemon skins for a few minutes to whiten them.
● **Milk bath** Sprinkle some powdered milk into running bath water for a relaxing bath that will soften the skin.

HOME FACIALS

Treat yourself to a home facial when you have time to enjoy it. Lie down and relax, perhaps listening to soothing music. You can make your own face masks and lotions from natural ingredients found in the kitchen. They are inexpensive and beneficial to your skin.

CARING FOR YOUR SKIN

● **Facial scrub** Make your own exfoliating scrub for your face by mixing cornmeal, honey, and ground walnuts. Rub it on your face with your fingertips and leave for five minutes before rinsing the scrub off.
● **Foundation** Wipe a wet sponge over your face before putting on liquid make-up. This will prevent the make-up from dragging on your skin.
● **Skin freshener** Make your own skin freshener from equal parts of rosewater and witch hazel, and apply it to your face with a cotton-wool pad. Because it contains no alcohol, this mixture will not leave your skin feeling taut.

HOMEMADE FACE TREATMENTS

FOR DRY SKIN

● **Cucumber and yoghurt** Cut up an unpeeled cucumber and liquidize with a carton of natural yoghurt. Spread this on your face, then rinse off.
● **Egg yolk, oil, and lemon** Mix one egg yolk with 2.5 ml (½ tsp) each of olive oil and lemon juice. Wash your face and spread on well, avoiding the eyes. Leave for 10 minutes, then rinse off.

FOR OILY SKIN

● **Egg white and cornflour** Mix one egg white with 30 g (2 tbsp) of cornflour. Spread the mixture over your clean face and leave for several minutes until it feels dry and tight. Brush off what you can of the face pack with a dry cloth, and rinse thoroughly with cold water. Apply beaten egg white on its own to tone the skin and tighten the pores.

HEALTHY HAIR

There are all sorts of natural treatments for healthy, shiny hair, so you should be able to find one that suits your hair type. Regular cutting is essential for getting rid of split ends. Diet can also affect the way your hair looks, as can stress, mood, smoking, and air pollution.

FINAL RINSING
● **Adding shine** Shine up brunette or red hair by rinsing in coffee or cider vinegar before the final water rinse.

Blonde hair
Pour 300 ml (½ pint) of boiling water over 10 g (2 tsp) of dried chamomile leaves or a handful of fresh ones. Leave to infuse, then strain. Use the liquid as a rinse for shining blonde hair.

CARING FOR HAIR
● **Conditioner** Mayonnaise is a good conditioner for dry hair. Apply 100 ml (4 fl oz) to unwashed hair, cover with foil or plastic film, and leave for 15 minutes. Rinse off the mayonnaise, then shampoo.
● **Hot oil** For a professional-style hot-oil treatment, run very hot water over two bath towels, then spin them in your washing machine. Saturate hair with olive or corn oil, and wrap your head in foil or plastic film. Wrap the towels around this covering, so that they will not get dirty. Wait for 20 minutes before shampooing and rinsing.
● **Fine hair** Rinse very fine hair with beer to give it body.

RECIPE FOR NATURAL HAIR CONDITIONER

● **Almond and rosemary** Heat chopped rosemary and 15 ml (1 tbsp) each of almond oil, glycerine, and lanolin. Remove the mixture from the heat and beat in an egg (but do not allow it to scramble). Shampoo your hair, then massage the mixture into the head. Leave for 10 minutes, then rinse hair thoroughly.

MONEY-SAVING TREATMENTS

Economize where you can so that you can splash out occasionally on treatments such as facials, manicures, or even a visit to a health farm. Buy large sizes of products you use frequently, and make sure you use the last bits in containers and jars before you discard them.

UNUSED PERFUME

Scenting the home
If you do not like a particular perfume enough to wear it, wipe a small amount over light bulbs. They will produce scent when heated up. Do not put on too much if the scent is strong.

LEFTOVER SOAP

Add boiling water to soap ends

Saving old soap
Save soap pieces in a screwtop jar. Add the juice of a lemon and fill up the jar with boiling water. Stir to dissolve, then add 5 ml (1 tsp) of glycerine. Allow to cool, and use for washing hands.

OTHER ECONOMIES
● **Shampoo** Put a few drops of water in an almost-empty shampoo bottle, and shake it well. Stand the bottle upside down for a few minutes. Use in showers as liquid soap.
● **Cotton wool** Buy surgical cotton wool, which is cheaper than other types. Break it into pieces and store it in a plastic bag in an airing cupboard. The pieces will then swell ready for use.
● **Lip gloss** Use petroleum jelly as a lip gloss, or rub a little over your lipstick.
● **Talcum powder** Make talcum powder last longer by taping over all but three holes. This also saves mess.

CARS AND GARAGES

Y OUR CAR IS A VALUABLE ASSET, so keep it clean and well maintained. Check it regularly for faults and dirt, especially before setting out on long journeys. Have the car serviced at regular intervals. Keep your garage in order as well.

CLEANING YOUR CAR AND GARAGE

If you do not have time to clean your car yourself, use a valeting service, or take it through a do-it-yourself car wash at a garage. Do not forget to clean the interior. Bear in mind that keeping your car clean will prolong its useful life and help to maintain its value.

CLEAN SCREEN

Wiping off insects
Use plastic net bags to wipe windscreens on which insects have accumulated. Tie a few bags into one and rub well until the insects are gone. Then wash the windscreen thoroughly. Wipe with white vinegar.

CLEANING TIPS
● **Rinsing** Add 225 ml (8 fl oz) of kerosene to the car wash water, so that no rinsing will be necessary. It also prevents rust and helps water bead on the car when it is raining.
● **Windscreen wipers** If your wipers are doing more smearing than cleaning, wash the windscreen, and clean the wipers with rubbing alcohol.
● **Carpet** If salt from road gritting leaves marks on the carpet, wash with an equal amount of warm water and vinegar. Let dry, then vacuum.
● **Stickers** Use nail-varnish remover to take off stickers.

GREEN TIP

Removing tar
Wipe tar spots on cars with a little linseed oil or eucalyptus oil. Leave the oil to soak until the tar softens, then wipe it off with a paper towel moistened in some fresh oil.

CLEANING GARAGES

Provided you keep the garage swept clear of leaves and debris, there will be little else to do except remove grease and oil stains from the floor.

● **Fresh stains** Sprinkle fresh oil stains on garage floors with plenty of cat litter, then grind the litter in with your foot. Sweep the litter up when it has absorbed the oil, and discard it.

● **Using sugar soap** First scrape off as much of the stain deposit as you can, using a putty knife. Wet the remaining oil stains, then sprinkle on sugar-soap crystals (available from hardware stores). As these dissolve, use a bristle brush to rub at the stains for 15–20 minutes. Add more sugar soap and continue to scrub. Rinse off the stains with clean water.
● **Old stains** For old stains, apply a spray-and-wash product and leave it for five minutes. Sprinkle with laundry detergent, scrub with a stiff broom, and hose the area down.
● **Tough stains** For really tough stains, use oven cleaner. Let it set, then rinse it away.

OTHER CARE TIPS
● **Scenting cars** Keep a sheet of fabric softener underneath your car seat to keep the whole car smelling fresh.
● **Stain guard** Before long trips, spray the front of your car with cooking oil to stop bugs from sticking to the grill.
● **Air conditioners** Run the air conditioner for five minutes each week during winter to keep it functioning smoothly.
● **Keeping oil clean** Keep open cans of motor oil clean by sealing them with the plastic tops from used cans of coffee.
● **Chrome** Clean car chrome with damp aluminium foil.
● **Windscreens** Add a splash of white vinegar to a wet, lint-free rag to clean windscreens.

WEATHER-RELATED PROBLEMS

Be prepared for when things go wrong with your car, particularly in cold weather. Carry an emergency kit consisting of a blanket, water, mint cake, torch, and book. A mobile telephone is useful in case you break down on a stretch of road that has no telephone.

FROZEN LOCKS

● **Heating locks** If your car is in a garage, use a hairdryer on the lock at a low setting to thaw it out. Alternatively, spray the lock with de-icer.

Heating the key
Heat the key (not the lock) with a match or cigarette lighter until it is warm. Insert it in the lock and leave for a couple minutes before turning it. Repeat.

STUCK IN SNOW

● **Using cat litter** Keep a bag of cat litter in your boot during the winter. If your car gets stuck on ice or in snow, it will provide traction.

Using floor mats
Remove the rubber mats from your car and place them behind the rear wheels. They might just provide enough traction to get your car moving again.

PRECAUTIONS

● **Washer** Check the level of windscreen-washer water, particularly in hot weather, when it tends to evaporate.
● **Preventing frozen doors** Wipe the rubber gaskets of your car doors with vegetable oil to prevent them from freezing up in winter.
● **Morning starts** Reverse your car into the garage at night – it is easier to drive forwards than to reverse when the engine has not warmed up.
● **Cold engine** If the car will not start on a cold morning, try blowing hot air from a hairdryer on the carburettor.
● **Full tank** A full fuel tank will give extra weight and traction when driving on icy roads.

GENERAL MAINTENANCE

Simple problems can give you as much trouble with your car as getting stuck in a traffic jam and missing a vital appointment. Regular checks on items such as lights will help you avoid minor problems and may save you from calling out the emergency services.

REGULAR MAINTENANCE

● **Spare fuel** Keep the spare petrol can full, especially when going on long journeys.
● **Spare tyre** When checking tyre pressure, always check the pressure on the spare tyre. Inflate the spare each time you put air in the other tyres.
● **Lights** Enlist the help of a second party to check that all lights are working. Always carry spare light bulbs.
● **Tyres** Regularly inspect the tyres and remove any stones or nails lodged in the treads.
● **Wipers** Carry a set of spare wiper blades in the car.
● **Jump leads** If your battery is not in good condition, keep jump leads in the car.

CAR AERIALS

● **Retractable aerials** If your aerial is retractable, put it in when you leave the car. This will prevent damage to it.

Temporary aerial
Use a coat hanger as a substitute for an aerial. Cut off the hook, shape into a diamond, and wedge into the aerial socket.

BRIGHT IDEA

Safe garage parking
When you are parked in your garage, measure the distance from the rear wall to your windscreen. Suspend a ball from the ceiling at this point; it will touch the windscreen, warning you to stop the next time you park in the garage.

ENTERTAINING

HAVING FRIENDS AROUND to your home for food and friendship requires proper planning. The guests will not enjoy themselves if the hosts are run ragged trying to serve drinks, get food on the table, and make conversation.

DINNER PARTIES

This type of entertaining is usually a bit more formal than a supper or buffet party, or asking people around to take pot luck. Make sure everything is prepared well in advance to avoid a last minute rush and to give yourself plenty of time to greet your guests.

THE GUESTS
● **Choosing** Select guests carefully so that they are all compatible. Do not invite more people than you can seat, and avoid people who may argue or dominate the conversation. Indicate both an arrival time and a dinner time when you invite guests.

THE FOOD
● **Planning a menu** Do not aim to have all the courses hot, otherwise you will never get out of the kitchen. Give yourself plenty of time to get all the ingredients you will require. Be careful not to experiment with dishes that you have never tried before.

PREPARATIONS
● **Lists** Make a full list of everything required for the event – this includes not only food and drink, but also table linen, candles, and flowers.
● **Timetable** Make a timetable of what to do. Do not leave everything to the last minute.

LAYING A DINNER TABLE

Correct place settings
Lay the dinner table according to what you are going to eat, starting from the outside. This setting is laid for a four course meal that will include soup, fish, a main course, and a dessert. Place all the glasses you are going to use to the right of the place setting.

White wine glass

Red wine glass

Dessert utensils sit at top of plate

Fish fork sits on outside, since it will be used first

Tumbler for water

Use a special knife if serving fish

Place soup spoon with knives, to right of plate

Place bread knife on bread plate, or with other knives

SEATING
● **Pre-dinner** If you are sitting down for pre-dinner drinks, make sure there are enough chairs – if necessary, moving some from the dining area.
● **Table plan** Work out the seating plan in advance and put place names around the table to avoid embarrassment.

CLOTHES
● **Dress code** Decide what you will be wearing for the occasion, in case any guests telephone and want to know in advance how to dress.
● **Coats** Make sure you have somewhere to put guests' coats where they will not be squashed or creased.

ETIQUETTE
● **Timing** Be ready on time. It is embarrassing for guests if their hostess is in the bath, getting dressed, or making up.
● **Avoid cliques** Try and stop people who will be sitting next to each other at dinner talking to each other during pre-dinner drinks.

CHILDREN'S PARTIES

These can be hell for parents, but are usually much enjoyed by children. With younger children, do not invite too many guests, or they may be overwhelmed and unhappy. Do not allow children to overeat, or to become overly excited or boisterous.

PARTY GAMES

● **Planning ahead** Decide what the activities will be – games, magic, film, or swimming – and make a rough timetable.
● **Games helpers** Enlist a helper (teenagers are good) to supervise activities while you deal with food, visits to the toilet, accidents, and so on.
● **Prizes** Buy prizes for games and sports and try to make sure everyone wins one.

PARTY FOOD

● **Kid's treats** Choose simple foods that can be eaten with the fingers. It does not matter if it is not particularly healthy. That can be remedied at other meals taken with the family.

PROTECTING FURNITURE

Lining food tables
Protect table surfaces by putting clingfilm under the tablecloths. Do the same for piano tops and anywhere else that food and drinks are likely to be placed or spilled. Ideally, eat in the kitchen, where spills can be mopped up.

BRIGHT IDEA

Party invitations
Inflate large, brightly coloured balloons, and write the invitation details on them with a felt-tip pen. Deflate the balloons, put them in envelopes, and deliver them.

OTHER SOCIAL OCCASIONS

Most social occasions are less formal than dinner parties – apart from weddings, christenings, and funerals. Pre-planning is the key to everyone enjoying themselves. If you plan ahead, you will have time to prepare properly and to enjoy the occasion as well.

DRINKS PARTIES

● **Seating** If you want to invite a lot of people, provide food that can be eaten standing up. Allow a few chairs and tables for those who prefer to sit down, such as the elderly.
● **Serving buffet food** Invest in a set of drinks clips that attach to plates and make handling a plate and fork easier while standing up. Try not to use paper plates – they bend and cannot take hot food.
● **Drinks** Provide plenty of soft drinks for those driving.
● **Food preparation** Prepare as much hot food in advance as possible, and keep it warm. Keep cold desserts and salads in the fridge, ready to receive dressings and sauces.

PICNICS

● **Food** Wrap sandwiches and portions individually, then label them with each person's name to make serving easy.
● **Picnic dressings** Empty pill bottles, thoroughly washed, make ideal containers for salad dressings at a picnic.

SPECIAL EVENTS

● **Christmas** Buy wrapping paper and cards in sales after Christmas, and gifts when you see them during the year. This prevents a huge hole in your budget at Christmas time.
● **Weddings** Use any leftover fabric from the wedding dress to make a large bow. Hang on the entrance to the reception to welcome your guests.

ESTIMATING DRINKS QUANTITIES

Use the guidelines below to work out how much drink to buy for a party. People drink more at small parties than they do at large ones.

● **Wine** A 750 ml (24 fl oz) bottle of wine or champagne gives six glasses. If serving wine at a party, allow about one-half bottle per person.
● **Sherry and port** A standard bottle will yield 16 glasses.
● **Spirits** A standard bottle of spirits gives 30 measures.
● **Soft drinks** Drunk alone, a 500 ml (16 fl oz) bottle gives three servings; mixed with spirits, it gives five servings.

MOVING HOUSE

MOVING HOME IS A TRAUMATIC EXPERIENCE for most people, especially if they have a lot of possessions to be packed and transported. Whether you are going just around the corner or across the country, there is a lot to think about.

BEFORE YOU MOVE

Plan the removal carefully. There are things to do in both your old and new homes. Time spent in organization will reduce the chaos, particularly where children and pets are concerned. Hire a reputable removal firm so that you benefit from their experience.

PACKING UP
- **Thinning** Go through your possessions, discarding those you do not want or never use. Give them away to charity, or hold a garage sale.
- **Insurance** You will be insured for damage only if the removers, rather than you, have packed everything. They are professionals, so trust them with delicate items.
- **Children** Arrange for young children who would get in the way to stay with friends. Put pets in a kennel or cattery for a few days while you get the new home sorted out.

MOVING PLANTS

Plant carrier
Transport plants yourself instead of leaving them for the movers. Water them well two days in advance. Put them in tea chests, wedge the pots with newspaper, and cover with polythene.

MOVING PICTURES

Protecting picture glass
Reinforce picture glass with criss-crossed masking tape – this also prevents the glass from splintering if broken. When you remove the tape, clean the glass with methylated spirit.

CHANGE OF ADDRESS

People will need to be informed of your change of address. Local ameneties will also need to be told if you are moving far away.

- **Utilities** Arrange for the utility meters to be read at a specific time, and make sure the bills are sent to your new address. Arrange for utilities to be supplied at your new home, checking well in advance whether a deposit is required.
- **Doctors** Tell your doctor, dentist, and any other medical advisers where you are moving to, and ask them to recommend local practitioners.
- **Banks** Inform your banks and building societies, as well as any professional financial advisers, of your new address.

- **Schools** Give notice to your children's schools, and check out where you can send your children in the new area – and whether they will be accepted. In addition, check how they can get to the new school.
- **Local commitments** Cancel library tickets and subscriptions to local clubs. Resign from local commitments such as the school board or Neighbourhood Watch.
- **Insurance** Tell all your insurance companies your new address, and check if premiums increase or decrease according to the new area.
- **Investments** Inform your tax office of your move, and also any companies in which you hold shares and any government investments.

- **Mail order** Change your address with any mail-order suppliers with whom you wish to stay in touch. (They will probably find you anyway.)
- **Post Office** Arrange with the Post Office for your mail to be redirected for a year, after which everyone who needs it should have your new address.
- **Companies** Inform any companies with whom you have local contracts – burglar-alarm or mobile-phone companies, for example.
- **Credit cards** Make sure you send your new address to your credit-card companies.
- **Telephone** Tell the telephone company of your move several weeks in advance, so that a final bill can be sent to you.

MOVING DAY

It helps if one person can go to the new home and await the removal van, while another stays in the old place to check on the packing. With self-removals, make a similar arrangement, enlisting the help of friends if necessary. This helps to facilitate the move.

SURVIVAL KIT

Make up a "kit" of what you will need when you arrive at your new home. You do not want to wait for the removal van to arrive to have a cup of tea.

● **Bedding** Take enough sheets and blankets or duvets for all family members so that when the beds arrive they can be made up immediately. Making up the beds is a priority, since you will be tired after moving into the new house and will not feel like doing it later on.
● **Food and equipment** Take tea or coffee, milk, sugar, something to eat, cups or mugs, plates, a kettle, a can opener, a saucepan, and some cutlery.

● **Emergency supplies** Do not forget to take toilet paper, washing-up liquid and a kitchen cloth, soap, a self-seating plug, electric light bulbs, and a first-aid kit.
● **Tool kit** Take a basic tool kit in case things need fixing, and to assist in plugging in electrical equipment when it arrives. This kit could include an adjustable spanner, a hammer, a pair of pliers, and a screwdriver. Take a torch and candles in case the electricity is not turned on.
● **Clothes** Take enough clothes for the following day in case you are too tired to unpack.
● **Keys** Of course, do not forget the keys to your new home.

ON ARRIVAL

● **New home** Check your new home, making sure that the previous owners have not removed anything they said they would leave behind, or left you with a pile of junk. If there is a problem, call your solicitor immediately.
● **Furniture** When the removal van arrives, take the foreman around the house, explaining where you want major pieces of furniture to go. Ask him to leave breakable items on surfaces where you can inspect them straight away.
● **Damages** Check for any damage and make any necessary insurance claim as soon as you possibly can.

YOUR NEW HOME

Do not imagine that you will be able to put your feet up until everything is unpacked and the removal team has left. You need to be constantly vigilant to ensure that everything is under control. Check that all your belongings have arrived, and that there are no breakages.

ACTION PLAN
● **Protect carpets** Protect carpets from muddy boots by putting newspapers over the carpets. Give the removers a plan of the house and tell them how you have labelled the boxes for each area.
● **Drinks** Be prepared to make endless supplies of drinks for the removers – but no alcohol. Moving furniture is physically demanding and thirsty work.
● **Children** If there are small children with you, keep them well out of the way of the removers. Take toys with you to keep the children amused.
● **Pets** If pets have travelled with you, shut them in one room and ask the removers to deal with that one last.

MOVING BY YOURSELF
● **Hiring a van** Consider hiring a van to move house by yourself. It will be cheaper than getting a removal firm.

Labelling boxes
Put different coloured pieces of tape on boxes and items of furniture to indicate in which room they should go. Stick the relevant colour tape on the door of the room when you arrive.

REMOVERS
● **Tipping** Expect to tip the removers in addition to paying the amount agreed when you signed the contract for the job.

Using a floor plan
Give the foreman a floor plan of the house, showing where you want the major pieces of furniture to go. This way you will not have to move heavy items around afterwards.

HEALTH & SAFETY

QUICK REFERENCE

Emergencies, p. 166

Resuscitation, p. 168

Treating Injuries, p. 170

Common Injuries, p. 173

Common Ailments, p. 179

Health and safety should take top priority in a home, especially one that has small children, or elderly or disabled people. Try to look at your home as a stranger would to spot possible danger areas. Bear in mind that learning first-aid techniques from a book, although useful, is not a substitute for the practical training of a first-aid course.

FIRST-AID KIT

Keep all first-aid items together in a box that is easily accessible for adults but out of reach of small children. Replace items as you use them, and dispose of any that are past their best. Your pharmacist will do this for you. Supplement the first-aid kit with a supply of painkillers such as aspirin or paracetamol. Do not, however, keep medicines in the first-aid box; they should be locked in a medicine cabinet. The items shown here comprise a basic first-aid kit for the home.

● **Creams and lotions** Keep antihistamine cream for insect bites and stings, and calamine lotion for sunburn.
● **Dressings** Your kit should contain two sterile pads, one sterile dressing with bandage, two sterile eye pads with bandages, and gauze swabs. Keep a selection of adhesive plasters for minor wounds.
● **Bandages** Keep two folded, triangular bandages, small and large roller bandages (crêpe or conforming), and a finger bandage with an applicator.
● **Fastenings and tools** Keep hypoallergenic tape or safety pins for securing dressings, tweezers for removing splinters, and blunt scissors for cutting dressings and bandages.

Folded triangular bandage

Large roller bandage

Small roller bandage

Sterile eye pad with bandage

Hypoallergenic tape

Finger bandage with applicator

Sterile non-adhesive pad

Sterile dressing with bandage

Blunt scissors

Tweezers

Gauze swabs

Plasters

SAFETY IN THE HOME

Simple precautions can prevent accidents and even save lives. The kitchen is the most dangerous room in the home, followed by the bathroom. Always mop up spills that could cause people to slip, especially on tiled floors. Put a safety rail on the bath if necessary.

KITCHEN SAFETY

Fit kitchen cupboards with safety catches

Point pot handles inwards

Preventing accidents
Turn pan handles away from the cooker edge, and keep children away from hot oven doors. Fit safety catches on cupboards, and store matches out of reach. Teach children about safety.

GENERAL SAFETY

● **Glass doors** Replace ordinary glass panels fitted into doors with safety or laminated glass, which does not splinter when broken.
● **Fireguards** Always use a fireguard when you leave an open fire unattended. This also applies to flame-effect fires, which get very hot.
● **Rugs** Fix any loose rugs or mats into position with anti-slip pads or tape.
● **Lighting** Ensure hazardous areas of the house, such as stairways and landings, are well lit at all times.
● **Irons** Always switch off an electric iron if you have to answer the door or telephone.
● **Adaptors** Unused plug sockets should be covered with plastic safety covers.

FIRE PRECAUTIONS

● **Smoke alarms** Fit a smoke alarm on each floor of your home. Check them regularly.
● **Fire blankets** Install a fire blanket in the kitchen.
● **Ashtrays** Keep ashtrays for the smouldering cigarette or cigar stubs of smokers.
● **Hinges** Fit self-closing hinges to doors in a home with a high fire risk.
● **Fire drills** Conduct regular family fire practices so that everyone knows the escape routes. Make sure that children know not to return to a burning building, even for family pets (see p. 166).
● **Furniture** Avoid buying old furniture that is stuffed with polyurethane foam. This can burst into flames in a fire and release poisonous fumes.

CALLING EMERGENCY SERVICES

Make a list of important telephone numbers, and keep the master in your home log book and a copy near to each telephone. Stick the copies where they will not be moved, for example inside cupboard doors. Add written instructions to the list in case the caller panics.

EMERGENCY NUMBERS

Keep the telephone numbers of the following services and people on your list:

● Emergency services (fire, police, and ambulance).
● Doctor and dentist (include the office opening hours).
● The nearest hospital with emergency services.
● Immediate family members (include workplace numbers).
● Late-night chemist.
● Emergency numbers for the electricity board, gas board, and water board.
● Taxi service.
● Vet.

MAKING THE CALL

● **Relevant information** When making an emergency call, you will need to give your telephone number, the exact location, the severity of the emergency, the age, sex, and condition of anyone involved, and details of any hazards, such as a gas leak.
● **Teaching children** Drill your children in the basics of calling the emergency services so that if you are injured they will know what to do.
● **Fires** If your house is on fire, ring the emergency services from a neighbour's house or a public telephone.

STAYING IN CONTROL

Keeping calm
In an emergency, it is important to stay calm so that you think clearly. When calling emergency services, try to answer questions and give details precisely. Allow the dispatcher to hang up first.

ACTION IN EMERGENCIES

K NOWING WHAT TO DO IN AN EMERGENCY can contribute greatly to preventing and limiting casualties and damage to property. See pages 108 and 111 for what to do in the event of flooding in the home or a gas leak respectively.

ACTION IN CASE OF FIRE

F ire is frightening and moves very quickly. If you cannot put out a small fire yourself, the most important thing to do is to evacuate the entire building. If you live in an apartment block, sound the fire alarm, then save yourself and your family. Do not let anyone panic.

SMALL FIRES
● **Chimney fires** If an open fire is out of control, dowse it with water. If the chimney is alight, call the fire brigade. Pull furniture and carpets away from the fireplace.
● **Electrical fires** Do not use water on electrical fires. If an appliance such as a television or computer is on fire, turn off the electricity at the mains, and smother the flames with a heavy blanket or coat.
● **Kitchen fires** If a frying pan catches fire, immediately turn off the fryer or the hob ring. Cover the pan with a fire blanket, a damp kitchen cloth, or a large saucepan lid.
● **Controlling small fires** Shut doors and windows to isolate the fire in one room. Air will cause fire to spread.

BUILDINGS ON FIRE

Close door firmly

Block base of door with rug or towel

Open window to let in fresh air

Call for help out of window

Escaping a fire
If you are unable to get out of a burning building, shut yourself as far away from the fire as possible. Block the door with a roll of fabric, dampened if possible. Do not jump out of a window unless it is the only way of saving your life. Open a window and call for help.

WARNING
When evacuating a building, carry any babies and toddlers out with you. Never, for any reason, go back into a blazing building. Alert the emergency services if you know that someone is trapped.

CLOTHES ON FIRE

If a casualty's clothes are on fire, lay him down – burning side uppermost – and dowse him with water or any non-flammable liquid. Alternatively, wrap the casualty in heavy fabric to smother the flames. (Avoid using nylon or any other flammable material.)

Use a curtain, coat, rug, or blanket to wrap casualty

ACTIONS TO AVOID
● **Feeding flames** Do not allow the casualty to panic and rush outside, since movement or breeze will fan the flames.
● **Spreading burns** Do not roll the casualty on the ground – if you do the burns may spread to other parts of his body.

TREATING YOURSELF
● **Extinguishing flames** Wrap yourself in heavy fabric and lie down. Try to remain calm.

ELECTRICAL INJURIES

Many electrical injuries in the home result from faulty switches, frayed flexes, and defective appliances. Handling safe appliances with wet hands, or when standing on a wet floor, can greatly increase the risk of shock. See page 111 for Safety with Electricity.

BREAKING THE CONTACT

1 If someone has been injured by electricity, first break the current by switching off the supply at the mains or meter. If this is difficult, pull the cable free from the socket.

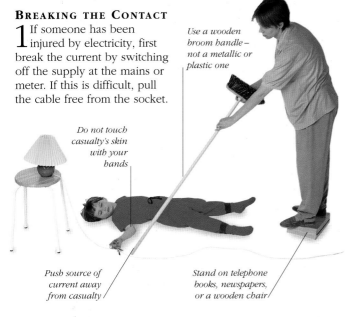

Use a wooden broom handle – not a metallic or plastic one

Do not touch casualty's skin with your hands

Push source of current away from casualty

Stand on telephone books, newspapers, or a wooden chair

2 If you cannot cut the power, stand on insulating material, and use a wooden broom handle to disconnect the current from the casualty.

3 Wrap a dry towel around the casualty's feet, and drag him away from the appliance. As a last resort, pull on his clothes (if they are dry).

4 Check for breathing and pulse if the casualty is unconscious. Resuscitate if necessary (see p. 168). If the casualty seems unharmed, make him rest, and call a doctor. Treat for shock and burns if necessary (see p. 170).

DROWNING

Take particular care with young children near water, and encourage all members of the household to learn to swim as early and as strongly as possible. Remember: a child can drown in 2.5 cm (1 in) of water. Minimize the dangers by watching children near water.

RESCUING A CASUALTY FROM DROWNING

Conscious casualty

To rescue a drowning child, lift her out of the water, holding her head lower than her chest. If she is conscious, dry her, keep her warm, and take her to hospital, even if she seems to have recovered - she will need to be checked for water in the lungs. Never leave babies or small children unattended in baths, or near ponds or swimming pools.

Keep child's head lower than chest after removing her from water

UNCONSCIOUSNESS
● **Administering CPR** If a casualty is unconscious after being rescued from drowning, check for breathing and pulse. Restart the breathing with artificial ventilation and chest compressions (see p. 168). Proceed slowly because of possible water in the lungs.

RELATED PROBLEMS
● **Hypothermia** A drowning victim may possibly develop hypothermia. Remove all wet clothes, dry the casualty, and keep him or her warm.
● **Water in the lungs** Take the casualty to hospital to check that water has not been inhaled – this could cause secondary drowning later on.

RESUSCITATION

W HEN TREATING AN UNCONSCIOUS CASUALTY, the priority is to check whether the lungs and heart are working. Open the airway, then check for breathing and a pulse. If you suspect back or neck injury, treat the casualty with care.

A, B, C OF RESUSCITATION

These letters stand for Airway, Breathing, and Circulation – three areas that you must immediately assess in an unconscious casualty.

If an unconscious casualty is breathing and has a pulse, place him or her in the recovery position (see below) and call an ambulance.

ASSESSING THE CASUALTY

Lift chin to tilt head back

Opening the airway
Open the casualty's mouth, and carefully remove anything inside it that could obstruct the airway. Open the airway by placing one hand on the casualty's forehead and two fingers of the other hand under the casualty's chin to tilt his head back slightly.

Look and listen for breathing

Checking for breathing
Keeping the airway open, place your cheek beside the casualty's mouth and nose for five seconds, and listen and feel for any breath being exhaled. At the same time, carefully look along the casualty's chest to see if there is any sign of movement of the lungs.

Checking circulation
Place a finger at the side of the windpipe for five seconds. If there is a pulse but no breathing, begin artificial ventilation (see opposite). If there is no pulse or breathing, call an ambulunce, then start cardiopulmonary resuscitation (see opposite).

THE RECOVERY POSITION

The position shown below is the safest for someone who is unconscious, because the tongue cannot block the throat, and liquids can drain from the mouth. This greatly reduces the risk of the casualty inhaling stomach contents, then choking on vomit as a result.

PLACING A CASUALTY IN THE RECOVERY POSITION

1 Bend the casualty's near arm at a right angle to the body. Place the back of her far hand to her near cheek. With her near leg straight, bend the other leg so that the knee is at a right angle.

2 Holding the casualty's hand against her cheek, pull the thigh of the bent leg towards you, and roll her on to her side. Working from this position, you should even be able to roll someone heavy.

3 Guide the casualty's head as you turn her. Tilt her head back, and pull the jaw forwards to open the airway. Continue to check the A, B, C of resuscitation (see above) until an ambulance arrives.

Upper hand supports head

Lower arm stabilizes body

Lower leg is straight

Upper leg is at right angles, with knee bent

ARTIFICIAL VENTILATION

If an unconscious casualty is not breathing, you will need to blow air into his or her lungs. Give 10 breaths per minute, and check for a pulse after every 10 breaths. Continue for as long as you can – until the casualty starts to breathe again, or until help arrives.

ADMINISTERING MOUTH-TO-MOUTH VENTILATION

Cover casualty's mouth completely, so that no air escapes

Look to see that chest is deflating

1 Lay the casualty on his back. Remove obstructions from his mouth. Place your hand on his forehead, and pinch his nose while placing two fingers under his chin and tilting his head back.

2 Place your mouth over the casualty's mouth, sealing it firmly. Blow steadily until the chest rises, then remove your mouth. Inhale fresh air, and repeat this step, administering 10 breaths per minute.

3 Continue Step 2 until the casualty is breathing unaided or professional help arrives. Stop every 10 breaths and check for a pulse. Start cardiopulmonary resuscitation if the casualty's pulse fails.

CARDIOPULMONARY RESUSCITATION

Cardiopulmonary resuscitation (CPR) is a combination of artifical respiration and chest compressions. If there is no breathing or pulse, administer first two breaths of artificial ventilation, then fifteen chest compressions. Alternate these actions until help arrives.

ADMINISTERING CHEST COMPRESSIONS

Follow lowest rib up to breastbone

Tilt head back so that airway is open

Apply compressions here

1 Lay the casualty on a firm surface. To locate the area for applying compressions, feel for the casualty's lowest rib with your first and middle fingers. Slide your fingers upwards until your middle finger reaches where the rib meets the breastbone – there may be a slight hollow here.

2 Your first finger should now be lying on the casualty's breastbone. Slide the heel of your other hand down the breastbone until it reaches the point where your first finger is resting. The heel of your hand is now sitting in the exact area to which the compressions will be applied.

3 Keep the heel of your hand in position. Place the other hand on top, then interlock your fingers. Lean over the casualty, keeping your arms straight. Press down 5 cm (2 in) and release, without removing your hands. Stop and check if you suspect pulse and breathing have returned.

169

TREATING INJURIES

EVEN IF YOU KNOW THAT A CASUALTY needs medical or hospital treatment, you can keep him or her comfortable, reduce the risk of shock, and prevent any injuries from getting worse. Prompt, efficient action may save a life.

BLEEDING

It is important to stop all bleeding as quickly as possible. Remove clothing from around the wound, and wash away blood and dirt. You may need to apply pressure to control the bleeding. Reassure the casualty, and be aware that you may have to treat for shock.

TREATING MAJOR WOUNDS

Raise wound above level of heart

Lay casualty down so that wound can be easily elevated

1 Make a pad from a piece of clean cloth, and hold it over the wound, pressing firmly with the palm of your hand. Raise the wound above the level of the casualty's heart to reduce bleeding. Do not try to remove anything embedded in the wound.

2 Lay the casualty down, taking care to keep the wound above the level of the heart. Keep him as flat as possible, using only a thin pad under the head for comfort. Continue to press the wound firmly, until the bleeding begins to lessen.

3 Leave the pad in place, and cover the wound with a sterile dressing. Bandage this into place, keeping the wound above heart level. The bandage should be tight but should not cut off the blood supply. If blood starts to seep through the dressing, place another pad on top.

4 When the bleeding seems under control, keep the injured part elevated, and take the casualty to hospital. If there is an object embedded in the wound, place rolls of gauze around the wound – this will stop the bandage from pressing on the object.

RECOGNIZING AND TREATING SHOCK

Shock occurs when not enough oxygen circulates around the body. This may occur as a result of failure of the circulatory system, as in the case of heart attack, or loss of fluid through bleeding, burns, vomiting, or diarrhoea. As the body responds by withdrawing the blood supply from the surface to the core of the body, the casualty's skin may become grey and clammy, and the pulse may begin to race. To treat a casualty for shock, keep her still, and raise the legs to increase the blood flow to vital organs. Loosen any tight clothing, and keep her warm. Call an ambulance, and be prepared to resuscitate (see p. 168). Do not give any food or drink.

Raise legs to improve circulation

Elevate any wounded limb to minimize loss of blood

CUTS AND GRAZES

Minor cuts and abrasions can be treated without medical help, unless there is a foreign body or a risk of infection.

1 Wash dirt out of a cut or graze gently, using soap and water on a gauze pad. Avoid fluffy cloths, since they may stick to the wound.

2 Press firmly on the wound with a clean gauze pad to stop the flow of bleeding.

3 Cover the wound with a plaster or dressing that is large enough to cover the entire area. (If necessary, apply antiseptic cream first.)

BURNS AND SCALDS

Cool burns and scalds at once to prevent further tissue damage and reduce pain. If a fire is the cause of the casualty's burn injury, make sure that both you and the casualty are safe before attempting treatment. See page 167 for rescuing a casualty from electric shock.

TREATING MAJOR BURNS AND SCALDS

1 Remove the casualty from the source of the burn. Pour cold water on to the burn for at least 10 minutes.

2 Carefully remove clothing and jewellery from the burn area, cutting around any cloth sticking to the wound.

3 Continue to cool the burn if necessary, by immersing it in cold water or any other cool liquid, such as milk.

4 Cover the burn with a clean, sterile dressing, or a piece of clean plastic. If the burn is large, use a clean sheet or pillowcase. Do not apply any fats or creams.

5 Get medical attention as quickly as possible. Treat the casualty for shock if necessary (see opposite). Do not offer her food or drink. Continue to reassure her.

Cool burn with cold water

Do not remove clothing until burn has been cooled

Avoid touching burn

MINOR BURNS
● **Treating** Cool the burn for at least 10 minutes, as above. Remove any jewellery and clothing from around the burn before the area starts to swell.
● **Dressing** Cover minor burns with any clean, non-fluffy material. Burns are susceptible to infection, so clingfilm or a polythene bag make good temporary coverings.

CHEMICAL BURNS
● **Detection** These can be caused by toxic household substances. They are less obvious than heat burns, and may take time to develop.

Removing chemicals
Hold the burned area under cool, running water at once, and wash away all traces of the chemical. Wear rubber gloves to prevent the chemical from splashing on to your own hands. Treat the affected area as for major burns (see above).

ELECTRICAL BURNS
● **Causes** Electrical burns are caused by lightning, or high- or low-voltage current. In the home, low-voltage current can cause scorching to the skin.

Treating the injury
Make sure the current is off (see p. 167). Hold the burn under cool, running water for at least 10 minutes. Cover with a sterile dressing. Seek medical help, as electrical current can cause internal injury. Treat for cardiac arrest or shock if necessary.

BURNS TO THE AIRWAY

Administering water
Burns to the mouth or throat are dangerous, since they can cause the airway to become blocked by swelling. Loosen the casualty's clothing around the neck, and administer sips of cold water. Go at once to hospital. Reassure the casualty.

POISONING

Household chemicals can be poisonous if ingested, as can certain plants and drugs. Seek medical attention as soon as possible. Try to identify the type of poison involved. Keep a sample of the substance ingested, any vomit, or containers or pill bottles found nearby.

TREATING CHEMICAL POISONING

Empty containers are clues to what type of poison has been swallowed

1 Wipe away any chemical residue from around the casualty's mouth and face, taking care not to contaminate yourself. Wash the area gently with cold water. Remove any contaminated clothing.

2 Give the casualty frequent sips of cold water or milk to reduce burning on the lips and in the mouth. Do not try to make her vomit, since this will bring back the chemical and cause further burns.

3 Take the casualty to hospital. Make sure you take the chemical container, so that doctors can give the correct treatment. See below for the appropriate action if the casualty is unconscious.

TREATING DRUG POISONING

Tell emergency services what drug has been taken, and how much

Save container to pass to emergency services

Keep a conscious casualty close to you until help arrives

1 If the casualty is conscious, try to find out which drug has been taken, how much, and when it was ingested. Do not induce vomiting, since this may cause further injury.
If he has vomited, keep a sample for the doctor.

2 Take the casualty to hospital, talking to him calmly to keep him conscious. Take the drug bottle with you. Be prepared to treat for shock (see p. 170). See below for the appropriate action if the casualty is unconscious.

WARNING
Do not give the casualty anything to drink. This will dilute the drug and cause it to be absorbed more readily.

IF THE CASUALTY IS UNCONSCIOUS

BREATHING AND PULSE PRESENT

1 If breathing and pulse are present, place the casualty in the recovery position (see p. 168) to keep the airway open, and call an amubulance.

2 Treat any related injuries such as chemical burns (see p. 171) if necessary.

NO BREATHING, BUT PULSE PRESENT

1 Give 10 breaths of artificial ventilation (see p. 169). Call for an ambulance, and repeat.

2 Continue to give artificial ventilation to the casualty until an ambulance arrives. Check the pulse every minute (after every 10 breaths).

NO BREATHING, NO PULSE

1 Get someone to call an ambulance. Administer five chest compressions, followed by one breath of artificial ventilation (see p. 169).

2 Continue administering CPR until the heartbeat and breathing resume as normal.

COMMON INJURIES

T HE HOME IS A DANGEROUS PLACE. Accidents can happen even if every safety precaution has been taken. Children in particular are at risk because they have less of a sense of danger than adults. Be prepared for any emergency.

ANIMAL BITES

A ll animals, including humans, have germs in their mouths, and bites can not only break the skin but can also cause infection. Always treat animal bites immediately – start by cleaning the wound thoroughly. Take every precaution to avoid being bitten yourself.

TETANUS AND RABIES

● **Tetanus** This produces poisons in the nervous system and is a serious illness. It can be caused by organisms in the soil getting into cuts and bites. Immunization against tetanus is part of a baby's vaccination programme. Adults should have boosters every 10 years.

● **Rabies** This is a potentially fatal disease that is spread by infected animals. If you are bitten in an area where rabies is a danger, seek medical help, even if it appears that the animal has not been infected.

TREATING MINOR ANIMAL BITES

Run wound under water

1 Wash a minor bite wound in soap and water. Then hold it under a running tap for at least five minutes to rinse away any dirt and reduce the risk of germs.

2 Pat the wound dry with a clean gauze pad or tissues. Do not apply an ointment or tincture. Cover with a plaster or sterile dressing. Visit a doctor to explain what has happened, in case there is any infection in the wound.

WARNING

Rabies can be fatal. Treat all animal bites that occur in areas where rabies exists as dangerous, and seek medical attention immediately.

TREATING SERIOUS ANIMAL BITES

1 Wash the wound in soap and water. Hold it under a running tap for five minutes to remove as much dirt and as many germs as possible.

2 Press a clean dressing or pad firmly on the wound. Raise the affected part above the level of the heart. If the bleeding is severe, follow the treatment for major wounds shown on page 170.

3 When the bleeding stops, cover the wound with a sterile dressing or with a pad bandaged firmly in place. Take the casualty to hospital. Do not assume that the wound will heal on its own – it may have been infected by germs from the animal.

Cover wound with dressing and bandage

Keep casualty calm as you work

SNAKE BITES

Wash bite wound

Indications of a snake bite include a pair of puncture marks, severe pain, redness and swelling around the wound, vomiting, and breathing difficulties. Seek medical help immediately.

● **Treating snake bite** Wash the wound with soap and water. Bandage it firmly, holding it below the level of the heart. Keep the casualty calm. Do not cut the wound or try to suck out the venom.

INSECT STINGS

For some people, insect stings can be dangerous and require immediate medical attention or treatment for anaphylactic shock (see below). For other people, the treatments described below are sufficient. Treat stings immediately. Do not let the casualty panic.

INSECT STINGS

1 If the sting is still present, carefully remove it with a pair of tweezers, grasping the sting at the base. Take care that the sting does not break while you are extracting it. Do not squeeze the poison sac at the top of the sting.

2 Apply a cold compress to the area to reduce pain and swelling. Use a cloth wrung out in cold water, or a bag of frozen peas or ice cubes, wrapped in a cloth. Leave the compress on the wound for 10 minutes.

MOUTH AND THROAT

1 If a casualty has been stung in the mouth or throat, reduce the swelling by giving him or her an ice cube or an ice lolly to suck, or some cold water to drink.

2 Take the casualty to a doctor. Call an ambulance if the casualty's breathing becomes difficult because of swelling. If the casualty loses consciousness, treat immediately for anaphylactic shock (see below).

TICK BITES

● **Treatment** Ticks burrow underneath the skin to feed on blood, and can cause infection. Grasp a tick with a pair of tweezers, taking care not to leave any part of the tick in the skin. Keep the tick to show a doctor in case the victim begins to feel unwell.

NETTLE RASH

● **Description** This is a rash of red spots that both itches and hurts. A traditional remedy is to apply dock leaves, which can usually be found growing close to nettles; alternatively, use the treatment below.

Treating nettle rash
The pain and itching of nettle rash can be relieved by applying a cold compress or calamine lotion. Leave on for 10 minutes. Reapply until the itching and pain have ceased. If the rash is extensive, call a doctor.

RECOGNIZING ANAPHYLACTIC SHOCK

Support a conscious casualty in a comfortable position

Anaphylactic shock is caused by a severe allergic reaction to a particular food, an insect sting, or a marine sting. Swelling of the face and neck may block the airways, causing breathing difficulties and, possibly, suffocation. Anxiety, red, blotchy skin, and a rapid pulse may also occur. The casualty urgently needs oxygen and a life-saving injection of adrenaline. Call an ambulance immediately.

The following measures will help to minimize shock until medical help arrives.

● **Loosen clothing** Ensure that any tight clothing is loosened – this will aid breathing.
● **Medication** If the casualty is a known sufferer from this condition, administer any regular medication.
● **Avoiding panic** Anaphylactic shock can cause panic in the sufferer. Try to keep him calm and warm until help arrives.
● **Conscious casualty** Help the casualty to sit up in a position that he finds comfortable.
● **Unconsciousness** Place an unconscious casualty in the recovery position (see p. 168).

BRUISES AND SWELLING

Bruising may be caused by a blunt blow rupturing blood capilliaries beneath the skin, and blood leaking into the tissues. Severe bruising may indicate deep injury, such as a fracture. Likewise, swellings should always be examined, in case they indicate serious injury.

TREATING BRUISES

1 Sit the casualty down, with the injured limb supported. Elevate the injured area on a cushion in order to rest it.

2 Apply a cold compress to the injury. Hold the compress against the injury for 30 minutes to reduce the swelling.

Make sure casualty is comfortable

Elevate injured limb

COLD COMPRESSES

● **Making a cold compress** Wring out a clean cloth in very cold water, or wrap it around ice cubes. Keep it pressed on the swelling for about 30 minutes.

TIME-SAVING TIP

Instant compress
If you need a cold compress in a hurry, a package of frozen peas is an excellent alternative to ice cubes. Wrap it in a light towel and lay it on the injury. Remove when the swelling has gone down.

BONE AND MUSCLE INJURIES

Treat all bone and muscle injuries as serious until you have discovered the extent of the damage. Look for bruises and swelling, and if you think there may be a fracture, take or send the casualty to hospital for an X-ray. Prevent movements that may aggravate the problem.

COMMON BONE AND MUSCLE INJURIES

● **Sprain** Elevate the injured area, and apply a cold compress. Wrap with cotton wool and bandage firmly. Take or send the casualty to hospital as soon as possible.
● **Dislocated shoulder** This occurs when the head of the arm comes out of the shoulder-joint socket. Support the arm in a sling with the hand across the chest. Get the casualty to hospital as soon as possible. Do not give the casualty any food or drink.
● **Broken collar bone** Put the arm on the side of the collar bone in a sling, and take or send the casualty to hospital.

IMMOBILIZING BONE INJURIES

Keep injury immobile

Support injured limb

Make a sling with triangular bandage

Supporting limbs
The immediate action for bone injuries is to support the injury. For an injured arm, seat the casualty, and ask her to support her arm across her chest. For leg injuries, lay the casualty down. Support the leg in your hands.

Securing limbs
Keep the injured part supported by securing it properly. Support an injured arm in a sling, then bandage it to the chest, and take the casualty to hospital. Tie a damaged leg to the uninjured one. Call an ambulance.

CHOKING

Choking can frighten both the person undergoing the fit and those around him or her. Action must be quick, otherwise the casualty may suffocate. Choking is usually caused by eating too fast, or when children put small, inedible objects in their mouths.

RECOGNIZING AND AVOIDING CHOKING

● **Symptoms** The casualty may have difficulty speaking and breathing, and the skin may be blue. The casualty may point at the throat or neck.

● **Prevention** Encourage family members to chew their food thoroughly. Make sure children do not put foreign objects in their mouths.

TREATING CHOKING IN CONSCIOUS ADULTS

1 Lean the casualty forwards, and slap him between the shoulder-blades five times to dislodge the foreign object.

2 If this fails, stand behind the casualty, and place your arms around his abdomen. Interlock your hands, and pull them inwards and upwards against his diaphragm five times.

3 Continue to administer five back slaps and a few abdominal thrusts alternately, until you dislodge the object. (If this fails to dislodge the object and the casualty becomes unconscious, follow the treatment below.)

4 Once the object has been dislodged, encourage the casualty to sit down. Advise him to see a doctor because of the risk of internal damage from abdominal thrusts.

CHOKING IN CHILDREN

The treatment for choking in children differs from the treatment for adults. The following steps are a quick outline; if your household includes small children, you are strongly recommended to take a first-aid course.

1 Encourage the child to cough up the object.

2 If coughing does not remove the object, turn the child over your knee, and slap the area between the shoulder-blades five times.

3 If this still does not dislodge the blockage, turn the child on his or her back, and press hard on the lower breastbone with the heel of one hand. Repeat this action five times.

4 Continue pressing on the breastbone, first pushing downwards, then upwards five times each. If the child loses consciousness, begin resuscitation (see p. 169). Continue until help arrives.

TREATING CHOKING IN UNCONSCIOUS ADULTS

1 If choking has caused loss of consciousness, check whether the casualty is breathing. If not, roll him on to his side and administer five sharp slaps between the shoulder-blades. The muscle spasms may be relieved by losing consciousness.

2 If the casualty remains unconscious, turn him over on his back, and kneel astride his body. Use the heels of your hands to press down five times, just below the casualty's ribcage (see p. 169).

3 If the casualty's breathing does not resume, call an ambulance, and begin resuscitation (see p. 169). Once breathing resumes, place the casualty in the recovery position (see p. 168). Even if the casualty appears to have recovered fully, have him checked by a doctor.

Keep your arms straight as you press on abdomen

Press down firmly below ribcage

FOREIGN BODIES

Foreign bodies in the eyes, ears, nose, or throat are unpleasant, can be frightening, and may be dangerous. Use the appropriate technique below to deal with the obstruction, taking care not to cause harm to the casualty. Get medical help as soon as possible.

IN THE EYE

1 Hold the eyelids apart with two fingers and get the casualty to look up, down, left, then right. Do not touch a foreign body that is sticking to or embedded in the eye – take the casualty to a doctor.

2 Pour clean water into the inner corner of the eye to try to wash out the object. If the object does not wash out, provided it is not embedded, lift it out with a moist swab or the corner of a handkerchief.

IN THE EAR

● **Looking for objects** With a torch, try to see what is in the ear. If it is embedded, do not try to remove it – you may damage the eardrum. An adult or older child may be able to tell you what the object is. Keep the casualty calm, and take him or her to hospital.

INSECT IN THE EAR

1 Place the casualty in a chair with the affected ear upwards. Flood the ear with tepid water so that the insect floats out. Use a towel to catch any overflow.

2 If the insect does not come out, or if it is a wasp that might sting inside the ear, keep the casualty calm, and take him or her to hospital. Never put anything in the ear to remove a foreign body.

IN THE NOSE

● **Recognition and treatment** A foreign object inside the nose may cause difficult breathing, a bloody discharge, or swelling. Encourage the casualty to breathe through the mouth. Keep the casualty calm, and take him or her to hospital. Do not attempt to remove the object yourself.

SWALLOWED OBJECTS

● **Identifying objects** Ask the casualty what object has been swallowed. If it is small and smooth, it will work through the system. Large, sharp items must be removed by a doctor.

> ### WARNING
> Do not allow the casualty to eat or drink if the swallowed object is large or sharp. Take the casualty to hospital.

SPLINTERS AND BLISTERS

Splinters and burst blisters may cause infection if they are not treated properly. Remove splinters as soon as possible, but do not try to treat deeply embedded objects. Seat the casualty while removing splinters, so that the affected area remains steady.

REMOVING SPLINTERS

Hold ends of tweezers over flame

1 Wash your hands, then clean the area around the splinter with soap and warm water. Sterilize a pair of tweezers by passing them through a flame. Alternatively, boil them in water for about 10 minutes. Leave them to cool before you use them.

Pull splinter out in direction it went in

2 Grasp the splinter with the pair of tweezers, as close to the skin as possible. Draw the splinter out at the angle at which it went in. Squeeze the wound so that it bleeds a little to flush out any dirt. Wash the area again, pat dry, and cover with an adhesive plaster.

TREATING BLISTERS

● **Cleaning blisters** Wash the blistered area with soap and warm water. Rinse with clear water. Pat thoroughly with tissues or a clean gauze pad to dry. Cover the area with an adhesive plaster.
● **Burn blisters** Burns often cause fluid to collect under the skin. Never break a blister caused by a burn – you may cause even more damage than the burn itself. See page 171 for treating burns and scalds.

NOSEBLEEDS

Nosebleeds often occur unexpectedly, and can be frightening if the blood flow is copious. Use a towel to mop up blood and protect the casualty's clothes. Frequent, serious nosebleeds may indicate a deeper problem, and the nose may have to be cauterized.

TREATING NOSEBLEEDS

1 Seat the casualty with the head tilted forwards. Tell her to breathe through her mouth. Meanwhile, pinch the fleshy part of the nose so that the nostrils stay tightly together for 10 minutes.

Tilt casualty's head forwards

Pinch nostrils together

Lean casualty over bowl to catch any fluid

WARNING
If there is a watery discharge from the nose or if the bleeding lasts for more than 30 minutes, take the casualty to hospital at once.

2 Holding the head tilted over a bowl, encourage the casualty to spit out excess fluid in the mouth. Pinch the nostrils for 10 more minutes. Repeat for another 10 minutes if necessary. If the bleeding persists, take her to hospital.

3 Once the bleeding has stopped, clean around the nose and mouth with a damp towel or cotton wool and tepid water. Instruct her not to blow her nose, since this may cause the nosebleed to start again.

BLEEDING MOUTH AND EAR

Cuts to the tongue, lips, or lining of the mouth may bleed profusely and cause alarm. If an adult's tooth is knocked out, it can be replanted in its socket – but a child's tooth cannot be replanted. Bleeding from inside an ear usually follows a rupture to the eardrum.

MOUTH WOUNDS

Make casualty lean forwards over bowl

Applying pressure
Lean the casualty over a bowl to catch the blood. Press the mouth wound with a gauze pad, and pinch it between your thumb and forefinger for about 10 minutes. Do not wash out the casualty's mouth – this may disturb a blood clot.

TOOTH LOSS

Saving teeth
If the casualty is an adult, you can replant the tooth in its socket. Alternatively, store the tooth in milk, and place a pad over the socket, making sure it is higher than surrounding teeth so that the casualty can bite on it. Take him to a dentist.

EAR INJURIES
● **Ear wounds** Place a gauze pad over the wound. Pinch the wound for about 10 minutes. When the bleeding stops, cover the wound with a sterile dressing lightly held in place with a bandage.
● **Bleeding from inside the ear** Seat the casualty in a semi-upright position with the head turned towards the injured side so that blood drains off. Put an absorbent pad over the ear, and bandage it in place. Do not plug the ear. Take the casualty to a doctor.
● **Danger signs** If bleeding from inside an ear follows a head injury, and the blood is watery, fluid may be leaking from around the brain. Take the casualty to hospital.

COMMON AILMENTS

COLDS AND FEVERS MAY not seem like serious complaints, because they occur to people fairly frequently. However, they can have dangerous consequences if not treated correctly, especially for small children and elderly people.

FEVER AND COLDS

The common cold can often become more serious and produce a high temperature and fever because of infection. If someone develops a fever, you should try to bring his or her temperature down as quickly as possible, particularly if it rises above 40°C (102°F).

FEBRILE CONVULSIONS

Undress child so that you can reach as much body area as possible

Cooling a child
In babies and children under four years of age, fever can produce febrile convulsions. If a child's temperature rises above 40°C (102°F), call a doctor. Undress the child and cool her by sponging with tepid water for up to 30 minutes. Keep the child calm.

TREATING FEVER IN ADULTS AND CHILDREN

1 Take the temperature of the casualty. It should be approximately 37°C (98.6°F); anything above 40°C (102°F) indicates a fever. Make the casualty comfortable – let him or her rest in bed in a room that is evenly warm.

2 Give the casualty plenty of water or diluted fruit juice to drink to help bring down the temperature. An adult may take two paracetamol tablets; a child may be given a dose of paracetamol syrup. Sponge with water if the fever is high.

TREATING COLDS

● **Avoiding overheating** Colds usually result in a raised temperature, so be careful not to become overheated in excess clothes or blankets.
● **Using a humidifier** Installing a humidifier in your home and workplace may reduce your incidence of winter colds. Many bacteria and viruses cannot survive as long in a more humid atmosphere.
● **Clearing breathing** Clear a congested nose by inhaling a few drops of eucalyptus oil sprinkled on a handkerchief at regular intervals. Fresh air may also help clear breathing.

● **Easing a sore throat** If you have a sore throat, gargle with warm water mixed with a little cider vinegar and cayenne or hot pepper. The vinegar creates a mild acidic environment to kill bacteria, and the heat from the warm water and pepper helps to speed extra blood to the irritated tissues. A warm water and salt gargle may also help to relieve a sore throat.
● **Taking exercise** Some light exercise may help to clear a congested head through producing sweat. You should also drink plenty of fluids.

TREATING MENINGITIS

This is an inflammation of the tissues surrounding the brain. It usually occurs in children and must be treated promptly, since it can be fatal.

● **Recognition** Symptoms of meningitis are: sensitivity to light, fever, loss of appetite, listlessnes, vomiting, stiffness and pain in the neck, a rash of red or purple spots, and convulsions. A change for the worse in a child who has recently had an infection may also indicate meningitis.
● **Medical attention** Make the casualty comfortable, and call a doctor urgently. Immediate admission to hospital will probably be recommended.

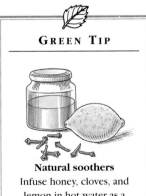

GREEN TIP

Natural soothers
Infuse honey, cloves, and lemon in hot water as a natural remedy for coughs and sore throats. Sucking a whole clove will quiet tickles in the throat.

STOMACH ACHE

Pain in the stomach can be relatively trivial indigestion, or it can indicate a damaged intestine – particularly if the pain fluctates in intensity, and is accompanied by vomiting. Stomach pain may also indicate inflammation of the appendix, particurly in older children.

TREATING STOMACH ACHES

1 Ensure that the casualty is comfortable in a bed or on a sofa, propped up on pillows. Leave a bowl nearby in case she wants to vomit.

2 Give her a covered hot-water bottle, or wrap one in a towel, to hold against her stomach. Do not give her medication or anything to eat.

3 If this fails to alleviate the pain after 30 minutes, or if the pain is severe, call a doctor. Severe pain could indicate a serious condition.

WARNING

Do not wait more than 30 minutes before calling a doctor if the pain continues. It could indicate appendicitis.

APPENDICITIS

● **Symptoms** Appendicitis tends to affect older children, particularly teenagers. The symptoms include pains in the middle of the abdomen, acute pain in the right lower abdomen, loss of appetite, raised temperature, nausea, vomiting, and diarrhoea.
● **Medical help** Do not give food or drink to a casualty with appendicitis symptoms. Call a doctor at once.

VOMITING

Adults can usually cope with their own vomiting, but children will need assistance and care. Vomiting can cause children to panic, so reassurance is important. If vomiting occurs together with diarrhoea, call a doctor – these may be symptoms of a serious illness.

TREATING VOMITING IN CHILDREN

1 Hold the casualty's head over a bowl and support her upper body with your free hand while she vomits. Constantly reassure her.

2 When she has finished vomiting, wipe her face and around her mouth with a sponge or cloth wrung out in tepid water.

3 Give her plenty of water to drink. This will replace lost fluid and remove any unpleasant taste. Encourage her to sip it slowly.

4 Encourage the casualty to rest on a sofa or in bed. If the vomiting persists, call a doctor. Do not give her milk to drink, since this may make the vomiting worse.

Let casualty vomit into a bowl

Hold casualty and continue to reassure her

WARNING

A baby or small child can become very dehydrated when vomiting. Give him or her sips of cooled, boiled water – do not give milk. Call a doctor if necessary.

EARACHE AND TOOTHACHE

Earaches may be caused by an infection, a cold, a boil in the ear canal, or a foreign body in the ear. Toothaches may be the result of a cavity, an abscess, or a mouth infection. Children may need a lot of attention while the pain of an earache or toothache is present.

TREATING TOOTHACHE

1 Give the casualty the recommended dose of paracetamol tablets or syrup to ease the pain and make him or her more comfortable. If the pain persists, make an appointment with a dentist.

2 Lay the casualty down, or prop him or her up with pillows. Place a covered, warm hot-water bottle under the affected cheek. Give the casualty a small measure of spirits to hold in the mouth – this helps to allieviate pain.

TREATING EARACHE

1 Encourage the casualty to lie down, or seat him or her in a propped up position. Give the recommended dose of paracetamol tablets or syrup to ease the pain and discomfort in the ear.

2 Cover a hot-water bottle, and give it to the casualty to lean the painful ear against. Advise the casualty to see a doctor. If you are worried about the casualty's condition, or if the earache does not subside, call a doctor.

WARNING
When treating a toothache, if the jaw is affected or swollen, call a doctor. When treating an earache, call a doctor if there is discharge from the ear, fever, or hearing loss.

TRADITIONAL TIP

Temporary filling
If you need a tooth filled but cannot get to a dentist immediately, soak a small piece of cotton wool in oil of cloves. Pack it into the cavity to relieve the discomfort.

TREATING A PRESSURE-CHANGE EARACHE

Clearing the ears
Blocked ears may occur on flights during take-off and landing, or when travelling through tunnels, particularly in trains. Tell the casualty to make the ears "pop" by closing the mouth, pinching the nostrils, and blowing out hard through the nose. Yawning widely or sucking a sweet will also help.

Ask casualty to pinch her nose and blow out

HICCUPS

Hiccups are contractions of the diaphragm against a partially closed windpipe. They occur unexpectedly and can be frightening for children, particularly if they will not go away. See a doctor for advice if the hiccups persist or last more than a few hours.

VARIOUS CURES FOR HICCUPS

● **Drinking water** To cure hiccups, try drinking water from the wrong side of a cup. This awkward task will take your mind off the hiccups, which should then stop.
● **Breath holding** Try holding your breath for as long as possible. Repeat until the hiccups have stopped and you can breathe properly.

● **Relaxation** It is best to stand or sit quietly while trying to cure hiccups – moving around may only make the hiccups worse.

Breathing expired air
Hold a paper bag over the mouth and nose and rebreathe your expired air for one minute. Never use a plastic bag.

INDEX

A

accessories, caring for:
  clothes, 67
  household, 86–87
acetate fabrics, care, 57
acrylic fabrics, care, 57
acrylic baths, 24
adhesive tape, storing, 143
adhesives, 70
  removing marks, 51
  using, 80
aerials, car, 159
ailments, treating, 151, 179–181
air conditioners
  car, 158
  economy, 114
air fresheners, 17
air vents, cleaning, 21
airing:
  bedding, 13, 60
  clothes, 60
  homemade rack, 63
airlocks, curing, 108
alabaster, cleaning, 81
alarm systems, 118
alcohol:
  serving, 141
  stains, 39–40, 72
aluminium foil:
  cake tins, lining with, 136
  on ironing board, 64
  reusing, 30
aluminium pans, cleaning, 29
ammonia:
  solvent, 70
  stain remover, 11, 33
anaphylactic shock, treating, 174
animal bites, treating, 173
answering machines, 84
antique furniture:
  cleaning, 22
  polish for, 71
ants, deterring, 30
appendicitis, symptoms, 180
apple sauce, 134
apples:
  cooking, 125
  storing, 122
arm injuries, treating, 175

artificial ventilation, 169
ashes, removing from grates, 21
ashtrays:
  cleaning, 77
  fire safety, 165
aubergines, preparing, 123
avocados, ripening, 122

B

babies, 150
baby formula stains, 55
bacon, cooking, 126
baking, 136–139
ballpoint-pen ink:
  stains, 47
  on leather furniture, 82
bananas:
  ripening, 122
  preserving, 125
bandages, 164
baths:
  blocked drain, 109
  cleaning, 24
  rust marks, 54
  scented, 155
bath plugs, removing, 25
bathroom:
  cleaning, 13, 24–25
  repairs, 107–110
bed linen:
  laundering, 61
  moth proofing, 68
  storing, 68, 83
bedding:
  airing, 13, 60
  laundering, 61
  moving house, 163
beer stains, 40
beeswax polish, 22
  recipe for, 71
beetroot:
  cooking, 124
  stains, 38
belts:
  drying, 62
  storing, 67
beverages:
  estimating quantities, 161
  making and serving, 140–141
  stains, 39–41, 72

biological detergent:
  laundering, 56
  stain removal, 35
biological stains, 42–45
birds:
  bird-dropping stains, 45
  feeding, 153
biscuits, 139
blacking, applying, 21
blankets:
  electric, 83
  moth proofing, 68
bleach, 11
  laundering, 56, 58
  stain removal, 35
bleeding, 170
blenders, cleaning, 29
blind baking, 138
blinds, cleaning and care, 23
blisters, treating, 177
blood stains, 42
body lotions, 155–156
  removing stains, 50
  storing, 154
bone, ornamental, 75, 81
bone injuries, 175
books, caring for, 85
boots:
  care, 69
  children's, 151
bottles, baby's, 150
bouquet garnis, making 127
boxes:
  for storage, 142
  wooden, 73
brass, cleaning and care, 77
bread, 130–131
bread bins, cleaning, 29
breadcrumbs, making, 130
breath fresheners, 155
brick surfaces:
  cleaning, 21, 31
  painting, 93, 96
  sealing, 19
  soot stains, 54
brocade, care, 57
broccoli, preparing, 124
bronze, cleaning and care, 77
brooms:
  cleaning and storing, 12

improving tools, 14, 19
bruises, treating, 175
brushes:
    household, 12, 70
    hairbrushes, 81
    paint brushes, 92, 98–99
buckets, 13
buffets, 161
bulbs, watering, 145
    see also light bulbs
burglaries, preventing, 118–119
burn marks:
    on brick surfaces, 21, 31
    on flooring, 16, 53
    on polished wood, 53, 72
burned food:
    rescuing, 121, 136
    cleaning off pans, 27, 29
burns:
    preventing, 120
    treating, 171
butter, 128
buttonholes, making, 149
buttons, 66, 149

C

cabbage, 124
cake tins, 136, 137
cakes, 136–137
    freezing, 135
cameras, cleaning and care, 84
candied flowers, making, 137
candle wax:
    on fabric and carpet, 51
    on wood floors, 16
candles:
    caring for, 85
    for emergencies, 112
candlesticks:
    pewter, cleaning, 76
    silver, cleaning, 75
cane furniture:
    cleaning, 22
    fixing sagging seats, 73
canvas shoes:
    cleaning, 69
    removing grass stains, 44
carbon paper stains, 55
cardiopulmonary resuscitation,
    169
care symbols, 56
    drying, 62
    ironing, 64
    washing, 59
carpet beetles, eradicating, 17
carpet shampoo, 17

for stain removal, 33
carpets:
    car, 158
    cleaning, 17, 34
    laying, 105
    stain removal, 33–55
carrots, cooking with, 124
cars, 158–159
    holiday precautions, 119
    pets in, 153
cashmere, care, 57
casserole dishes, 80, 127
cast-iron pans:
    cleaning, 29
    seasoning, 76
cats, caring for, 152–153
cauliflower, 124
cedar chests, 104
ceilings:
    cleaning, 18–21
    painting, 96
    papering, 101, 102
ceramic tiles:
    cleaning, 19, 31
    fire surround, 21
    flooring, 15
    painting, 93
    repairs, 16, 104
chains:
    cleaning, 77
    untangling, 86, 87
chamois leather, 12, 154
champagne, 141
chandeliers, cleaning, 79
cheese, 128
cheese sauce, 134
chemicals:
    burns, 171
    fumes, 11
    poisoning, 172
chest compressions, 169
chestnuts, preparing, 132
chewing gum, stains, 48
chicken, see poultry
chickens, caring for, 153
children, 150–151
    choking, 178
    parties, 161
    safety, 11, 150
chimney fires, 113, 166
china:
    care and repair, 80
    washing, 28
    packing, 143
chintz, cleaning, 23
chisels, 89, 90

chocolate, 139
    shapes, 137
    stains, 38
choking, treating, 176
chopping boards:
    cleaning, 29
    sealing splits, 73
Christmas, cards and paper, 161
chrome:
    caring for, 76
    on cars, 158
    taps, cleaning, 25
chutney stains, 55
cider, 141
cigarette burns, 53
cigarette smoke, 17
cisterns, overflowing, 110
citrus fruit, 125
    squeezing, 141
citrus peel, 125
    moth proofing, 68
    scenting, 21
cleaners, household, 11
cleaning, 10–31
    methods and routine, 13
    safety aspects, 11
    various surfaces, 31
cleaning equipment:
    kit, 10
    care and storage, 12
    bathroom, 24
    kitchen, 26
cleansing scrub, 156
clingfilm, storing, 142
closets, see cupboards
clothes:
    children's, 151
    laundering and care, 56–65
    mildew, removing, 52
    minor repairs, 66
    stain removal, 34–54
    storage, 67–68
clothes pegs, 62
cloves:
    moth deterrent, 68
    oil of, 181
    treating coughs, 137
coal:
    fires, 21
    stains, 55
coats:
    dry cleaning, 60
    children's, 151
cockroaches, eradicating, 30
cocoa stains, 41
coconuts, opening, 132

coffee, 140
    stains, 41
coffee makers:
    cleaning, 29
    using, 140
cola-drink stains, 55
cold compresses, 175
colds, treating, 179
collar bone, broken, 175
collars:
    dirty, 61
    ironing, 64
colour runs, in laundry:
    preventing, 59
    removing, 46
coloured fabrics:
    colourfast test, 60
    machine washing, 59
    preventing fading, 58, 62
    stains, 35
combs, cleaning, 87
compact discs, cleaning, 84
computers, caring for, 84
concrete surfaces, 14, 31
condensation, reducing, 24, 117
cookbooks, 121
cookers:
    cleaning, 27
    economy, 113
    safety, 120, 165
cooking oils, 132
cooling:
    fevers, 179
    houses, 114–115
copier toner powder stains, 55
copper, cleaning and care, 77
    pans, 29, 77
cord, storing, 90
corduroy:
    care, 57
    ironing, 65
cork flooring:
    burn marks, treating, 16
    cleaning, 15
    laying, 105
corn:
    preparing, 123
    cooking, 124
correction-fluid stains, 48
cosmetics:
    stains, 50
    storage and care, 154, 157
costume jewellery, 86, 87
cotton fabric, care, 57
    discoloured, 58
cotton wool, storing, 157

coughs, soothing, 179
crayon marks, 48
cream, 128
    stains, 55
creosote stains, 51
crockery, see china
crystal:
    glasses, 28, 78
    vases, 79
cucumbers, 122
cuffs:
    dirty, 61
    reshaping, 60
cupboards, 68
curry stains, 38
curtains:
    drawing, 115, 119
    hooks, 23
    laundering, 23
    lengthening, 83
    rings and rods, 83
    weighting, 83
    window cleaning, 20
cuticles, 155
cutlery:
    egg stains, 31, 37
    silver, 75
    washing, 28
cuts and grazes, 170

D

dairy foods, 128
damp:
    carpets, 17
    cupboards, 68
    prints, 85
    wallpaper, 103
    wood floors, 16
decanters, cleaning, 79
decorating cakes, 137
deep frying, 132
delicate fabrics:
    flat drying, 63
    ironing, 64
    laundering, 59, 60
    removing stains, 35, 36
denim, caring for, 57
    preserving colour, 58
dents in wood, 72
deodorant:
    for shoes, 69
    stains, 50
detergent, 11
    laundering, 56
    quantities, 59
    stain removal, 35

dinner parties, 160
dishwashers, 28
    overflowing, 110
    silver items, 75
distemper, 93
documents, storing, 8, 143
dogs, caring for, 152–153
doormats, 14, 106
doors:
    cleaning, 19
    glass, 150, 165
    painting, 97
    security, 118–119
    sticking, 116
    warning bell, 150
double glazing, 114
    temporary, 115
drainholes, cleaning, 24
drainpipes, and security, 118
drains, unblocking, 109
draughts, preventing, 115
drawers:
    clothes storage, 67
    greasing runners, 73
    scenting, 68, 154
dressings, see bandages
dried flowers, 147
dried fruit, in cakes, 136
drinks, see beverages
drip-dry clothes, 62, 65
driveways, cleaning, 110, 158
drowning, rescue from, 167
drug poisoning, treating, 172
dry cleaning, 60
    curtains, 23
    duvets, 61
dry skin, treatments for, 156
drying:
    laundry, 57, 62–63
    mattresses, 43
    shoes, 69
duck, roasting, 127
duplicating-ink stains, 55
dust, 16, 21
duster, time-saving, 13
dusting, two-handed, 13
duvets, 83
    laundering, 61
dye stains, 46

E

ears:
    earache, 181
    foreign bodies, 177
    injuries, 178
    popping, 181

earrings:
cleaning, 86
silver, 75
ebony, caring for, 71
eggs, 129
stains, 37
electric appliances:
cleaning, 28–29
on fire, 166
safety, 111, 112
electric blankets, 83
electric fixtures, cleaning, 20
electric sockets:
cleaning, 20
overloading, 112
safety, 150, 165
electrical injuries:
rescuing a casualty, 167
treating burns, 171
electricity, 111–112
electronic equipment:
cleaning and care, 84
energy-saving tips, 113
embroidery:
ironing, 65
transfers, 55
emergency services, 165
emulsion paint, 94
cleaning brushes, 98
painting over, 93
enamel baths, 24
energy efficiency, 113
entertaining, 160–161
environmentally friendly:
carpet shampoo, 17
household cleaners, 11
leather polish, 82
equipment kits:
care and repair, 70, 74
cleaning, 10–11
decorating, 92, 100
first-aid, 164
laundry, 56
maintenance, 107, 111
stain-removal, 32
tool kit, 88–89
extension leads, storing, 142
eyes:
foreign bodies in, 177
beauty tips, 154, 155

F

fabric:
laundering, 56–65
sewing, 148
stain removal, 34–55

fabric protector, 37, 151
fabric softener, 56, 63
face cloth, soapy, 61
facials, 156
faecal stains, 45
fats, 121
in pastry-making, 138
removing stains, 36
fax machines, cleaning, 84
felt-tip ink stains, 48
festoon blinds, cleaning, 23
fever, reducing, 179
finger nails, caring for, 155
fire blankets, 106, 165
fire precautions, 165
fireguards, 165
fires, 166
electrical, 111, 166
house, 165, 166
oil and fat, 120, 126
open, 113
fireplaces, cleaning, 21
first-aid kit, 164
fish, preparing, 127
fish stock, 127
fleas, deterring, 152
flexes:
safety, 150, 153
repairs to, 111
floor polish, 14, 15
floorboards, repairs to, 116
flooring:
cleaning, 14–15
laying, 105
special treatments, 16
floors:
insulation, 114, 116
repairs, 116
see also wooden floors
flowers, 146–147
candied, 137
fly specks, removing, 45
food, 120–139
parties and picnics, 160–161
pet foods, 152
stains, 36–38
food processors, cleaning, 29
foreign bodies, removing, 177
foundation, applying, 156
stains, 50
fountain-pens:
cleaning, 87
ink stains, 47
freezers:
cleaning and defrosting, 27
freezing tips, 135

saving energy, 113
French polish, 22
frozen pipes, 109
fruit-juice:
making, 125, 141
stains, 40
fruit, 122–125
stains, 55
frying:
fish, 127
frying pans, 29, 132
oils for, 132
meat, 126
fumes:
chemical, 11
paint, 94, 98
furniture:
cleaning, 22
fire risk, 165
mildew, 52
moving, 16
stain removal, 36–54
see also upholstery
furniture polish, 11, 22
homemade, 71
furs, caring for, 67
fuses, faulty, 112

G

garages, 158–159
security, 118, 119
garlic, storing, 133
gas leaks, 113
gelatine, 139
gilt frames, restoring, 77
glass:
broken, 117
chipped, 78
cleaning, 31, 78–79
grease marks, 55
picture glass, 85
glass doors, safety, 150, 165
glass-fibre baths, 24
glass shelves, 105
glasses, 78
child's, 151
decorative, 141
washing, 28, 78
gloss paint, 94
gloves, 67, 151
glycerine, 11, 33
gold, caring for, 77
goose, roasting, 127
grass stains, 44
grasscloth, cleaning, 18
graters, cleaning, 29

grates, clearing, 21
gravy, making, 134
    stains, 37
grazes, 170
grease:
    disposing of, 30
    on fabric and carpets, 36–37
    on garage floor, 158
    on glass, 31
    on paper, 55, 85
    on wall coverings, 18, 101
    on wood, 72
grease solvent, 33
grill:
    cleaning grills, 27
    grilling meat, 126
grooming:
    personal, 154–157
    pets, 152
grouting, 15, 19

H

hair:
    baby's, washing, 150
    hair-oil stains, 55
    natural treatments for, 157
    paint in, 55
hair ribbons, 65
hairbrushes, bone, 81
hairspray stains, 50
ham, preparing, 128
hamburgers, frying, 126
hammers:
    cleaning, 90
    types of, 88, 89
hand washing, 60
handbags:
    caring for, 87
    removing mildew, 52
hands, caring for, 155
hangers, adapting, 67
hanging baskets, watering, 145
hanging pictures, 85
hats, storing, 67
heat marks, 55, 72
heaters, cleaning, 21
heating, 114–115
heavy fabrics, care, 65, 149
hems, ironing, 64
herbs, 133
    freezing, 135
hessian wall coverings, 18
hiccups, cures for, 181
hinges:
    protecting during painting, 97
    sticking, 116

hobs, cleaning, 27
holidays:
    packing for, 68
    security, 119
    watering plants during, 145
home log book:
    making a log book, 11
    decorating log, 99
    freezer log, 135
honey:
    cold cure, 179
    softening, 133
hot chocolate:
    making, 140
    stains, 41
hot-water bottles, reusing, 142
household cleaners, 11
household product stains, 49–54
house plants:
    caring for, 144–145
    transporting, 162
humidifiers, 17, 71
    cold treatment, 179
humidity, 115, 144
hydrogen peroxide, 33
hypothermia, preventing, 167

I

ice cream:
    stains, 37
    storing, 128
ice cubes:
    decorative, 135
    large quantities, 141
    watering with, 145
icing cakes, 137
injuries, treating, 170–178
ink stains:
    duplicating ink stains, 55
    on fabric and carpets, 47–48
    on leather furniture, 82
    on skin, 55
    on wood floor, 16
insects:
    in ear, 177
    deterring, 17, 30
    stings from, 174
insulation, 114, 116
iodine stains, 49
iron mould, see rust
ironing, 57, 64–65
ironing boards, 64
irons:
    cleaning and care, 64
    safety, 165
ivory, cleaning and care, 81

JK

jade, cleaning, 81, 86
jam:
    making, 135
    stains, 38
jars:
    for jam making, 135
    removing smells, 78
    unscrewing, 120
jelly, making, 139
jewellery:
    cleaning and care, 86–87
    gold jewellery, 77,
    security, 119
    silver jewellery, 74–75
jumpers:
    drying, 62, 63
    storing, 68
    washing, 60
kettles:
    safety, 150
    saving energy, 113
keys:
    and security, 119
    frozen car locks, 159
    oiling locks with, 116
kitchen:
    cleaning, 13, 26–30
    cookery tips, 120–121
    fires, 120, 166
    safety, 165
    utensils, care, 73
    waste, 30
kitchen appliances:
    cleaning, 29
    energy-saving, 113
    faults, 110
kitchen cloths:
    laundering, 61, 63
    worn, 83
knitting, tips, 149
knives:
    caring for, 76
    decorative handles, 75
    silver, 74–75

L

labels:
    gummed, 142
    jam jars, 135
    nail and screw cans, 90
    see also care symbols
lace:
    laundering, 57, 60
    mildew on, 52

ladders:
    for household chores, 89, 91
    for painting, 96
    security risk, 118
lagging pipes, 114
lamb, serving, 126
lampshades, cleaning, 83
laundry, 56–67
laundry aids, 56
    stain removal, 33, 35
laundry borax, 11, 56
    stain removal, 33, 35
lavender sachets, making, 68
lead, caring for, 77
leather:
    care, 31
    mildew, 52
    stain removal, 55
    washability check, 82
    water marks on, 53
leather-bound books, 85
leather fabric, 57
leather furniture:
    cleaning and care, 23, 82
    removing ink stains, 82
leather shoes, cleaning, 69
    stain removal, 36, 43
leg injuries, treating, 175
lemon juice, removing stains
    with, 11, 33
lemons:
    storing, 122
    using, 125
lettuce, preparing, 123
light bulbs, 112
    cleaning, 20
    scented, 20, 157
light switches:
    cleaning, 20
    wallpapering around, 103
lights, 112
    car, 159
    safety, 165
    saving energy, 113
    security, 118–119
lilies, as cut flowers, 147
limescale, removing:
    from irons, 64
    from showers, 24, 25
    from sinks, 26
    from taps, 25
    from toilets, 25
line drying, 62
linen, care, 57
    discoloured, 58
linen cupboard, 68

linoleum flooring:
    cleaning, 15
    cracks in, 16
    laying, 105
    paint stains, 16
linseed oil, uses, 70
lint:
    in sewing machine, 148
    on clothes, 67
    on upholstery, 23
lipstick, tips, 154
    stains, 50
liqueur stains, 40
litter trays, reducing smells, 152
locks, 116
    car, frozen, 159
loft insulation, 114
log book, see home log book
long dresses, hanging, 67
loose covers, cleaning, 82
luggage labels, 119

M

machine washing, 59
mahogany, caring for, 71
make-up, tips, 154
    stains, 50
marble:
    cleaning, 21, 31
    stain removal, 81
marinades, 126
marshmallows, 139
mascara, 154
    stains, 50
mats and matting, cleaning, 17
mattress:
    drying, 43
    pressing clothes under, 65
    stain removal, 42
mayonnaise, making, 129
    stains, 37
meat, preparing, 126
medicine stains, 49
melons, storing and serving, 125
mending, see repairs
meningitis, symptoms, 179
meringue, making, 139
metal polish, 11, 70
    stains, 49
metals, caring for, 74–77
    furniture, 22
microwave ovens:
    cleaning, 27
    using, 113
mildew, removing 52
    from books, 85

    from bread bins, 29
    from shower curtains, 24, 52
milk:
    baths, 156
    boil overs, 121, 128
    stains, 41
mirrors:
    cleaning, 20, 79
    hairspray marks, 50
mopping floors, 14
moth proofing, 68
motor oil, 158
mouth wounds, treating, 178
mouth-to-mouth ventilation, 169
moving house, 162–163
mud:
    on shoes, 69
    stains, 44
muscle injuries, treating, 175
mushrooms:
    storing, 122
    preparing, 124
musical instruments, care, 73
mustard stains, 38

N

nails:
    storing, 90
    using, 91
    see also finger nails
nail varnish, 154, 155
    stains, 50
napkin rings, silver, 75
nappies, fastening, 150
natural fabrics, care, 35
natural floor coverings, 17
necklaces, storage and care, 87
nettle rash, treating, 174
newspapers:
    and shoe care, 69
    and window cleaning, 20
    newsprint stains, 55
    preserving clippings, 142
    storing, 142
nose:
    bleeding, 178
    congested, 179
    foreign bodies in, 177
nuts, storing and shelling, 132
nylon, care, 58

O

oak, caring for, 71
odours, removing:
    from bathrooms, 25
    from bottles and jars, 78

odours, removing, *continued*
  from hands, 28, 127
  from refrigerators, 27
  from pans, 29
  from plastic containers, 31
odours, types of:
  cigarette smoke, 17
  fish, 127
  food, 30
  pets, 152
  urine, 43
office equipment, cleaning, 84
oil stains:
  on fabric and carpet, 36
  on garage floors, 158
oily skin, treatments for, 156
ointment spills, 49
onions, slicing, 123
oranges, 125
ormolu, caring for, 77
ovens:
  cleaning, 27
  energy-saving, 113
  using, 121

P

packing:
  for holidays, 68
  moving house, 162
  parcels, 143
paint, 94
  estimating quantities, 95
  storage, 98, 99
  types of, 94
paint brushes, 92
  cleaning, 98
  storing, 98–99
paint kettles, 92, 94
paint pads, 92, 95
paint stains, 46
  on linoleum, 16
  on skin and hair, 55
paint tray, 92
painting, 92–99
  cleaning up, 98–99
  preparing surfaces, 93
  special areas, 96–97
  techniques, 94–95
paintwork:
  cleaning, 19, 22
  flaking, 93
pancakes, 134, 136
pans, *see* pots and pans
paper:
  grease marks, 55, 85
  removing from wood, 73

paper towels, 32
parasites, on pets, 152
parsley, 133
parties, 160–161
pasta, preparing, 131
pastry, preparing, 138
patching:
  flooring, 16
  upholstery, 82
  wallpaper, 18
patent leather, cleaning, 69
peanut butter, storing, 132
pearls, caring for, 86
pencil marks, 48
peppers, 123, 124
perfume, 154, 157
  stains, 50
perspiration stains, 45
pests:
  household, 17, 30
  house plants, 145
pets, 26, 152–153
  hairs, 23
  stains, 45
pewter, cleaning and care, 76
pianos:
  cleaning and care, 81
  safety and children, 150
pictures, cleaning and care, 85
  restoring gilt frames, 77
  protecting picture glass, 162
pie funnels, improvised, 138
pillows, laundering, 61
pin cushions, 148
pins, storing and finding, 148
pipes:
  frozen, 109
  painting, 96
  repairs to, 108–109
piping bag, making, 137
place settings, 160
plaster:
  nailing into, 91
  painting, 93
plasters:
  in first-aid kit, 164
  removing, 151
plastic, cleaning, 31
plastic containers:
  reusing, 30
  removing smells from, 31
plastic-putty stains, 48
plates:
  displaying, 105
  heating, 121
  securing, 151

stacking, 80
platforms, for painting, 96
platinum, caring for, 77
playing cards, cleaning, 87
pleated skirts:
  drying, 62
  ironing, 65
pliers, 88
plugs, electric, 111
plumbing, 107–108
plumblines, 100, 103
plungers, 109
plywood, sawing, 91
poisoning, treating, 172
polish, 11
  build up, 19, 73
  reviving, 73
  stains, 49
polishing:
  fireplaces, 21
  floors, 14, 15
  wood, 22, 71
pollen stains, 45
porcelain baths, 24
porcelain sinks, 26
pork, preparing, 126
possessions, protecting, 119
post, 143
  change of address, 162
potatoes:
  storing, 122
  cooking, 124
pots and pans:
  energy-saving, 113
  non-stick, 132
  replacing knob, 120
  washing, 28, 29
poultry, preparing, 127
power cuts and failures, 112
precious stones, cleaning, 86
preserves, making, 135
  stains, 38
primer, 94
protein stains, 35
pulses, preparing, 124
punch, making and serving, 141
putty repairs, 117

QR

quarry tiles:
  care, 15, 16
  laying, 105
rabbits, caring for, 153
radiators:
  cleaning, 21
  painting, 96

reflecting heat, 115
radios, cleaning, 84
recovery position, 168
recycling:
    fabric items, 66
    plastic pots and bags, 30
    zips and buttons, 149
red-wine stains, 39
refrigerators, cleaning, 27
repairs:
    clothes, 66, 149
    house, 116–117
    household items, 70–87
    plumbing, 107–110
resuscitation, 168
rice, preparing, 131
ring marks, removing, 66
rings:
    cleaning and care, 86
    stuck, 87
rocking chairs, 16
rollers:
    painting with, 92
    cleaning, 98
    pasting wallpaper, 101
    using, 95
roller blinds, cleaning, 23
rolling pins:
    cleaning, 29
    improvised, 138
rope, storing, 90
roses, as cut flowers, 147
rubber gloves, 11, 32
rugs:
    cleaning, 17
    securing, 165
rust:
    cake tins, 136
    metal furniture, 22
    on tools, 90
    pins, 148
    removing marks, 24, 54

S

safety, 165
    and children, 150
    cleaning materials, 11
    electrical equipment, 84
    electricity, 20, 111
    irons, 64
    lighting, 112
    pets, 153
safety pins, storing, 148
salad bowls, cleaning, 73
salads, preparing, 123
salt, using, 121, 133

salt shakers, silver, 75
sanding wood, 91
sandpaper, 70
sandwiches, preparing, 130
sauce bottles, 120
sauces, preparing, 134
sausages, frying, 126
sawing wood, 91
saws, 89, 90
scalds, treating, 171
scarves, storing, 67, 143
scorch marks:
    on fabric and carpet, 53
    on wood, 72
scouring pads, using, 26
scratches:
    on baths, 24
    on watch glass, 79
    on wood, 16, 72
screwdrivers, 88, 89
screwholes:
    filling, 91
    wallpapering over, 103
screws:
    storing, 90
    using, 91
seams:
    fabric, ironing, 64
    wallpaper, 103
seat covers, upholstery, 82
security, 106, 118–119
sewing, 148–149
sewing machines, 148
sheets:
    ironing, 65
    laundering, 61
    quick-drying, 62
shellac stains, 55
shelves, 105
    above radiators, 21, 115
shock, treating, 170
    anaphylactic shock, 174
shoe containers, 67
shoe polish, 69
    stains, 49
shoes:
    cleaning and care, 69
    children's, 151
    grass stains, 44
    grease stains, 36
    tar stains, 51
    urine stains, 43
shoulder, dislocated, 175
shower curtains, 24, 52
shower heads, cleaning, 25
showers, cleaning, 24

silk, care, 57
    drying, 65
    hand washing, 60
silk flowers, cleaning, 147
silver, cleaning, 74–75
    tarnished, 129
silverplate, cleaning, 75
sinks:
    blocked drain, 109
    cleaning, 24, 26
    outlets, 30
sink plugs, tightening, 30
skin:
    care, 11, 156
    foreign bodies in, 177
    paint removal, 55, 99
    softening, 155, 156
    stains, 47, 155
skirting boards:
    cleaning, 19
    painting, 96
skirts:
    pleated, 62, 65
    storing, 67
slate, cleaning, 31
slip covers:
    cleaning, 23
    using, 82
smells, see odours
smoke alarms, 165
snake bites, treating, 173
soaking clothes, 58
soap:
    in face cloths, 61
    storing, 68
    using leftover pieces, 25, 157
soapflakes:
    laundering, 56
    ink stains, 35
socks:
    keeping in pairs, 59
    line drying, 62
    storing, 67
    white cotton, 58
soft drinks, 141
    stains, 40
soft furnishings, 23, 82–83
solvents, 70
soot marks, 21, 54
sorbet stains, 55
sore throats, soothing, 179
sorting washing, 59
soufflés, making, 134
soup, 121, 127
    freezing, 135
    stains, 55

soy-sauce stains, 55
spanners, 88, 89
spectacles, cleaning, 79
spin drying, 63
spinach, preparing, 124
spirits of salts, 54
spirits stains, 40
splinters, removing, 151, 177
sponge mop, storing, 12
sponges, 32
  slimy, 24
sprains, treating, 175
stain removers, 11, 33
stainless-steel:
  cleaning, 31, 76
  shining, 26, 76
stain removal, 32–55
  baths and sinks, 24
  china, 28
  furnishings, 22
  laundry, 61
  marble, 81
  skin, 47, 155
stairs:
  creaking, 117
  laying carpet, 105
stamps, storing, 142
starch, 56
  using, 63
steam irons, cleaning 64
steel-wool pads, 12, 26
stews, 127
  freezing, 135
  over-salted, 125
stock, 127
  freezing, 135
stomach ache, treating, 180
stone surfaces:
  cleaning, 81
  removing soot marks, 54
  stone floors, 14
stoppers, stuck, 154
storage, household, 142
stoves, see cookers
strawberries:
  preparing, 125
  cleaning teeth with, 155
stretching shoes, 69
string:
  storing, 143
  watering aid, 145
succulents, caring for, 145
suede:
  erasing marks, 69
  fabric care, 57
  grease marks, 36

ink marks, 47
  removing fluff, 67
  stain removal, 43, 55
  water marks, 53
sugar:
  brown, 133
  coloured, 137
sugar soap, 11, 19
suitcases:
  removing mildew, 52
  storing, 68
sunburn, treating, 156
swallowed objects, 177
sweeping floors, 14, 15
  damping down dust, 16
swelling, treating, 175
synthetic fabrics:
  care, 57
  stains, 35
  tumble drying, 65
syrup, measuring and using, 133

T

tables:
  kitchen tables, 27
  laying a table, 160
  repairing wobbly tables, 73
  party tables, 161
tablecloths:
  ironing, 65
  plastic, storing, 142
  red-wine stains, 39
tableware:
  silver, 75
  wood, 73
talcum powder:
  economizing, 157
  on stains, 36, 39
  squeaky floors, 116
tapestry furniture, cleaning, 82
taps:
  cleaning, 25
  dripping, 107, 110
  repairs, 107
  shining, 76
tar stains, 51, 158
tarragon, using, 133
tea, 140
  iced, 141
  stains, 41
  watering plants with, 145
teak, caring for, 22, 71
teapots, cleaning, 75, 80
teeth:
  cleaning, 155
  knocked out, 178

temporary filling, 181
toothache, 181
telephones:
  cleaning, 84
  emergency calls, 165
  moving house, 162
televisions:
  cleaning, 84
  saving energy, 113
tetanus, preventing, 173
textured paints, 94
textured wallpaper, 100
thermos flasks, storing, 140
thermostats, 114
thimbles, 148
threads, 148
ticks, 152, 174
tidemarks on bath, 24
ties:
  fabric-protector, 36
  ironing, 65
tights:
  line drying, 62
  prolonging life of, 66
tiles, see ceramic tiles; quarry
  tiles
tiling, 104
timer switches, 119
toast, making, 130
tobacco stains:
  on hands, 45
  on paintwork, 19
toddlers, tips for, 151
toilet:
  cleaning, 25
  plumbing repairs, 110
toilet brush, 24
toilet cleaner, 24
tomato-sauce stains, 38
tomatoes:
  peeling, 123
  ripening, 122
  stains, 55
tongue-and-groove boards, 116
tools:
  care and storage, 90
  kit, 88–89, 163
  tips on use, 91
toothbrushes, 12, 70
towels, laundering, 61
treacle stains, 55
trellis, for house plants, 145
tulips, as cut flowers, 147
tumble drying, 63, 65
tumblers:
  for children, 151

in place settings, 160
unsticking, 78
turmeric stains, 38
two-bucket cleaning method, 13

U

U-bend, unblocking, 109
unconscious casualties, 168–169, 172
undercoat, paint, 94
upholstery:
  cleaning, 23
  and pets, 153
  renovations, 82
  stain removal, 33–54
urine stains, 43, 153

V

vacuum cleaners, using, 12
vacuum cleaning, 10
  behind radiators, 21
  carpets, 17
  lampshades, 83
varnishing woodwork, 97
vases:
  cleaning, 79, 80
  deep, 80, 146
vegetables, 122–125
velvet, care, 65
Venetian blinds, cleaning, 23
verdigris, removing, 77
video players and tapes, 84
vinegar, 11, 33
  air freshener, 17
  cleaning windows, 20
  cutting grease, 28
vinyl flooring:
  cleaning, 15
  laying, 105
  marks, 15, 16
  paint stains, 16
vinyl surfaces:
  cleaning, 23
  pen and ink stains, 47, 48
vinyl wall coverings, 100
  cleaning, 18
  pen and ink stains, 47, 48
  removing, 101
viscose rayon, care, 65
vomiting, 180
  stains, 43

W

wall coverings:
  cleaning, 18
  hanging, 100–103

pen and ink stains, 47, 48
wallpaper:
  candlewax stains, 51
  cleaning, 18
  felt-tip pen marks, 48
  hanging, 100–103
  painting over, 93
  patching, 18
  removing, 101
  sealing, 103
  types, 100
wallpapering, 100–103
  curing faults, 103
  order of work, 102
  useful techniques, 103
walls:
  cleaning, 18–21
  mildew, 52
  painting, 95
  papering, 102
walnuts, 132
wardrobes, storage, 67
washers, replacing, 107
washing clothes, 57–60
washing lines, 62
washing machines, 59
  overflowing, 110
  water-economy, 110
washing powder, see detergent
washing-up, 28
  silver cutlery, 75
  water-economy, 110
washing-up brushes, 26
washing-up liquid, 11, 26
waste-disposal units, 30
watches, caring for, 79
water economy, 110
water marks, removing:
  on hides and clothes, 53
  on wood, 72
watering plants, 145
wax floor polish, 14, 15
weather stripping, 114
white fabrics:
  cotton socks, 58
  discoloured, 58
  flannel, 44
  removing stains from, 35
white sauce, making, 134
white spirit, 11, 33
wicker furniture, cleaning, 22
windows:
  cleaning, 20
  painting, 97
  repairs, 117
  security, 118, 119

windscreens, cleaning, 158
wine:
  estimating quantities, 161
  stains, 39
  storing and serving, 141
wire wool, 70
wiring, and safety, 111
wood:
  bare, painting, 93
  burn marks, 53
  caring for, 71–73
  cleaning, 31
  conditioning, 71
  removing marks, 72
  untreated, 42, 55
  varnishing, 97
wood panelling, 19
wooden floors, 14–16
  cleaning, 15, 105
  rising damp, 16
  removing candle wax, 16
  removing ink stains, 16
  removing scratches, 16
wooden furniture:
  care and repair, 71–73
  cleaning, 22
wooden objects, caring for, 73
woodwork:
  painting, 97, 104
  stripping, 104
  varnishing, 97
woodworm, 104
wool, care, 57
  discoloured, 58
  drying, 60
  ironing, 65
work surfaces, cleaning, 12, 26
wrapping packages, 143
wrapping paper, 143, 161

XYZ

yoghurt, 128
  stains, 55
zips:
  common problems, 66
  repairs, 149

ACKNOWLEDGMENTS

AUTHOR'S ACKNOWLEDGMENTS

I would like to thank my husband Michael Taylor for his
unfailing patience and support while I have been writing this
book, and my son Damian and daughter Flavia for, over the
years, providing a fair number of the problems it aims to solve.

I would also like to thank my editor Victoria Sorzano for her
continued charm and calmness in the face of missed deadlines
and writer's block. Thanks, too, to art editor Jayne Carter and
her assistant Darren Hill, and to the management by
Stephanie Jackson and Nigel Duffield.

PUBLISHER'S ACKNOWLEDGMENTS

Dorling Kindersley would like to thank the following:

Consultation The British Red Cross for consultation and
approval of the Health & Safety chapter. Special thanks to
Joe Mulligan for planning and checking text, and to
Robert Spigel of the British Red Cross.

Prop loan Elizabeth David Cookshop, Covent Garden, for props
used in the Food & Drink chapter. Thanks also to Churches
Shoes and Hugo Boss at Moss Bros, Covent Garden.

Reference Rentokil Ltd (for mildew reference).

Editorial and design Adèle Hayward and Lynn Parr for
editorial assistance; Chacasta Pritlove for data entry;
Chris Bernstein for the index.
Jackie Dollar and Jan Richter for design assistance;
Harvey De Roemer for DTP assistance.

ILLUSTRATIONS

Illustrators All illustrations by Kuo Kang Chen and
John Woodcock. Additional illustrations on pages 106–119
and 165–181 by David Ashby.

PHOTOGRAPHY

Photographer Andy Crawford.
Assistant Gary Ombler.
Additional photography Steve Gorton, Tim Ridley,
Colin Keates, Steve Shott, and Harry Taylor.

Hand models Linda Birungy, Lisa Broomhead,
Duncan Horastead, Helen Oyo, Victoria Sorzano,
and Nick Turpin.